ELEMENTS OF
FOOD ENGINEERING

other AVI books

Food Science

ELEMENTS OF
FOOD ENGINEERING

---

by JOHN C. HARPER, Sc.D., B.D.

Professor, Emeritus
Department of Agricultural Engineering,
University of California
Davis, California

THE AVI PUBLISHING COMPANY, INC.
WESTPORT, CONNECTICUT

© Copyright 1976 by
THE AVI PUBLISHING COMPANY, INC.
Westport, Connecticut

Library of Congress Catalog Card Number: 76-27460
ISBN-0-87055-218-X

Printed in the United States of America
BY MACK PRINTING COMPANY, EASTON, PENNSYLVANIA

Foreword

This book is a memorial to John Cline Harper who received his Sc.D degree in Chemical Engineering from the Massachusetts Institute of Technology in 1944. Four years earlier he had graduated from the California Institute of Technology with a B.D. degree in Applied Chemistry. From 1944 to 1950 he was project research engineer in petroleum engineering with the California Research Corporation. He was appointed as an Associate Professor in the College of Engineering at UCLA in 1953 and transferred to the Department of Agricultural Engineering at the Davis campus of the University to teach and do research in food engineering. After twenty years of faculty service he elected early retirement as a professor on October 31, 1973. Just two months and a day later, on January 1, 1974, he was killed on U.S. Highway 50 east of Placerville, California while assisting with an auto accident.

This book is published to make Dr. Harper's approach to presenting engineering fundamentals as applied to basic food processing available to students majoring in food science. The chapters in this book were in manuscript form and used in several food engineering courses in the U.S. and Canada prior to his death. It was Dr. Harper's plan to have several of his colleagues prepare additional chapters and then later publish their joint work as a textbook generally following the report of the Institute of Food Technologists Task Force on subject matter for the course in food engineering. The full report of the Task Force as it was published in the March, 1969 issue of *Food Technology* is reprinted as Appendix II in this book. Instructors using this text are encouraged to provide supplementary lecture material and laboratories for a year long course as outlined in the Task Force report.

We are pleased to have had a part in preparing this memorial for John Harper, our colleague and close personal friend. There are many whom John Harper would have thanked for their contributions to what he had written had he lived to publish this book. With only sketchy records and his remarkable memory now silent, we sincerely thank each of his contributing colleagues, whomever they may be. We have succeeded in fulfilling a deep and patient desire of his wife—Jeanette; publishing his book and should there be any royalties from its sale, making them available through the Cal Aggie Foundation on the Davis Campus for students majoring in food engineering.

JOHN R. GOSS
University of California, Davis
DENNIS R. HELDMAN
Michigan State University
RICHARD L. MERSON
University of California, Davis
ERNEST L. WATSON
University of British Columbia

July 1976

Contents

CHAPTER 1

Engineering Dimensions and Units[1]

INTRODUCTION

Quantitative results of any engineering investigation must ultimately be expressed in terms of numbers. Before any intelligent study of engineering can be undertaken, it is therefore necessary to have a clear understanding of the dimensions and units in which the physical quantities commonly used in engineering are expressed and to be able to convert among different sets of units.

Dimensions

A dimension is a term describing the kind of physical quantity under consideration. For example, length, area, volume, time, force, mass, velocity, temperature, energy, electric charge, etc. are all different dimensions. It is, of course, possible to express certain of these dimensions in terms of others. Thus, area has the dimensions of length squared; velocity has the dimensions of length divided by time. In equational form, we would write

$$\text{area } [A] = [L^2]$$

$$\text{velocity } [V] = [L/\theta]$$

The symbol θ is used to represent time so that T can be reserved for absolute temperature.

Units

A unit is a term used to measure the size or amount of a quantity of a certain dimension. Thus, inches, feet, centimeters and miles are all units measuring the dimension, length. Engineering data are given in a variety of units, and it is frequently necessary to convert from one to another. These conversions may be conveniently effected by using the defining relationships.

Example 1.—Convert a velocity of 60 miles/hr to ft/sec. We write

$$5280 \text{ ft} = 1 \text{ mile and } 3600 \text{ sec} = 1 \text{ hr}$$

Alternatively, these equations can be expressed as

$$5280 \, \frac{\text{ft}}{\text{mile}} = 1 \text{ and } 3600 \, \frac{\text{sec}}{\text{hr}} = 1$$

---

[1] Symbols used in this chapter are listed and defined at the end of the chapter.

Since each of these conversion factors is equal to unity, any quantity can be multiplied or divided by them without changing its value. If the factors are arranged so that unwanted units cancel, the desired result will be obtained.

$$\left(60\,\frac{\text{miles}}{\text{hr}}\right)\left(5280\,\frac{\text{ft}}{\text{mile}}\right)\left(\frac{1}{3600}\,\frac{\text{hr}}{\text{sec}}\right) = \frac{60\,(5280)}{3600}\,\frac{\text{ft}}{\text{sec}} = 88\,\frac{\text{ft}}{\text{sec}}$$

Tables of unit conversion factors are given in all the scientific and engineering handbooks. If used in the above manner, no difficulty will be encountered in deciding whether to multiply or divide by the factor. Some selected conversion factors are given in Table A.4 of the Appendix.

UNITS FOR COMMON DIMENSIONS

The most important dimensions in working with problems in mechanics are mass, length, time, and force. These dimensions are related by Newton's second law of motion, which may be stated as: "The force acting on a body is proportional to the product of its mass and acceleration." In the form of an equation, this law is written as

$$f = Kma$$

The dimensions of force, mass, and acceleration can be expressed in a wide variety of units. The numerical value of the constant K is fixed by the particular set of units being used. The units of length and time are well enough understood that they need not be further discussed here.

Mass

Mass is a measure of the quantity of matter. It should be clearly distinguished from weight, which is the force exerted on a body by the Earth's gravitational attraction. For any material, a given mass represents a definite number of molecules and is independent of any changes in volume or gravitational attraction. Mass may also be defined in terms of the inertia of a body, that is, its resistance to a change in motion. Consider, for example two doors, one of steel and the other of wood. If properly hung, the doors do not assume any different positions because of their different weights, which are represented by the downward pull of gravity. Yet it requires a great deal more effort to set in motion the steel door than the wooden one. Clearly, some property other than weight is involved, and this *property* is *mass*.

By international agreement, a kilogram (kg) is defined as the mass of a certain block of platinum-iridium preserved in Sevres, France. The pound mass (lb_m) is the mass of a block of platinum preserved in London and is equal to 0.45359 kilogram. The slug is a unit of mass sometimes used in engineering calculations and is equal to 32.17 pounds mass.

Acceleration

Acceleration is the rate at which the velocity of a body is changing. Thus, we may write for velocity

$$v = ds/d\theta$$

where s and θ represent distance and time, respectively. For acceleration

$$a = dv/d\theta = d(ds/d\theta) = d^2s/d\theta^2$$

Acceleration thus has the dimensions $[L]/[\theta^2]$. Any free body in the earth's gravitational field will be accelerated according to the law of gravitational attraction. This acceleration, represented by the symbol g, varies with local position on the earth and with altitude. By international agreement, the standard value is taken as 32.1739 ft/sec^2 or 980.665 cm/sec^2. For simplicity, these numbers will be rounded off to 32.17 and 980.7 in the remainder of this book.

Force

The resultant force on an object is given by Newton's second law, as stated above. In selecting units of force, it would be possible to set arbitrarily the size of the unit, thereby fixing the value of the proportionality constant, K. Another procedure is to establish the size of the unit by assigning some convenient numerical value to K. The simplest choice of a numerical value of K is unity, and this value is the one most commonly used in physics and in some branches of engineering. In the CGS (centimeter-gram-second) system, with mass in grams mass, acceleration in cm/sec^2, and K equal to unity, the force is given in dynes. Clearly, one dyne is the force necessary to give one gram mass an acceleration of one cm/sec^2. The corresponding unit in the English system is the poundal which is the force necessary to give one pound of mass an acceleration of one ft/sec^2. The poundal is rarely used and need not be given further consideration for engineering purposes. Electrical engineers now extensively use the MKS (meter-kilogram-second) system. This system has the advantage of the unity conversion factors of the CGS system, but results in standard units of a more convenient size. The newton is the force required to give one kilogram of mass an acceleration of one meter/sec^2.

As an alternative to assigning K a value of unity, unit force may be defined as the *weight* of unit mass at a location where the acceleration due to gravity has the standard value. As explained above, the weight of a body is the force exerted on it by the earth's gravitational attraction. If the body is placed on a spring scale, the spring must exert a restraining force just equal to that resulting from the accelerating force of gravity. This restraining force can be measured by the extension of the spring. The commonly used English engineering unit for force is called the pound force (lb_f) and is defined as the weight of one pound mass at a location where g equals 32.17 ft/sec². Alternatively, it can be said that one pound force is the force necessary to give one pound mass an acceleration of 32.17 ft/sec². With these units, the weight of a body in lb_f is numerically equal to its mass in lb_m wherever the local acceleration of gravity is 32.17 ft/sec². If g is lower, as at a high altitude, the weight of the body will be less. A properly calibrated spring scale measures weights, whereas a beam balance compares masses.

In order to be able to use a value of K equal to unity in Newton's second law and retain the pound force as the unit for force, the slug is sometimes used as a unit of mass. The slug is then defined as that mass which will be given an acceleration of one ft/sec² by a force of one lb_f. Since one lb_f will give one lb_m an acceleration of 32.17 ft/sec², the slug clearly represents a larger quantity of matter than the lb_m, and numerically, one slug equals 32.17 lb_m. The slug-lb_f combination is widely used in fluid mechanics.

Considerable confusion is caused among many students (and practicing engineers) by the use of the name "pound" for the common engineering unit of both mass and force. To obtain correct numerical answers and correct dimensional checks in many engineering calculations, it is necessary to distinguish carefully between these two quantities. As an aid, it is customary to use the symbol lb_m for pound mass and lb_f for pound force.

SYSTEMS OF UNITS AND DIMENSIONS

All equations must be dimensionally consistent. In other words, each term on both sides of an equation must represent the same kind of quantity and thus have the same net dimensions. If an equation does not check dimensionally, then it cannot be correct. Whenever an equation or expression is derived, it should be given a dimensional check, and any one making engineering calculations should develop some facility in handling dimensions. It is important to note that in making a dimensional check of an equation, the *units* in which the quantities are expressed need not be considered. If a general equation has been derived, the result will usually be expressed in terms of certain symbols, which represent quantities of different dimensions. Frequently, however, no specific units are attached to these symbols. Thus, the symbol L would indicate length, but the units might be feet, inches, centimeters, meters, or one of many other possibilities. *It must be emphasized that when substituting numbers into equations, the necessary conversion factors must be used so that all terms have consistent units.*

It was stated earlier that many dimensions can be expressed in terms of other dimensions. It is found that a minimum of three independent dimensions are necessary and sufficient to express all quantities encountered in ordinary mechanics. For thermal and electromagnetic quantities, it is necessary to include additional dimensions. The three fundamental dimensions can then be related by the laws of mechanics to give all other dimensions.

It is entirely permissible to use more than the minimum of three dimensions in establishing a system. In physics, a three dimensional system of mass, length, and time, with the proportionality constant in Newton's second law taken as unity, is commonly used. Because of the wide variety of units employed in engineering calculations and the large number of conversion factors therefore encountered, certain problems are simplified if force is defined as a fourth fundamental dimension.

Three Dimensional System

In the three dimensional system commonly employed in physics courses, the basic dimensions are taken as mass, length, and time. Force is obtained as a derived dimension from Newton's second law. Thus, remembering that acceleration is the time rate of change of velocity, $dv/d\theta$, and has the dimensions $[L]/[\theta^2]$, force is

$$f = Kma,$$

with dimensions

$$[F] = [M][L]/[\theta^2]$$

In this system, the proportionality constant K must be dimensionless. Work or energy, which is given by a product of force and distance, has the dimensions

$$[E] = [F][L] = [M][L^2]/[\theta^2]$$

Other dimensions can be built up in a similar manner, but do not necessarily convey a physical meaning.

Four Dimensional System

Many engineers prefer to use a four dimensional system as it somewhat facilitates the task of keeping units in order and emphasizes the distinction between mass and force. Numerical answers must, of course, be the same regardless of which system is used. Force is given a separate dimension instead of being expressed in terms of $[M]$, $[L]$, and $[\theta]$. In order that Newton's second law be dimensionally consistent, it is therefore necessary to assign dimensions (and units) to the proportionality constant, K. Rearranging the equation for force, we find that

$$K = \frac{f}{ma}$$

$$[K] = \frac{[F][\theta^2]}{[M][L]}$$

The numerical value of K depends on the units used for mass, force, length, and time. Consider that a mass of one pound is subjected to the standard accelerating force of gravity. From the definitions of force units given above, we know that the force must be one pound force. Substituting into Newton's second law,

$$f = Kma \text{ for which } 1 \text{ lb}_f = K(1 \text{ lb}_m)(32.17 \text{ ft/sec}^2)$$

For consistency of dimensions and units on both sides of the equal sign, the equation is solved for $1/K$, thus

$$\frac{1}{K} = 32.17 \frac{\text{lb}_m \text{ ft}}{\text{lb}_f \text{ sec}^2} = g_c$$

Because the reciprocal of the proportionality constant is numerically equal to the standard acceleration of gravity in this case, it is given the symbol g_c. The constant g_c has the units shown and the dimensions

$$\frac{[M][L]}{[F][\theta^2]}$$

The constant g_c appears in the same place in a three dimensional system, but there it is dimensionless. *It should be emphasized that in no case does g_c have either the units or dimensions of acceleration.* In the CGS system

$$1 \text{ dyne} = K(1 \text{ gram-mass})(1 \text{ cm/sec}^2)$$

$$\frac{1}{K} = 1 \frac{\text{gram-mass cm}}{\text{dyne sec}^2}$$

In following Table 1.1, some of the more commonly used sets of units are shown, together with the corresponding values of the proportionality constant. The unit of time for all units is the second. It will be noted that the units of mass and force are selected so that $1/K$ is *numerically* equal either to unity or to the standard acceleration of gravity. The former has the advantage of giving simpler conversion factors. The latter has the advantage that, under the acceleration of gravity, the weight of an object is numerically equal to the mass. It is this equality that frequently allows a correct numerical answer to be calculated even though a clear distinction may not be made between a pound mass and a pound force.

Example 2.—Determine the force necessary to give 5 lb_m an acceleration of 8 ft/sec². If we want the answer in lb_f, $1/g_c$ must be used for the proportionality constant K.

$$f = \frac{1}{g_c} ma = \left(\frac{1}{32.17} \frac{\text{lb}_f \text{ sec}^2}{\text{lb}_m \text{ ft}}\right)(5 \text{ lb}_m)\left(8 \frac{\text{ft}}{\text{sec}^2}\right) = 1.2 \text{ lb}_f$$

TABLE 1.1

SETS OF UNITS COMMONLY USED

Force	Mass	Length	Proportionality Constant, $1/K$
dyne	gram-mass	cm	$1 \dfrac{\text{gram cm}}{\text{dyne sec}^2}$
gram-force	gram-mass	cm	$g_c = 980.7 \dfrac{\text{gram-mass cm}}{\text{gram-force sec}^2}$
newton	kilogram	meter	$1 \dfrac{\text{kg meter}}{\text{Newton sec}^2}$
poundal	pound-mass	ft	$1 \dfrac{\text{lb}_m \text{ ft}}{\text{poundal sec}^2}$
pound-force	pound-mass	ft	$g_c = 32.17 \dfrac{\text{lb}_m \text{ ft}}{\text{lb}_f \text{ sec}^2}$
pound-force	slug	ft	$1 \dfrac{\text{slug ft}}{\text{lb}_f \text{ sec}^2}$

Example 3.—At a location where $g = 30$ ft/sec^2, how much mass must be used on a vertical piston to exert a force of 6 lb$_f$? Give answer in lb$_m$ and in slugs.

$$m = \frac{g_c f}{a} = \left(32.17 \frac{\text{lb}_m \text{ ft}}{\text{lb}_f \text{ sec}^2} \right) (6 \text{ lb}_f) \left(\frac{1}{30} \frac{\text{sec}^2}{\text{ft}} \right) = 6.4 \text{ lb}_m$$

$$m = \frac{f}{Ka} = \left(1 \frac{\text{slug ft}}{\text{lb}_f \text{ sec}^2} \right) (6 \text{ lb}_f) \left(\frac{1}{30} \frac{\text{sec}^2}{\text{ft}} \right) = 0.2 \text{ slugs}$$

OTHER PHYSICAL QUANTITIES

Several other quantities that are of importance in processing calculations can be defined in terms of the units and dimensions discussed above.

Density

Density is defined as mass per unit volume (not weight per unit volume), and has the dimensions $[M]/[L^3]$. Customary units are lb$_m$/ft^3 or gram/cm^3. The density of water at 4°C is 1.000 gram/cm^3. Specific gravity is defined as the ratio of the density of a liquid or solid to the density of water. Because of thermal expansion effects, in stating specific gravity it is necessary to specify both the temperature of the material and the temperature of water to which it is referred. Since specific gravity is a simple ratio, it is a dimensionless number and has the same value in any set of units. The density of a substance in gram/cm^3 is approximately equal numerically to its specific gravity, but the two values are quite different in English units. It is therefore desirable to avoid the common practice of using density and specific gravity as synonyms.

Pressure

Pressure is force per unit area, with dimensions of $[F]/[L^2]$. In processing calculations, we are concerned with a hydrostatic, or fluid pressure, which is a pressure that exists uniformly in all directions. Thus, an object surrounded by fluid (either liquid or gas) will be subject to the same pressure on all sides. The most common engineering unit of pressure is the $lb_f/in.^2$, frequently referred to as psi.

Work and Energy

Work is done when a force acts through a distance. If a man pushes a car along a street, for example, the work he does is equal to the product of the force he exerts and the distance the car moves. If the car does not move, he does no work in a mechanical sense, even though he may be expending a great deal of effort. Since work can be expressed as the product of a force and a distance, it obviously has the dimensions $[FL]$. The engineering unit is the $ft\text{-}lb_f$, commonly called the foot-pound. In using this latter term, it must be remembered that it is a pound of force, not a pound of mass. The fundamental CGS unit of work is the dyne-cm, or erg. Since an erg represents a very small quantity of work, the joule, equal to 10^7 ergs, is frequently used.

Work is one form of energy, and energy is frequently defined as the ability to do work. Energy thus has the same units and dimensions as work. Kinetic and potential energy are two types of particular importance. Kinetic energy is energy that an object possesses because of its velocity, or the work required to impart a given velocity to an object initially at rest. To develop an expression for kinetic energy, let us consider a body of mass m whose velocity, v, is increased by a differential amount dv in a length of time $d\theta$. The distance traveled is the product of velocity and time, or $vd\theta$; and the acceleration is the rate of change of velocity, or $dv/d\theta$. The force acting on the body is given by Newton's second law

$$f = km(dv/d\theta)$$

and

$$\text{Work} = f \times s = Km(dv/d\theta)(vd\theta) = Kmvdv$$

In order to obtain the total kinetic energy acquired in going from rest to a final velocity v, we must integrate the above expression between the limits of zero and v

$$\text{Kinetic Energy } (KE) = \text{Work} = \int_0^v Kmvdv = Kmv^2/2$$

where the constant K is selected according to the units desired.

Example 4.—A mass of 3 lb_m has a velocity of 15 ft/sec. What is its kinetic energy? If we use the kinetic energy expression as it is commonly written with the factor K equal to unity,

$$KE = mv^2/2 = 3(15)^2/2 = 337.5(lb_m)(ft^2)/(sec^2)$$

Although this is a valid answer, it is not given in the usual units. In order to obtain the desired units, we must divide by the proportionality constant g_c

$$KE = \left(337.5 \frac{(lb_m)(ft^2)}{(sec^2)} \right) \left(\frac{1}{32.17} \frac{(lb_f)(sec^2)}{(lb_m)(ft)} \right) = 10.5 \text{ ft-lb}_f$$

This example illustrates the necessity of making a clear distinction between mass and force. Overlooking the difference can result in serious numerical errors.

The potential energy of a body is represented by the amount of work required to raise it to a given elevation above some reference level. Here, the force is given by the product of the mass and the gravitational acceleration, and the distance is the height, z. As before, we must divide by g_c to obtain the conventional engineering units.

$$PE = mgz/g_c$$

Power

Power is the rate of doing work, or the rate of expenditure of energy, and has the dimensions $[FL]/[\theta]$. In the English system, power can be expressed in ft-lb$_f$/sec or ft-lb$_f$/min. A more commonly used unit is the horsepower which, by definition, is equal to 550 ft-lb$_f$/sec. In the metric system, the most common unit is the watt, which is one joule/sec.

CONVERSION OF DIMENSIONS

As explained at the beginning of this chapter, dimension designates the kind of a physical quantity, and it is not ordinarily possible to convert one dimension to another. For example, a length could never be made equivalent to a velocity. In any equation that correctly expresses a relationship among physical quantities, it must be possible to reduce all terms to the same dimensions.

Mass and force in a 4-dimensional system represent an exception to the above statement regarding conversion. Newton's second law gives a direct relationship between mass and force that can be used to eliminate one in terms of the other. In the usual 3-dimensional system, this relationship is always used, and force is not considered to be a separate dimension. In eliminating either mass or force, it is helpful to look upon the constant g_c

as a dimensional conversion factor to be used in the same way as unit conversion factors. Recalling that 1 lb$_f$ = 32.17 (lb$_m$)(ft)/)sec^2, the ratio

$$32.17 \frac{(lb_m)(ft)}{(lb_f)(sec^2)} = g_c$$

can be considered to be identically equivalent to unity, just as the ratio 60 sec/min is equivalent to unity. Accordingly, any term in an equation can be multiplied or divided by g_c without changing the relative values of the terms, although the numerical magnitude and units of the terms will change. If the units of all terms are clearly set down, it becomes immediately obvious whether one should multiply or divide by g_c in order to eliminate an unwanted unit of either lb$_m$ or lb$_f$, just as in the example of kinetic energy above.

PROBLEMS

1. Make the following conversions, using standard values for the relationship of length and mass units. Derive force-unit conversions on the basis of the definitions given in Table A.4 in the Appendix rather than using values listed in tables.

a) 925 cm/sec to miles/hr
b) 480 cm/sec^2 to ft/hr^2
c) 62.4 lb$_m$/ft^3 to gram/cm^3
d) 1.013 × 10^6 dyne/cm^2 to lb$_f$/in.^{2}
e) 8750 ft-lb$_f$ to joules and to kilowatt-hours
f) 10 kw to ft lb$_f$/sec and to horsepower

2. Using the following information, compute a factor to convert pressure in millimeters of mercury to lb$_f$/in.^{2}. Remember that the pressure at the bottom of a column of liquid is equal to the weight of the liquid divided by the cross-sectional area. Use your factor to find the standard atmospheric pressure in lb$_f$/in.^{2}.

density of mercury = 13.6 gram-mass/cm^3
2.54 cm = 1 inch
454 gram-mass = 1 lb$_m$
standard acceleration of gravity = 980 cm/sec^2 = 32.17 ft/sec^2
standard atmospheric pressure = 760 mm Hg

3. The gravitational force on the surface of the moon is about 1/6 of that on the earth. In the cargo of a space craft that has landed on the moon is a beam balance with a set of weights, a spring scale that was calibrated on the earth, and a one pound mass of iron. What would be the indicated weight of the iron on the beam balance? On the spring scale? What is the true weight and mass of the iron on the moon? If the iron is in a space ship

in orbit around the earth, what is its true weight and mass? Give reasons for your answers.

4. Thermal energy quantities are usually measured in calories or Btu. Calculate a factor to convert Btu to ft-lb$_f$, using only the following information:

4.185 joules = 1 calorie (a joule is 10^7 dyne-cm)
252 calories = 1 Btu
454 gram-mass = 1 lb$_m$
1 ft = 12 in. = 30.48 cm
g = 980 cm/sec^2 = 32.2 ft/sec^2
g_c = 980 (gram-mass)(cm)/(gram-force)(sec^2) = 32.2 (lb$_m$)(ft)/(lb$_f$) (sec^2)

5. A fluid of density ρ is flowing through a pipe with a velocity V and a pressure drop ΔP. Show that the kinetic energy per pound of fluid flowing has the same dimensions as ΔP divided by ρ. If the density is 70 lb$_m$/ft^3, the velocity 3 meter/sec, and the pressure drop 25 psi, calculate the ratio of the kinetic energy and pressure drop terms in consistent units.

SYMBOLS

$[A]$	dimensions of area
a	acceleration
°C	temperature in degrees Centigrade
CGS	centimeter-gram-second system of units
cm	centimeter
$[E]$	dimensions of energy or work
$[F]$	dimensions of force
f	force
ft	feet
g	gravitational acceleration
g_c	reciprocal of constant of proportionality (K) in Newton's second law, 32.17 lb$_m$ft/lb$_f$sec^2 of 980 gm-mass cm/gm-force sec^2
hr	hour
K	constant of proportionality in Newton's second law
$[K]$	dimensions of K
kg	kilogram
KE	kinetic energy
L	length
$[L]$	dimensions of length
lb$_f$	pound force
lb$_m$	pound mass
$[M]$	dimensions of mass
m	mass

MKS	meter-kilogram-second system of units
PE	potential energy
psi	pounds per square inch
s	distance
sec	second
T	absolute temperature
$[V]$	dimensions of velocity
v	velocity
z	height
θ	time
$[\theta]$	dimension of time

CHAPTER 2

Mass Balance

INTRODUCTION

Many food processes involve separating or combining constituents in order to achieve desired product characteristics. Such processes may be accompanied by chemical changes. Some examples of separation processes are evaporation, dehydration, distillation, absorption, and ion exchange. Most processed foods represent some blending of ingredients.

LAW OF CONSERVATION OF MASS

The basis for calculating the relative quantities of materials in such processes is the law of conservation of mass. This simply states that the quantity of material put into an operation must equal the quantity that comes out. It must apply to individual constituents as well as to the total. In the case of chemical change, the law is expressed in terms of chemical groups or elements.

The law can be written as

$$\text{input} - \text{output} = \text{accumulation}$$

As stated above, this relation must apply to the total, to individual constituents, and to chemical elements. In continuous, or steady state processes, there is by definition no accumulation, and the input is equal to the output. A continuous process is usually desired in large-scale operations because of the resulting simplifications in control of process variables and product quality. Particularly in smaller scale operations, it may be convenient to introduce the ingredients as a batch and to withdraw the entire quantity upon completion of the process. Sometimes a combination of continuous and batch processing may be used in which one or more feed or product streams flow continuously, but in which there is accumulation or depletion of some constituents within the operation until processing is completed. For example, if a material is dried in an oven, moisture will flow off continuously (but not at a constant rate), until the drying is completed, while the solid remains behind.

MAKING A MASS BALANCE

The first step in making a mass balance is to define a system to which the balance will be applied. A good way of visualizing a system is to imagine a large envelope placed around a piece of equipment or section of the processing operation. Any material that crosses this envelope must be accounted for in the mass balance. This envelope, which is called the boundary of the system, can be shown as a dotted line on a sketch of the operation. Any stream flow line that intersects this dotted line must enter into the balance. On the other hand, streams that do not cross the boundary do not enter into the balance. For example, within an over-all process, streams may divide, recirculate, and recombine. Any such activity that goes on entirely within the system boundary does not form a part of the mass balance. In batch or simple continuous operations, there will be no problem in deciding where to locate the system boundary. In more complex operations, with multiple streams and recirculation, considerable ingenuity may be required to select the most advantageous boundary location. Many times, solution of a problem will require that a complex system be divided into sections, with a separate balance around each section.

Following the definition of the system boundary, the next step is to choose a basis for calculation. A batch operation might have the total quantity of material in a batch as a basis. For continuous operation, the quantity of material flowing over a time period such as an hour or a day might be used. It will usually be most convenient, however, to select a unit quantity such as 100 pounds of a constituent or a stream as a basis. In particular, it is desirable to select a constituent that goes through the process unchanged in mass. In a dehydrator, for example, the solid stream continuously changes in mass as water is removed. The dry matter in the solid stream has the same mass entering and leaving and therefore provides a fixed basis for calculation. A constituent that goes through a process unchanged in this manner is called a "tie" substance, as it ties together the input and output streams. In semi-continuous operation, some streams flow continuously, but not necessarily at a constant rate, and there will be accumulation (or depletion) within the system. Here, the mass balance relationship must be applied to all constituents over some definite period of time.

The steps to be followed in making mass balances can be summarized as follows:

1. Draw a sketch or diagram representing the process, including all pertinent information on stream rates and compositions.
2. Show the boundaries of the system with a dotted line and select an appropriate basis for calculation.
3. Designate letters or other symbols to represent unknown quantities that are to be determined.
4. Write the mass balance relationships for the various constituents in terms of the known and unknown quantities.
5. Solve the resulting algebraic equations for the unknown quantities. Sometimes a solution of several simultaneous equations may be necessary.

These principles can be best understood by studying several examples. It should be emhasized that many times there will be more than one suitable choice of system and basis for a particular problem.

Example 1

One-half ton per hour of diced carrots are dehydrated in a parallel-flow dehydrator from 85% to 20% moisture content. Air with a moisture content of 0.013 lb water/lb dry air enters the dehydrator at a rate of 400 lb of dry air per lb of dry solid. Calculate the moisture content of the air leaving the dehydrator.

In a parallel-flow dehydrator, both the solid and the air streams enter at one end and flow in the same direction to the other end, as shown in the diagram. We will choose one lb of dry matter as the basis for calculation.

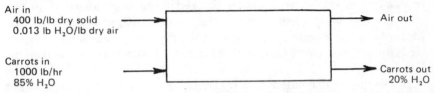

Air in
400 lb/lb dry solid
0.013 lb H_2O/lb dry air

Air out

Carrots in
1000 lb/hr
85% H_2O

Carrots out
20% H_2O

The entering solids contain 85 parts of moisture to 15 parts of dry matter, so the moisture entering with one lb of dry matter is 1.0(85/15) = 5.67 lb. Similarly, the moisture leaving in the solid stream is 1.0(20/80) = 0.25 lb. For one lb of dry matter, there are 400 lb of dry air with a moisture content of 400(0.013) = 5.2 lb. Since there is no accumulation in a continuous process, the total moisture in is equal to the total out. Letting m represent the moisture contained in the leaving air,

$$5.67 + 5.2 = 0.25 + m$$

$$m = 10.62 \text{ lb}$$

moisture content = 10.62/400 = 0.0266 lb water/lb dry air

To develop a more general relationship for this type of problem, we proceed in the following manner. Let X represent moisture in the solid per lb of dry matter and Y the moisture in the air per lb of dry air. The pounds per unit time of dry matter are S and the pounds per unit time of dry air are G. The subscripts 1 and 2 refer to the entering and leaving streams, respectively.

$$\text{moisture entering} = SX_1 + GY_1$$
$$\text{moisture leaving} = SX_2 + GY_2$$

Equating the entering and leaving moisture and rearranging,

$$SX_1 - SX_2 = GY_2 - GY_1$$
$$X_1 - X_2 = (G/S)(Y_2 - Y_1)$$

From the figures given, we see that $X_1 = 5.67$ lb, $X_2 = 0.25$ lb, $Y_1 = 0.013$ lb H_2O/lb dry air, and $G/S = 400$. Substituting these numbers into the above equation, we obtain

$$Y_2 = (X_1 - X_2)(S/G) + Y_1$$
$$= (5.67 - 0.25)/400 + 0.013 = 0.0266 \text{ lb water/lb dry air}$$

Moisture contents X and Y in the above general relationship are referred to as being on a dry basis, whereas the usual moisture percentage is expressed on a wet or total basis (as Example 1). Since the amount of dry matter remains constant, dry basis moisture contents have a basis that does not change throughout the process. Accordingly, the difference between the initial and final dry basis moisture contents is a direct measure of the amount of moisture lost or gained. Ordinary percentage moisture, or wet basis moisture contents are commonly used in reporting composition, but this value is based on a total weight that is constantly changing as drying proceeds. Consequently, the difference between the initial and final wet basis moisture contents has no direct significance in mass balance calculations.

If X is the water content on a dry basis and x is the water ratio content on a wet basis then, for one lb of dry matter,

$$\text{wt. of moisture} = X \text{ lb}$$

$$\text{total wt. of dry matter and moisture} = 1 + X \text{ lb}$$

$$x = \text{wt. of moisture/total wt.} = X/(1 + X)$$

$$100x = \text{wt. \% (percent moisture content, wet basis)}$$

Also

$$X = x/(1 - x)$$

Although the above discussion refers to moisture content, the same considerations apply any time there are variable constituents in some kind of constant carrier stream, whether solid, liquid, or gas. Absorption, adsorption, and extraction operations all fall in this category. The following example illustrates the necessity for selecting a proper basis.

Example 2

Hops are commonly dried by blowing heated air up through a bed about 3 feet deep in a batch operation. At the end of the drying period, the hops at the bottom will have the lowest moisture content, and the moisture content will increase continuously up through the bed. The hops are then mixed and placed in a tempering room where the moisture is allowed to equalize through the entire volume. After a particular drying run, samples

taken from succeeding 6-inch layers of a 36-inch bed showed the following
moisture contents on a wet basis:

Layer	Wt. % Water
1 (bottom)	1.1
2	2.3
3	3.9
4	7.5
5	12.9
6 (top)	19.4

What will the moisture content be after equalization? The volume (or
thickness) of a layer does not change as drying proceeds.

If the thickness does not change, each layer must contain the same
amount of dry matter, regardless of the moisture content. We will select
as a basis a vertical section through the bed that contains one lb of dry
matter in each layer, or a total of 6 lb. On this basis, the weight of moisture
in each layer is simply equal to X, and the sum of the X values is the total
moisture with 6 lb of dry matter in the final product. Calculating X from
the previous relation, we obtain the following results:

Layer	x	X
1	0.011	0.0111
2	0.023	0.0235
3	0.039	0.0406
4	0.075	0.0811
5	0.129	0.1481
6	0.194	0.2407
		0.5451 total moisture

For one lb of final dry matter, the moisture content is 0.5451/6 = 0.0908
lb.

Since $X = 0.0908$ lb, then

$x = 0.0908/(1 + 0.0908) = 0.0832$, or 8.32% moisture, wet basis

If we had merely taken an average of the original moisture percentages, we
would have obtained 7.85%.

Example 3

A winery produces a uniform sherry by blending to obtain the desired
alcohol and sugar contents. The compositions of the desired product and

the available blending wines are given in the following table.

	Wt. % Alcohol	Wt. % Sugar
wine A	14.6	0.2
wine B	16.7	1.0
wine C	17.0	12.0
blend	16.0	3.0

We will take as a basis 100 lb of blended product and let the letters A, B, and C represent the weights of the individual wines.

Alcohol balance: $0.146A + 0.167B + 0.170C = 16$ wt. %

Sugar balance: $0.002A + 0.01B + 0.12C = 3$ wt. %

Total balance: $A + B + C = 100$ lb

We have three equations and three unknowns and can solve for the quantities A, B, and C. The results are

$A = 36.4$ lb

$B = 42.8$ lb

$C = 20.8$ lb

Example 4

Tomato flakes are being dehydrated as shown in the diagram below. Parallel flow of air and tomatoes is used in the first stage and countercurrent flow in the second stage. Part of the air leaving the second stage is mixed with the air entering the first stage. In the diagram, x is wt. fraction moisture in the solid; Y, the pounds of moisture per pound of dry air; and G, the air rate in pounds of dry air per pound of dry solid. Determine the quantity of air returned from the second to the first stage and the moisture content of the tomatoes leaving the first stage.

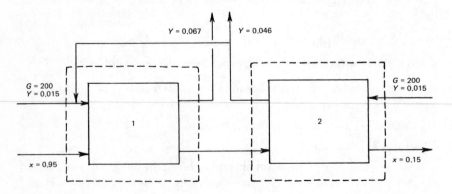

A basis of one lb of dry solid will be used. The dry-basis moisture contents of the tomatoes entering and leaving are

$$X_1 = 1.0(95/5) = 19 \text{ lb}$$

$$X_2 = 1.0(15/85) = 0.18 \text{ lb}$$

The moisture content of the intermediate stream is represented by X_i. Making a moisture balance around the second stage as shown by the dotted line,

$$\text{moisture in} = \text{moisture out}$$

$$X_i + 200(0.015) = 0.18 + 200(0.046)$$

$$X_i = 6.38 \text{ lb H}_2\text{O/lb dry matter}$$

It will be noted that the system boundary is drawn inside the point at which the recycle stream is taken off. Therefore, the amount of dry air leaving is the same as that entering the system. We will now make a balance around the first stage, letting R stand for the dry air in the recycle. The moisture content of the recycle is the same as that of the air leaving the second stage, and the total dry air leaving the first stage becomes 200 + R.

$$19 + 200(0.015) + 0.046R = 6.38 + 0.067(200 + R)$$

$$R = 106 \text{ lb dry air}$$

PROBLEMS

1. During formulation of a new food product, 30 lb of one component containing 30% solids are mixed with an unknown amount of another component containing 80% solids. If 250 lb of the food product are desired, compute the amount of 80% solids component necessary. What is the composition of the new food product?

2. In the manufacture of strawberry jam, the crushed fruit is mixed with sufficient sugar to give a mixture of 48 parts of fruit to 52 parts of sugar, and sufficient pectin is added (about 4 oz/100 lbs of sugar). The mixture is then evaporated until the refractometer indicates a soluble solids content of 67%. Determine the expected yield of jam from the fruit which has 20% soluble solids.

3. Vegetables leaving a dehydrator with a moisture content of 4 wt.% are to be put in packages containing 1 lb of dry matter. It is desired to reduce the moisture content to 1.5 wt.% by placing a desiccant in each package with the vegetable. The desiccant takes up moisture from the vegetable and when equilibrium is reached, the desiccant contains 9 times as much moisture as the vegetable, expressed as lb moisture/lb dry solid for each. If the des-

iccant initially has zero moisture, what weight of desiccant is required for each package?

4. The usual frozen orange juice concentrate is reconstituted by mixing one volume of concentrate with 3 volumes of water. In order to provide a fresh flavor character, the 3:1 concentrate is manufactured by mixing a 4:1 concentrate with fresh juice. Starting with 100 gallons of fresh juice, how much should be concentrated to a 4:1 ratio so that when the 4:1 concentrate is mixed with the remaining fresh juice, a 3:1 concentrate is obtained? Note that a 4:1 concentrate means that 4 volumes of water mixed with 1 volume of concentrate is equivalent to fresh juice. It may be assumed that the solids content of the juice in any concentration does not affect the volume.

5. The composition of ethanol-water solutions is frequently expressed as volume per cent. When ethanol and water are mixed, the volumes are not additive, and volume per cent ethanol is defined as the number of volumes of pure ethanol in 100 volumes of solution. In a certain distillation operation, the product contains 39.9 vol. % ethanol at 15°C. At this temperature, the specific gravity of the product of 0.952, the density of pure water is 0.999 gram/ml, and the density of pure ethanol is 0.794 gram/ml.

a) Calculate the weight percent and mole percent ethanol in the mixture.

b) How many ml of pure water must be mixed with 39.9 ml of pure ethanol to produce 100 ml of solution?

6. Studies have been made of the possibility of producing concentrated beer by freezing out a portion of the water. One such process is conducted as shown in the diagram below. From the information given, calculate the total quantity of each constituent (including water) in each of the streams. All concentrations are in weight percent.

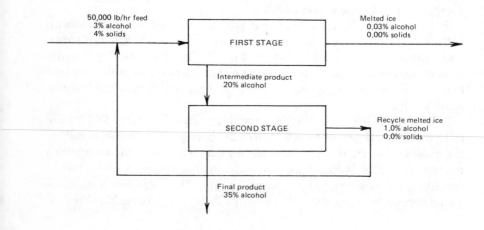

7. A milk evaporator producing feed for a spray dryer has a normal output of 25,000 lb per hour of concentrated milk, and the total daily production is 200,000 lb. The dryer feed rate is 20,000 lb/hr. In the daily operating procedure, the evaporator is started up first, and the dryer is put into operation when 30,000 lb of concentrated milk have accumulated in the tank. The two units are then operated at their normal capacities until the daily milk supply is consumed. It is desired that, at all times, there be sufficient excess storage capacity in the tank to handle the entire production from the evaporator in the event that the dryer must be shut down for a period of up to one hour to correct some operating difficulty. What storage tank volume is required to meet this condition?

8. In an experimental program, a pilot plant vacuum evaporator is being used to concentrate tomato pulp. In operation, the evaporator is first filled with fresh tomato pulp. As evaporation continues, fresh feed is continuously added so as to maintain a constant liquid level. When the material in the evaporator reaches the desired concentration, the operation is stopped and the product withdrawn. In one such test, samples taken at half-hour intervals had the following concentrations:

Time, hours	Wt. Fraction Total Solids (fresh pulp)
0	0.050
0.5	0.080
1.0	0.114
1.5	0.145
2.0	0.170
2.5	0.182
3.0	0.205
3.5	0.217
4.0	0.236
4.5	0.242
5.0	0.245
5.5	0.251

When full, the evaporator contains 28 gallons of liquid. The tomato pulp has a specific gravity equal to $1 + 0.428x$, where x is the wt. fraction total solids.

a) On the basis of the above data, make a plot of total pounds evaporated and the total pounds of feed vs. time.

b) Plot the rate of evaporation in pounds per hour vs. concentration.

   c) Assuming that the rate of evaporation can be expressed by the equation

$$dE/d\theta = a + bx + cx^2$$

determine the numerical values for the constants a, b, and c.

For adequate accuracy in this problem, plots should be carefully drawn on good graph paper. In making your plots, keep in mind that the actual behavior should be represented by smooth curves that will not necessarily pass through all of the experimental points.

CHAPTER 3

The First Law of Thermodynamics[1]

INTRODUCTION

The First Law of Thermodynamics is merely a quantitative expression of the principle of conservation of energy. It may be considered to be a method of accounting in which energy, rather than money, is balanced. Inasmuch as energy is associated with all material, mass, as well as energy, must be accounted for. The law has significance only where transfers of mass or energy are involved. In order to apply the law, the terms will be defined in the following sections.

THE SYSTEM

The system is that region in space or quantity of matter for which the transfers of mass and energy are to be accounted. The system must be clearly defined by its *boundaries*. The boundaries of a system may be physical, imaginary, or a combination of both. For example, if a process is being conducted in a closed tank, the walls of the tank would logically be the boundary of the system. In a study of weather phenomena, some region in the atmosphere, without any physical boundaries might be the system. The region outside the system is called the *surroundings*. A process which a system undergoes usually involves interchange of mass and/or energy with the surroundings. A *closed system* is one of constant mass, and only energy is interchanged with the surroundings. In an *open system,* both mass and energy are interchanged. A special case of the open system is the *steady state flow system.* In such a system, mass enters and leaves at the same rate, so that constant mass is contained within the system boundaries at all times. Furthermore, although properties such as temperature and pressure may be different at different points within the system, these properties do not change with time. A plate heat exchanger being used to pasteurize milk is an example of a steady state flow system. Milk flows through the exchanger at a constant rate. The temperatures are different at the entrance and discharge, but each of these remains constant. The steady flow system is the type most commonly encountered in engineering thermodynamics.

CHARACTERISTICS OF SYSTEMS

A *property* is any reproducible characteristic of a system. Some examples of properties are temperature, pressure, volume, density, viscosity, and heat

---

[1] Symbols used in this chapter are listed and defined at the end of the chapter.

capacity. Most of these are *intensive properties,* in that they do not depend on the mass, or extent, of the system. For example, the temperature of boiling water at normal atmospheric pressure is 212°F whether the container holds a gram or a pound. Volume is an *extensive property,* because its magnitude is directly proportional to the mass. It will be noted that any extensive property of a homogeneous substance can be converted to an intensive property by dividing by the mass. Thus, although two pounds of water has twice the volume of one pound at the same temperature and pressure, the *specific volume* in cu. ft. per lb. is the same regardless of the mass. In this case, specific volume is merely the reciprocal of density.

The *state* of a system is its condition, as fixed by values of its properties. If a system is allowed to pass through a variety of changes and is then brought to a condition in which its properties are the same as they were at some previous time, it is in the same state. If the state of a system is fixed, all its properties are fixed at some definite value. A *process* occurs whenever a system changes from one state to another.

ENERGY OF A SYSTEM

Energy quantities in thermodynamics may be divided into two broad categories: those associated with the state of the system, which are therefore properties; and those which comprise energy in transit and are recognizable only while the system is undergoing a process.

External energy is that form of energy which a system possesses because of its velocity or position. For present purposes, these may be considered to be kinetic energy and gravitational potential energy. It should be noted that values of these forms of energy depend on the selection of arbitrary frames of reference with respect to which velocities and elevations are measured. In many cases, selection of an appropriate frame of reference will allow changes in these energies to be eliminated.

Internal energy is that energy associated with the atomic and molecular structure of a substance. No arbitrary frame of reference can be found which will allow changes in internal energy to drop out. The forms in which internal energy can appear are as follows:

Nuclear energy—associated with the binding energies of nuclear particles.

Chemical energy—associated with the binding energies of atoms within a molecule.

Thermal energy—associated with translation, rotation, vibration and electron shifts of molecules. This form of energy is directly related to temperature.

Molecular energy—associated with forces of attraction or repulsion among molecules. A latent heat of vaporization, for example, represents the difference in molecular energy between a liquid and a vapor.

A substance in any state has a definite value of internal energy, which is usually designated by the letter U (or sometimes E). Strictly, the total energy of a substance is that given by the theory of relativity, mc^2, where m is the mass and c the velocity of light. In thermodynamics, we are interested only in changes in energy, not in absolute values of energy. Furthermore, ruling out nuclear reactions, the energy changes encountered are very small compared with the relativistic energy. Therefore, it is common practice to express energy quantities above some arbitrary reference state.

HEAT AND WORK

Energy in transit is defined as energy crossing the boundaries of a system during a process as a result of some difference between the properties of the system and its surroundings. All forms of energy in transit may be classified as either heat or work. Heat and work can never be properties of a system. They exist only during a process and show up only as a change in the energies of the system and the surroundings. Just as there are an infinite number of paths one can follow in going from one place to another on the earth, so there are an infinite number of paths (or processes) that a system can follow in passing from one state to another. Since all properties of the system depend only on the state, the difference in energy between any two states is the same regardless of the path followed by the system. However, heat and work, will, in general, be different for each path.

Heat is energy transferred across the boundary of a system as a result of a temperature difference between the system and the surroundings, and is usually represented by the letter Q. By established convention, we say that heat entering a system is positive and heat leaving is negative. Sometimes it is possible to determine the amount of heat transferred from changes in properties of the system and a knowledge of heat capacities and latent heats. If a material is heated without change in phase, we may write:

$$Q = \int_{t_1}^{t_2} c\,dt$$

If the heat capacity (or specific heat), c, is constant, this expression becomes

$$Q = c(t_2 - t_1) = c\,\Delta t$$

Because Q depends on the path followed, it is necessary to designate a heat capacity for each path. The commonest path is one of constant pressure, which occurs if a substance is heated while exposed to the atmosphere. In this case,

$$Q = \int c_p\,dt \qquad \text{Eq. 3-1}$$

On the other hand, if a cylinder of compressed gas were heated, the process would take place at constant volume, and

$$Q = \int c_v dt \qquad \text{Eq. 3-2}$$

For most solids and liquids, the numerical difference between c_p and c_v is negligible. For gases, the difference may be as much as 40%. Heat capacities of common substances are listed widely in tables of physical and chemical properties.

It is also possible to determine the quantity of heat transferred by other methods. For example, an instrument known as a heat flow transducer is available which, when placed on a surface, generates an electrical signal that is directly proportional to the rate of heat flow.

Work is energy crossing the boundary of a system as a result of any other agency than a temperature difference. Work can always be resolved into an action equivalent to a force moving through a distance. In many cases, the work effects associated with a process can be calculated by an examination of external conditions. For example, the work input to a pump may be obtained from the current drawn by the driving motor. This type of procedure is not always possible. Many times, it is necessary to estimate the work that would be required under some set of postulated conditions. It is therefore essential to have some expression for work based on the changes in the system rather than on external effects. Such an expression can be obtained by making what is frequently called a "mechanical energy balance." The validity of such a procedure does not depend on the law of conservation of energy, but on the laws of mechanics which state that work is given by the product of a force and the distance through which it moves. As stated previously, all work effects can be resolved into the action of a force acting through a distance. For convenience, it is desirable to classify these work effects in the groups given below. By convention, work done by a system is considered positive and work done on a system, negative.

Work of Changing Volume

Suppose a gas at pressure P is contained in the piston-cylinder arrangement shown. Let A be the area of the piston. The gas exerts a force on the piston

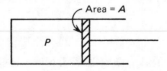

equal to the product of the pressure and area, or

$$f = PA$$

Suppose now that the piston is allowed to move out a very small distance, dL. The differential work done by the gas on the piston is therefore

$$dW = fdL = PAdL$$

The product AdL is merely the change in volume of the gas, dv. Therefore

$$dW = Pdv$$

$$W = \int Pdv$$

In this chapter, small v is used for volume and capital V for velocity. In order to integrate this expression and find the work for a finite change in volume, the relationship between P and v during the process must be known. This is another way of saying that the path of the process must be known in order to calculate the work.

Work of Changing Velocity

Work must be done in order to change the velocity of an object (or a system). In this case, the work is represented by the change in kinetic energy. If the kinetic energy increases (ΔKE is positive), work must have been done on the system, and W is negative. Therefore,

$$W = -\Delta KE$$

Work of Changing Elevation

If the elevation of an object is changed in the earth's gravitational field, there is an associated quantity of work which is equal to the change in potential energy. By the same reasoning as above, a negative sign appears, so that

$$W = -\Delta PE$$

Work to Overcome Friction

If any friction is present, in addition to the above work effects, a corresponding amount of work must be expended.

$$W = -F$$

It should be noted that friction is always a positive number. If work is done by the system (so that W is positive), the net work out put will be reduced by the amount of friction. If work is done on the system (W negative), friction will require that more work be added. The complete expression for work is given by the sum of all the above terms.

$$W = \int Pdv - \Delta KE - \Delta PE - F$$

or

$$W + F = \int Pdv - \Delta KE - \Delta PE \qquad \text{Eq. 3-3}$$

Certain work effects, such as those resulting from the action of electric and magnetic fields, have not been explicitly included in this discussion. Such work effects usually do not enter into applications of thermodynamics to chemical (or food) processing, and the expressions are simplified by omitting them.

First Law Expression for a Closed System

The law of conservation of energy states that the net energy added to the system during any process is equal to the increase in energy of the system. The change in energy of the system is the sum of its changes of internal, kinetic, and potential energies. In terms of the symbols defined above,

$$Q - W = \Delta U + \Delta KE + \Delta PE \qquad \text{Eq. 3-4}$$

If W is eliminated between Eq. 3-3 and 3-4, we obtain

$$(Q + F) - \int P dv = \Delta U \qquad \text{Eq. 3-5}$$

Clearly, the effect of friction is the same as though an equivalent amount of heat were added to the system, so that Q and F are logically grouped together. Suppose now that we heat a substance in a closed, rigid container, so that volume is constant. There is no friction, and the change in volume, dv, is zero, so that the expression becomes

$$Q = \Delta U \qquad \text{Eq. 3-6}$$

We now have an additional expression and a more general one than Eq. 3-1 for calculating constant volume heat quantities. To use this, of course, we must have a table of internal energies of the substance in question.

By an elementary theorem in calculus,

$$P dv + v dP = d(Pv)$$

or

$$\int P dv + \int v dP = \Delta Pv$$

Using this expression to eliminate $\int P dv$ from Eq. 3-5, we obtain

$$(Q + F) + \int v dP = \Delta U + \Delta Pv$$

$$= (U_2 - U_1) + (P_2 v_2 - P_1 v_1)$$

$$= (U_2 + P_2 v_2) - (U_1 + P_1 v_1)$$

The sum, $U + Pv$, appears so frequently in thermodynamics that it is given a separate symbol, H, and is commonly known by the name enthalpy. In process calculations with flow systems, enthalpy is a much more important property than internal energy, and tables and charts of enthalpies are available for many substances. For a heating process, we may now write

$$Q + \int v dP = \Delta H \qquad \text{Eq. 3-7}$$

If the heating is at constant pressure, dP is equal to zero, and

$$Q = \Delta H. \qquad \text{Eq. 3-8}$$

Because constant pressure heating is such a common process, enthalpy is called "heat content" in some textbooks on chemical thermodynamics.

First Law Applied to Steady-State Flow Systems

Consider a fluid in steady flow through some system as shown in the diagram. The box represents any kind of apparatus involving mechanical work and heat transfer. The boundaries of the system will be taken as the walls of the apparatus and two imaginary lines drawn across the entrance and discharge pipes. Note that the symbol W_s represents work transmitted by some kind of shaft through the walls of the apparatus. *If there is no such shaft in a system, there can be no shaft work.* (A magnetic or electric force could take the place of a mechanical shaft.)

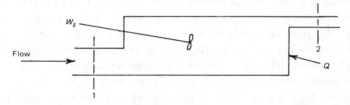

In treating a steady flow system, it is convenient to base equations and calculations on unit mass (usually one-pound-mass) of fluid flowing. By considering a unit mass to be surrounded by an imaginary membrane separating it from the surrounding fluid, we may apply Eq. 3-4 to the energy transfers that occur as the mass moves through the apparatus.

$$Q - W = U_2 - U_1 + KE_2 - KE_1 + PE_2 - PE_1$$

Note that subscripts 1 and 2 refer to conditions existing at the entrance and discharge of the apparatus, respectively. The total work done on the unit mass is given by Eq. 3-3. This total work is also equal to all the work done on the steady flow system for each unit mass that flows through. One component of this total work is the shaft work, W_s. Another component occurs at the entrance. When one unit mass is pushed into the system, work is done on the system. This work is equal to the product of the pressure at section 1 and the volume displaced, or $-P_1 v_1$. In this expression, v is the volume of a unit mass, or specific volume. By virtue of the definition of a steady state flow system, P_1 and v_1 are constant. The minus sign is used because work is done on the system. At the same time that a unit mass enters at section 1, another unit mass leaves at section 2. In order to push this unit mass out into the surroundings, the system must do work equal to $P_2 v_2$. The total work is therefore given by the expression

$$W = W_s - P_1 v_1 + P_2 v_2 \qquad \text{Eq. 3-9}$$

From Eq. 3-3 we can write

$$W = \int Pdv - \Delta KE - \Delta PE - F$$

or

$$W_s + F = \int Pdv - \Delta Pv - \Delta KE - \Delta PE$$

using the previous transformation for the pressure-volume integrals, we have

$$W_s + F = -\int vdP - \Delta KE - \Delta PE \qquad \text{Eq. 3-10}$$

remembering that the specific volume is the reciprocal of the density,

$$W_s + F = -\int dP/\rho - \Delta KE - \Delta PE \qquad \text{Eq. 3-11}$$

If the density is constant, Eq. 3-11 becomes the usual expression derived in chapters on fluid flow as an extension of Bernoulli's equation for incompressible fluids. If the density of the fluid changes during the flow process, the integral in Eq. 3-11 is not simply $\Delta P/\rho$. To perform the integration, the relationship between pressure and density for the specific process must be known. In handling flow processes, we are always interested in the shaft work, which is the work that must be supplied in order to drive the equipment, rather than the total work effect. For this reason, Eq. 3-10 rather than Eq. 3-3 is used in this situation. The power requirement for the shaft drive is obtained by multiplying the work per unit mass by the mass flow rate to give work per unit time.

Substituting Eq. 3-9 into Eq. 3-4, we obtain

$$Q - W_s = \Delta U + \Delta Pv + \Delta KE + \Delta PE$$

or

$$Q - W_s = \Delta H + \Delta KE + \Delta PE \qquad \text{Eq. 3-12}$$

Equation 3-12 shows that enthalpy, rather than internal energy, is the important energy property in steady flow processes. For example, in the compression of a gas, heat transfer and kinetic and potential energy effects are usually negligible. The work required is therefore equal to the change in enthalpy. If a fluid is being heated or cooled in a heat exchanger, there is no shaft work and changes in kinetic and potential energy will be negligible. In this case, the change in enthalpy is equal to the heat transferred.

SYMBOLS

A	area
c	specific heat when not dependent on process
c_p	specific heat at constant pressure

c_v specific heat at constant volume
f force
F friction work
H enthalpy of product
KE kinetic energy
L length
m mass
PE potential energy
P pressure
Q quantity of heat transferred
t temperature (not absolute)
U internal energy
v volume and specific volume, i.e., volume of a unit mass
V velocity
W work
W_s work transferred into a process or system, usually by a mechanical shaft
ρ density
Δ change in a property such as enthalpy, kinetic energy, etc.

CHAPTER 4

Thermodynamic Properties of Pure Substances[1]

INTRODUCTION

This chapter does not constitute a comprehensive treatment of the subject of thermodynamic properties. Rather, its purpose is to present in concise form the necessary background to serve as a basis for subsequent study of various processing operations. For a more complete treatment of this subject, the student should refer to one of the many available texts on engineering thermodynamics.

PRESSURE-VOLUME-TEMPERATURE RELATIONSHIPS

In the previous chapter, equations were derived for obtaining energy effects associated with processes, or changes in state, of materials. These changes in state must be specified in terms of properties of the material. As it turns out, the most important properties in the thermodynamic equations are also the simplest ones to measure in an actual process, namely, pressure, volume, and temperature. For a pure substance which may exist in gas, liquid, or solid phases, a knowledge of at most two of these properties is sufficient to establish the thermodynamic state of the material and therefore to establish values of all intensive properties.

Gases

The simplest representation for gases is the perfect gas law, which may be written

$$Pv = NRT \qquad \text{Eq. 4-1}$$

where P is pressure; v, volume; N, moles; T, absolute temperature; and R, the universal gas constant. Absolute temperatures are given in degrees Kelvin on the centigrade scale and degrees Rankine on the fahrenheit scale, where

$$°K = °C + 273.2 \text{ and } °R = °F + 459.7$$

For engineering purposes, these numerical values are usually rounded off to 273 and 460. A mole is a number of units of mass of a substance numerically equal to its molecular weight. For example, since oxygen has a molecular weight of 32, one gram-mole has a mass of 32 grams, and one pound-mole has a mass of 32 lb_m. The universal gas constant is a physical

---

[1] Symbols used in this chapter are listed and defined at the end of the chapter.

constant whose numerical value depends only on the units in which it is expressed. Values of R corresponding to some of the more commonly used units of pressure, volume and temperature are given in the Table 4.1.

TABLE 4.1

UNIVERSAL GAS CONSTANT (R) VALUES

Pressure	Volume	Temp.	N	R
lb_f/ft^2	ft^3	°R	lb-mole	1545
lb_f/in^2	ft^3	°R	lb-mole	10.73
atmospheres	ft^3	°R	lb-mole	0.7302
atmospheres	cm^3	°K	gram-mole	82.06

Engineering references occasionally list values of specific gas constants for individual gases. These are merely the universal gas constant divided by the molecular weight. The use of a specific gas constant means that the perfect-gas law is written for one pound rather than one mole.

To obtain the dimensions of R, we rearrange Eq. 4-1 to give

$$R = Pv/NT = \frac{[F][L^3]}{[L^2][M][T]} = \frac{[F][L]}{[M][T]}$$

The numerator of the above expression is the product of force and length, or energy, and can be converted to thermal energy units of calories or Btu. In thermal units of either cal/(gram-mole)(°K) or Btu/(lb_m-mole)(°R), R has the numerical value 1.986.

The perfect-gas law is an excellent approximation to the behavior of monatomic and diatomic gases such as helium, hydrogen, oxygen, nitrogen, etc. at reasonably low pressures and at temperatures well above the critical temperature. These conditions are well satisfied in any ordinary application to food processing operations. At the limit of zero pressure, all gases follow the perfect-gas law. The gases mentioned above show satisfactory agreement at pressures up to a few hundred psi, and more complex gases, such as the lower molecular weight hydrocarbons, agree reasonably well at pressures up to the vicinity of standard atmospheric pressure. There are various methods for improving upon the perfect-gas law, but these are unnecessary in any ordinary food processing application. For a discussion of such methods, a standard thermodynamics textbook should be consulted.

The perfect-gas law can be applied to mixtures as well as to pure gases. In this case, the value of N_t is the total number of moles of all gases present. It is convenient to define an average molecular weight that, when divided into the total mass, m_t, gives the total moles. Thus, if the symbol M_{av} represents average molecular weight,

$$N_t = N_a + N_b + N_c + \ldots$$

$$m_t = m_a + m_b + m_c + \ldots = N_a M_a + N_b M_b + N_c M_c + \ldots$$

$$M_{av} = m_t/N_t = (N_a/N_t)M_a + (N_b/N_t)M_b + (N_c/N_t)M_c + \ldots$$

Since the moles of any individual gas divided by the total moles is simply equal to the mole fraction, x,

$$M_{av} = x_a M_a + x_b M_b + x_c M_c + \ldots$$

For practical calculations, air is considered to consist of 0.21 mole fraction oxygen and 0.79 mole fraction nitrogen. Minor constituents, primarily argon and carbon dioxide, are lumped with the nitrogen. The average molecular weight of air, calculated on the basis of the true average composition, is 29.0.

Example 1.—Nitrogen gas from a cylinder is used to flush an apparatus. During a certain period of use, the pressure gage reading on the cylinder drops from 100 psi to 5 psi. If the cylinder has a volume of 1.0 ft³, how many cubic feet of nitrogen, measured at atmospheric pressure, were delivered in this period? The temperature remained constant throughout the operation.

At constant temperature, the product of pressure and volume remains constant, and we can write

$$(Pv)_{cylinder} = (Pv)_{atm.}$$

or,

$$v_a = (P_c/P_a)v_c$$

where subscripts a and c refer to atmospheric and cylinder. For the initial and final cylinder pressures, we have

$$v_a' = (P_c'/P_a)v_c$$

$$v_a'' = (P_c''/P_a)v_c$$

where v_a' and v_a'' represent the volumes of gas that would be obtained if the nitrogen were expanded from the cylinder pressures P_c' and P_c'' to atmospheric pressure. The net volume delivered is the difference between v_a' and v_a'', or

$$v_a' - v_a'' = (v_c/P_a)(P_c' - P_c'') = (1.0/14.7)(100 - 5) = 6.46 \text{ ft}^3$$

It should be noted that the values given for P_c are gage pressures and it is necessary to add 14.7 to these in order to obtain absolute pressures for use with the perfect-gas law. If only a difference in pressure is involved, as in the above calculation, the constant atmospheric pressure drops out, and the difference in gage pressures can be used.

Example 2.—What is the density of air in lb_m/ft^3 at 1 atm. pressure and 160°F as calculated from the perfect-gas law?

$$Pv = NRT = (m/M)RT$$

where m is mass and M is molecular weight. Density is mass divided by volume and, for the given conditions, $P = 14.7\ lb_f/in.^2$; $T = 460 + 160 = 620°R$; $M = 29.0$; and $R = 10.73$.

$$\rho = m/v = MP/RT = (29.0)(14.7)/(10.73)(620) = 0.0640\ lb_m/ft^3$$

Liquids

The volume (or density) of liquids is affected by both pressure and temperature. Extremely high pressures are needed to have an appreciable effect on the density of a liquid, and we will not encounter these in processing applications. The relatively small effect of temperature on the volume of a liquid can be satisfactorily expressed in terms of a constant coefficient of volumetric expansion. Values of such coefficients for various liquids are listed in handbooks of physical and chemical data, as well as extensive tables of densities as a function of temperature.

Vapor-Liquid Equilibrium

Consider an experiment in which pure water is introduced into a completely evacuated metal cylinder until it is about ¼ full. The space above the liquid will then be occupied by water vapor alone. The cylinder is fitted with a pressure gage, a thermometer, and a window for viewing the contents. The cylinder is now held in a constant-temperature bath until the temperature is uniform throughout. The readings of the pressure gage and thermometer are recorded at this equilibrium condition. If we raise the temperature of the bath and again wait for an equilibrium condition to be established, we will obtain another set of temperature and pressure readings. We will also observe that the level of water has dropped as a result of evaporation. Continuation of this process will yield a series of pressure and temperature readings that can be plotted as represented by the line ab in Fig. 4.1. Eventually, a temperature will be reached at which the liquid phase completely evaporates and only vapor remains. If the temperature is raised beyond this point, the plot will follow a new line as represented by bd. If the experiment is repeated with a somewhat larger amount of water in the cylinder, the points will fall on the same line except that the curve will extend to some point b' before the liquid completely evaporates. With the cylinder initially over half full, we will find that the volume occupied by the liquid actually increases as the temperature is raised and that at some

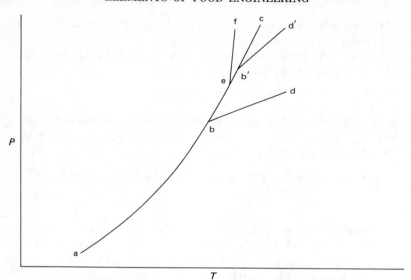

FIG. 4.1. LIQUID-VAPOR EQUILIBRIUM AT CONSTANT VOLUME

point e, no vapor remains. Further increase in temperature will give points falling along ef.

These results show that as long as vapor and liquid are in equilibrium, there is a fixed relationship between pressure and temperature. If the value of either one is specified, the value of the other is determined. All substances that can exist as liquid and vapor have vapor pressure curves similar to that of Fig. 4.1, and tables of vapor pressure data for many substances are listed in various handbooks and reference works. When a liquid being heated in an open container reaches a temperature at which its vapor pressure is equal to the pressure of the atmosphere, bubbles of vapor can form within the liquid, and boiling results.

If exactly the right amount of liquid is initially placed in the cylinder, the level will show little change as the temperature rises. At some temperature the liquid-vapor interface, which will be near the center of the cylinder, will suddenly disappear without either rising or falling. If the temperature is lowered, the interface will reappear in its former position. The explanation for this phenomenon is that the properties of the liquid and vapor phases have become identical, so that it is no longer possible to distinguish between them. As the temperature rises in this experiment, the density of the vapor increases because of the greatly increased pressure. On the other hand, temperature has a greater effect than pressure on the liquid density, which therefore decreases.

Eventually, the densities of the phases become the same, with the result noted above. The corresponding point on the vapor pressure curve is known

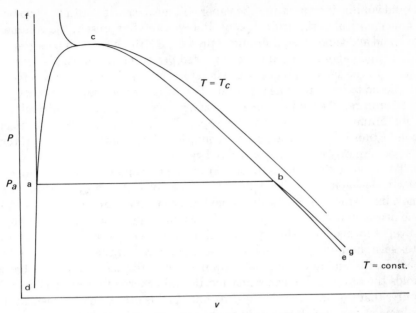

FIG. 4.2.   LIQUID-VAPOR EQUILIBRIUM

as the critical point and is designated by c in Fig. 4.1. Unless the correct amount of liquid is initially placed in the cylinder, a point such as b or e will be reached first, and the critical point phenomenon will not be observed. The critical point thus represents the upper limit of the vapor pressure curve. At temperatures above the critical, the substance is always in the vapor phase, and it is impossible for a liquid phase to exist, regardless of how much pressure is applied. Data on critical pressures and temperatures of many substances are readily available.

It should be noted that solids as well as liquids have vapor pressure curves. At temperatures below the freezing point, there will be equilibrium between solid and vapor rather than liquid and vapor. For any substance, there is one condition of temperature and pressure, called the triple point, at which solid, liquid, and vapor are all in equilibrium.

In the two-phase region, the equilibrium temperature and pressure are unaffected by the relative amounts of liquid and vapor present. A plot of pressure versus volume is more useful in giving a picture of the changes occurring on vaporization than is a vapor pressure curve. Let us suppose that in the previous experiment, we had also measured the specific volume in ft^3/lb_m of both the liquid and vapor at each temperature. A plot of these data would appear as in Fig. 4.2. Because vapor volumes at low pressures are so large, the volume scale in Fig. 4.2 has been compressed for purposes of illustration. It is seen that as the pressure and temperature increase the

liquid volume increases and the vapor volume decreases until the two become identical at the critical point. Points a and b represent the volumes
of liquid and vapor in equilibrium at pressure P_a. Because a and b represent
liquid and vapor in equilibrium at a fixed pressure, they must also correspond to the same temperature. Therefore, a horizontal line drawn from
the liquid to the vapor line represents both constant pressure and constant
temperature. The equilibrium liquid at a is called saturated liquid, and the
equilibrium vapor at b is saturated vapor. The line from d up to the critical
point c thus represents all possible conditions for saturated liquid, and the
line ec similarly represents saturated vapor.

To visualize the process involved in going from point a to b, consider a
new experiment in which 1 lb_m of water is placed in a cylinder with a
movable piston. The apparatus is held in a constant temperature bath and
the piston moved back (increasing the volume) until the first tiny bubble
of vapor forms. Since the liquid at this point is in equilibrium with vapor,
it is saturated liquid corresponding to a in Fig. 4.2. If the piston is moved
back further, more vapor must form in order to fill the volume. The bath
holds the temperature constant, and the vapor pressure relationship requires that the pressure also be constant. As this process of increasing the
volume at constant temperature continues, the material in the cylinder
follows a condition represented by the horizontal line from a to b, with the
proportion of vapor constantly increasing. When all of the liquid has
vaporized except for an infinitesimal droplet, the cylinder is completely
filled with saturated vapor corresponding to point b.

If the outward movement of the piston is continued after all the liquid
has vaporized, the process will consist of constant temperature expansion
of a gas, and the pressure will fall along the curve bg. The shape of this curve
is given qualitatively by the perfect gas relation, which states that the
product of pressure and volume is constant at constant temperature. Beyond point b, the vapor is no longer saturated, but is instead at a higher
temperature than that of saturated vapor at the same pressure. Vapor in
this region, to the right of the saturation curve, is called superheated vapor.
If the piston is compressed when the cylinder is filled with saturated liquid
at point a, the pressure will rise rapidly with little change in volume along
a line af. This liquid, to the left of the saturated liquid line, is called compressed or subcooled liquid.

The line fabg represents the relationship of pressure to volume as one
pound of water passes from a compressed liquid to a superheated vapor
state at constant temperature. If sufficient experimental data are available,
it is possible to draw a family of such constant temperature lines. The
constant temperature line for the critical temperature has no straight
section in the 2-phase region, as the saturated liquid and vapor lines coin-
cide at the critical point. However, the line has a point of inflection with
a horizontal tangent at c.

A plot such as Fig. 4.2 that includes a family of constant temperature lines provides complete information about the pressure-volume-temperature behavior of a substance. In the single phase regions, outside the saturation curve dce, the value of any two of these variables will allow the third to be obtained from the plot. A point lying within the saturation curve represents a mixture of saturated liquid and vapor at that pressure (and temperature). A simple relationship can be derived among the total volume of the mixture, the saturated liquid and vapor volumes, and relative amounts of liquid and vapor. Let x equal the wt. fraction of vapor. If the total weight is 1 pound, there are x pounds of vapor and $(1 - x)$ pounds of liquid. The volume occupied by the vapor is therefore xv_g, where v_g is the specific volume of saturated vapor in ft^3/lb_m. Likewise, the volume occupied by liquid is $(1 - x)v_f$, where v_f is the specific volume of saturated liquid. The total volume is the sum of the vapor and liquid volumes, or

$$v = xv_g + (1 - x)v_f$$

Solving for x, we obtain

$$x = \frac{v - v_f}{v_g - v_f} = \frac{v - v_f}{v_{fg}} \qquad \text{Eq. 4-2}$$

In this equation, v_{fg} represents the difference between the saturated vapor and liquid volumes.

The foregoing discussion has been primarily directed toward developing concepts and definitions concerning relationships among pressures, volume, and temperature for gases and liquids. The application of these ideas and the use of tabulations of data on these properties will be discussed in the final section of this chapter, following a treatment of thermal properties.

THERMAL PROPERTIES

Quantity of Heat

By thermodynamic definition, heat is energy that enters or leaves a system as a result of a temperature difference. In popular language, the term is loosely used and is frequently confused with temperature. For example, when someone says that he can't stand the heat, he really means that he can't stand the temperature. As was pointed out in the previous chapter, the properties of a system are affected by the addition or removal of heat, but heat is recognizable only as energy being transferred and is not a property.

Quantity of heat has traditionally been defined in terms of its effect on the temperature of a stated mass of water. On this basis, a calorie is the quantity of heat necessary to raise the temperature of one gram of water from 14.5 to 15.5°C, while a Btu refers to one lb_m of water going from 59.5 to 60.5°F. Because it is possible to measure electrical quantities with far greater precision than thermal quantities, primary energy units are now specified in terms of electrical measurements, and the calorie and Btu are defined in terms of the electrical units. From a physical point of view, however, it is convenient to think in terms of the older definitions.

As a result of improvements in accuracy of measurements and changes in primary standards, some variation in conversion factors for energy units is found throughout the literature. Furthermore, such factors may be based on absolute units derived from fundamental physical laws or on international units that are based on certain specified electrical measurements. For practical engineering purposes, these differences are inconsequential, and the following factors for the mechanical equivalent of heat will be considered satisfactory for applications in this text:

$$1 \text{ Btu} = 778 \text{ ft-lb}_f$$
$$1 \text{ cal} = 4.186 \text{ joule}$$

Heat Capacity

Consider an experiment in which a quantity of material is heated, without a change in phase such as melting or vaporization. If electrical heating is used, we can easily measure the amount of energy added, and we can also measure the temperature corresponding to any energy addition. Heat capacity refers to the quantity of heat that can be absorbed for a stated change in temperature. If the heat capacity of the material is constant, a plot of heat added versus temperature will be a straight line, the slope of which is equal to the heat capacity. In the usual case, the line is not straight, showing that heat capacity is temperature-dependent, and the value of the heat capacity at a particular temperature is given by the slope of the tangent at that point. The heat absorbed during this hypothetical experiment is obviously proportional to the quantity of material, and heat capacity is therefore expressed on the basis of unit mass.

As discussed in the previous chapter, the amount of heat transferred depends on the path of the process. Heat capacities are commonly defined only in terms of constant pressure and constant volume heating. Since the slope of a tangent to the heating curve is given by dQ/dt, we can write

$$c_p = (dQ/dt)_p$$
$$c_v = (dQ/dt)_v$$

where c is heat capacity and the subscripts p and v represent constant pressure and constant volume. The difference between c_p and c_v is related to the thermal expansion of the material. A constant volume process means that no expansion is permitted, and there consequently will be a rise in pressure as the temperature rises. With constant pressure heating, the volume increases, and there is an accompanying work of expansion for which energy must be supplied. Accordingly, more heat is required in the constant pressure than in the constant volume process, and c_p is larger than c_v. Thermal expansion of liquids and solids is so small that the difference between c_p and c_v can be neglected for engineering purposes. The difference is important for gases, but we will find very little occasion to use constant volume heat capacities in engineering calculations.

Heat capacities may be expressed in cal/(gram)(°C) or Btu/(lb$_m$)(°F). For gases, it is frequently advantageous to use a mole basis rather than a unit mass. From the definitions of the calorie and Btu given above, it is seen that the heat capacity of water is 1 cal/(gram)(°C) or 1 Btu/(lb$_m$)(°F). Heat capacities therefore have the same numerical value whichever set of units is used. The term specific heat, when used precisely, refers to the ratio of the heat capacity of a substance to that of water, analogous to the term specific gravity in relation to densities. Because numerical values of heat capacity are the same in CGS and English units, in contrast to the situation with density, confusing the terms specific heat and heat capacity does not lead to numerical errors.

Heat capacity is a property of a material, and values are widely listed in tables of physical and chemical data. For all materials, solid, liquid, or gas, heat capacity increases with increase in temperature. Any effect of pressure can be neglected for liquids and solids. Pressure has no effect on the heat capacity of a perfect gas. Since the perfect-gas law is generally suitable for food processing applications, the effect of pressure on gas heat capacity need not be considered here.

The primary application of heat capacities is to calculate the relation between quantity of heat and temperature change in a heating or cooling process. For a constant pressure process, for example, we can write

$$Q = \int_{t_1}^{t_2} c_p dt \qquad \text{Eq. 4-3}$$

If the temperature range is small enough that c_p can be considered constant, the heat is simply given by the product of c_p and the temperature change, or $Q = c_p(t_2 - t_1)$. For large temperature changes, it may be necessary to perform the integration in Eq. 4-3. In any event, information on the variation of c_p with temperature is needed. Table 4.2 lists heat capacities per mole as a function of temperature for common gases. For cases in which an exact integration of Eq. 4-3 is needed, the data in Table 4.2 have been integrated to give the mean heat capacities listed in Table 4.3. In this table, mean heat capacity is defined as

$$c_{pm} = \frac{1}{t - 77} \int_{77}^{t} c_p dt \qquad \text{Eq. 4-4}$$

where t is in °F. To find the heat necessary to raise the temperature of one

TABLE 4.2

HEAT CAPACITIES OF GASES AT CONSTANT PRESSURE

c_p in Btu/(lb Mole)(°F) at Zero Pressure

°F	O_2	N_2	H_2	CO	CO_2	H_2O	SO_2	CH_4	C_2H_4	C_2H_6	C_3H_6	C_3H_8
0	6.97	6.95	6.78	6.95	8.38	7.98	8.99	8.14	9.33	11.33	13.63	15.42
77	7.02	6.96	6.89	6.96	8.87	8.02	9.45	8.54	10.41	12.59	15.27	17.57
100	7.03	6.96	6.90	6.96	9.00	8.03	9.59	8.66	10.72	12.96	15.75	18.19
200	7.12	6.97	6.95	6.98	9.56	8.11	10.11	9.30	12.09	14.65	17.85	20.92
300	7.24	6.99	6.97	7.01	10.05	8.23	10.56	10.03	13.41	16.34	19.89	23.56
400	7.37	7.03	6.98	7.08	10.49	8.35	10.96	10.80	14.67	18.00	21.85	26.06
500	7.49	7.10	6.99	7.16	10.88	8.48	11.32	11.60	15.83	19.57	23.67	28.36
600	7.63	7.17	7.00	7.25	11.24	8.64	11.63	12.38	16.89	21.05	25.36	30.46
700	7.76	7.25	7.01	7.34	11.55	8.79	11.90	13.14	17.86	22.42	26.91	32.39
800	7.88	7.34	7.03	7.44	11.84	8.95	12.13	13.87	18.75	23.70	28.35	34.17
900	7.98	7.43	7.05	7.53	12.10	9.12	12.32	14.56	19.58	24.90	29.67	35.82
1000	8.07	7.52	7.07	7.62	12.34	9.28	12.49	15.21	20.34	26.03	30.89	37.35
1100	8.15	7.61	7.11	7.72	12.55	9.45	12.63	15.84	21.05	27.08	32.03	38.77
1200	8.23	7.69	7.15	7.81	12.75	9.62	12.76	16.42	21.71	28.05	33.09	40.10
1300	8.30	7.78	7.18	7.89	12.92	9.79	12.87	16.99	22.33	28.96	34.07	41.33
1400	8.36	7.85	7.23	7.96	13.08	9.96	12.96	17.50	22.90	29.81	34.97	42.47
1500	8.41	7.92	7.28	8.03	13.23	10.13	13.04	17.97	23.43	30.61	35.80	43.52
1600	8.47	7.99	7.33	8.10	13.36	10.30	13.12	18.42	23.92	31.33	36.58	44.49
1700	8.52	8.05	7.39	8.15	13.48	10.46	13.18	18.83	24.38	31.99	37.29	45.37
1800	8.57	8.11	7.45	8.21	13.59	10.62	13.23	19.23	24.81	32.62	37.96	46.21
1900	8.61	8.17	7.51	8.26	13.69	10.78	13.28	19.62	25.21	33.20	38.59	47.00
2000	8.65	8.21	7.56	8.31	13.79	10.92	13.34	19.94	25.58	33.74	39.16	47.71
2100	8.68	8.26	7.62	8.35	13.88	11.06	13.38	20.26	25.92	34.25	39.69	48.37
2200	8.72	8.31	7.68	8.40	13.95	11.20	13.41	20.56	26.23	34.70	40.18	48.99
2300	8.75	8.35	7.73	8.44	14.01	11.30	13.44					
2400	8.79	8.38	7.78	8.47	14.08	11.41	13.47					
2500	8.82	8.42	7.84	8.50	14.15	11.51	13.50					

2600	8.86	8.45	7.89	8.53	14.22	11.61	13.53
2700	8.89	8.48	7.94	8.56	14.27	11.71	13.55
2800	8.92	8.51	7.99	8.58	14.33	11.81	13.57
2900	8.96	8.53	8.05	8.60	14.38	11.91	13.59
3000	8.99	8.56	8.10	8.63	14.43	11.98	13.61
3200	9.05	8.61	8.21	8.67	14.54	12.15	13.64
3400	9.10	8.65	8.31	8.71	14.61	12.29	13.67
3600	9.15	8.69	8.40	8.74	14.68	12.44	13.69
3800	9.21	8.72	8.45	8.77	14.75	12.58	13.70
4000	9.26	8.75	8.49	8.80	14.81	12.71	13.72
4200	9.31	8.78	8.53	8.83	14.87	12.83	13.73
4400	9.35	8.81	8.57	8.86	14.92	12.94	13.74
4600	9.40	8.83	8.61	8.88	14.97	13.05	13.76
4800	9.45	8.85	8.66	8.90	15.01	13.16	13.77
5000	9.49	8.87	8.71	8.92	15.05	13.25	13.78

Sources: SO_2 from Justi and Luder, Forsch. Gebeite Ingenieurw. 6, 211 (1935). All others from Bureau of Standards Circular C 461, selected values of Properties of Hydrocarbons (1947). Values above 2200°F extrapolated with equations of Sweigert and Beardsley, Georgia School of Technology Engineering Experiment Station Bulletin 1 (No. 2) (June 1938).

TABLE 4.3

MEAN MOLAL HEAT CAPACITIES OF GASES AT CONSTANT PRESSURE

c_{pm} in Btu/(lb Mole)(°F) Between 77°F and t°F at Zero Pressure

°F	O_2	N_2	H_2	CO	CO_2	H_2O	SO_2	CH_4	C_2H_4	C_2H_6	C_3H_6	C_3H_8
77	7.02	6.96	6.89	6.96	8.87	8.02	9.52	8.54	10.41	12.59	15.27	17.57
100	7.03	6.96	6.90	6.97	8.94	8.03	9.58	8.61	10.57	12.75	15.51	17.88
200	7.07	6.97	6.92	6.98	9.22	8.07	9.84	8.91	11.24	13.47	16.58	19.25
300	7.12	6.98	6.93	6.99	9.49	8.12	10.06	9.24	11.91	14.28	17.61	20.60
400	7.18	6.99	6.96	7.01	9.74	8.17	10.28	9.60	12.56	15.24	18.61	21.90
500	7.24	7.01	6.97	7.04	9.97	8.23	10.48	9.98	13.20	16.12	19.58	23.15
600	7.31	7.04	6.97	7.07	10.18	8.30	10.67	10.36	13.81	16.93	20.52	24.34
700	7.37	7.07	6.98	7.11	10.37	8.37	10.84	10.75	14.38	17.71	21.42	25.46
800	7.43	7.10	6.99	7.15	10.56	8.44	11.00	11.14	14.93	18.46	22.29	26.54
900	7.49	7.14	7.00	7.19	10.73	8.51	11.15	11.51	15.45	19.17	23.11	27.58
1000	7.54	7.18	7.00	7.24	10.89	8.58	11.29	11.86	15.94	19.86	23.89	28.57
1100	7.60	7.21	7.01	7.28	11.04	8.66	11.41	12.19	16.41	20.51	24.62	29.50
1200	7.66	7.25	7.02	7.33	11.18	8.74	11.52	12.55	16.84	21.14	25.33	30.39
1300	7.71	7.29	7.04	7.37	11.32	8.82	11.63	12.91	17.26	21.74	26.01	31.23
1400	7.76	7.33	7.05	7.41	11.45	8.90	11.72	13.25	17.67	22.31	26.65	32.03
1500	7.81	7.37	7.07	7.46	11.57	8.99	11.81	13.57	18.06	22.86	27.26	32.79
1600	7.85	7.41	7.08	7.50	11.68	9.07	11.90	13.87	18.43	23.39	27.85	33.52
1700	7.89	7.45	7.10	7.54	11.79	9.15	11.98	14.17	18.78	23.90	28.41	34.22
1800	7.93	7.49	7.12	7.57	11.89	9.23	12.05	14.45	19.11	24.39	28.94	34.90
1900	7.97	7.53	7.14	7.61	11.99	9.31	12.12	14.73	19.44	24.86	29.45	35.55
2000	8.00	7.56	7.16	7.65	12.08	9.39	12.18	14.99	19.76	24.32	29.94	36.17
2100	8.03	7.60	7.18	7.68	12.17	9.47	12.23	15.24	20.06	25.75	30.41	36.76
2200	8.06	7.63	7.21	7.72	12.25	9.55	12.28	15.49	20.34	26.16	30.87	37.32
2300	8.09	7.66	7.23	7.75	12.32	9.62	12.34					
2400	8.12	7.69	7.25	7.78	12.39	9.70	12.39					
2500	8.15	7.72	7.28	7.80	12.47	9.77	12.43					

2600	8.18	7.75	7.30	7.83	12.55	9.84	12.47
2700	8.21	7.78	7.33	7.86	12.63	9.92	12.51
2800	8.23	7.81	7.35	7.89	12.68	9.99	12.55
2900	8.26	7.83	7.37	7.91	12.73	10.05	12.58
3000	8.28	7.86	7.40	7.94	12.78	10.12	12.62
3200	8.33	7.91	7.45	7.98	12.88	10.26	12.68
3400	8.37	7.95	7.49	8.03	12.99	10.38	12.74
3600	8.42	7.99	7.54	8.07	13.09	10.50	12.80
3800	8.46	8.03	7.59	8.10	13.18	10.62	12.85
4000	8.50	8.06	7.64	8.14	13.26	10.74	12.89
4200	8.54	8.10	7.68	8.17	13.34	10.84	12.93
4400	8.58	8.13	7.72	8.20	13.42	10.94	12.97
4600	8.61	8.16	7.76	8.23	13.49	11.03	13.00
4800	8.65	8.19	7.81	8.26	13.55	11.12	13.03
5000	8.68	8.22	7.85	8.28	13.60	11.20	13.06

Sources: SO_2 from Justi and Luder, Forsch. Gebiete Ingenieurw. 6, 211 (1935). All others from Bureau of Standards Circular C 461, Selected Values of Properties of Hydrocarbons (1947).

Example of use:

If one lb. mole of oxygen is heated at constant pressure from 77°F to 500°F

c_{pm} ($t = 500°F$) = 7.24

$Q = 7.24$ (500−77) = 3060 Btu

If one lb mole of oxygen is heated at constant pressure from 500°F to 1500°F

c_{pm} ($t = 1500$) = 7.81

Q (77°F−1500°F) = 7.81 (1500−77) = 11,110 Btu

Q (77°F−500°F) = 3060 Btu

Q (500°F−1500°F) = 11,110−3060 = 8050 Btu

lb-mole of a gas from 77°F to t°F, multiply the value of c_{pm} corresponding to t°F in Table 4.3 by the temperature difference $(t - 77)$. Table 4.3 can be used to find Q between any two temperatures as shown at the bottom of the table. This procedure makes use of the fact that the heat between two temperatures t_1 and t_2 is equal to the heat between t_2 and 77°F minus the heat between t_1 and 77°F. It should be noted that Table 4.3 is never used by taking the difference between mean heat capacities at two different temperatures. When the temperature change is relatively small, greatest accuracy is obtained by using Table 4.2 to get an average heat capacity for the temperature range. For larger temperature changes, the procedure outlined for Table 4.3 should be used.

Example 3.—A dehydration plant operation requires 15,000 ft³/min of air at 160°F and atmospheric pressure. If the air is initially at 70°F, how many Btu/min are required to raise the temperature to 160°F?

Using one minute of operation as a basis, the mass of air for the density calculated in Example 2 is

$$m = (15000)(0.0640) = 960 \text{ lb}_m$$

$$N = 960/29.0 = 33.1 \text{ moles}$$

Table 4.2 shows that heat capacities of oxygen and nitrogen change only slightly over the range of 70–160°F. It will therefore be satisfactory to use constant heat capacities corresponding to the average temperature of 115°F. Heat capacities at this temperature from Table 4.2 for O_2 and N_2 are 7.04 and 6.96, respectively. Separate calculations could be made for the heat required to raise the temperatures of the oxygen and nitrogen, and the two figures added to give the total heat. An equivalent procedure is to calculate an average molal heat capacity and apply this to the total moles of air. Thus,

$$c_{av} = (0.21)(7.04) + (0.79)(6.96) = 6.98 \text{ Btu/(lb-mole)(F°)}$$

$$Q = Nc_{av}(t_2 - t_1) = (33.1)(6.98)(90) = 20,800 \text{ Btu}$$

Example 4.—The heat for the air in Example 3 is provided by burning natural gas, which may be considered to consist of methane, with 25% more air than is theoretically required for complete combustion. If the total combustion gas stream leaves the burner at 2500°F and is cooled to 160°F in giving up its heat to the air, how many cubic feet of methane fuel per minute are required? It may be assumed that there is no condensation of water vapor.

Let us choose a basis of one mole of methane for the calculations. The reaction for complete combustion is

$$CH_4 + 2O_2 \rightarrow CO_2 + 2H_2O$$

For complete combustion, 2 moles of O_2 are required. The 25% excess amounts to another 0.5 mole for a total of 2.5 moles. The N_2 in the air with this amount of O_2 is $(79/21)(2.5)$, or 9.4 moles. The combustion gases therefore contain 1 mole of CO_2, 2 moles of H_2O, and 0.5 mole of excess O_2, and all the N_2. In order to calculate the heat given up when this gas mixture is cooled to 160°F, it is necessary to use the two-step procedure illustrated at the bottom of Table 4.3. The total quantity of heat is given by the sum of the quantities for the individual gases.

	moles	c_{pm} 2500°F	Nc_{pm} (2500–77)	c_{pm} 160°F	Nc_{pm} (160–77)
CO_2	1.0	12.47	30,200	9.11	760
H_2O	2.0	9.77	47,300	8.05	1340
O_2	0.5	8.15	9,900	7.05	290
N_2	9.4	7.72	176,000	6.97	5440
total	12.9		263,400		7830

For one mole of methane fuel,

$$Q = 263,400 - 7,800 = 255,600 \text{ Btu}$$

From Example 3, the required heat is 20,800 Btu/min

Methane required $= 20,800/255,600 = 0.0815$ moles/min.

If the fuel gas volume is measured at 1 atm and 70°F,

$$v = NRT/P = (0.0815)(10.73)(460 + 70)/14.7 = 31.5 \text{ ft}^3/\text{min}$$

Latent Heat

A heat quantity that can be obtained by the product of a heat capacity and a temperature change, as discussed above, is commonly called sensible heat. Latent heat is a heat quantity that accompanies a change in phase at constant temperature, such as melting or evaporation. For example, the latent heat of vaporization of a substance represented by Fig. 4.2 is given at pressure P_a by the heat required in going from a to b. Heat of vaporization is obviously a function of the temperature (or pressure). At the critical temperature, the liquid and vapor are identical, and the heat of vaporization is zero. Tables of latent heats of melting and vaporization for many substances are readily available in standard reference sources.

Enthalpy

In a process involving both sensible and latent heats, the total heat can be obtained by taking the sum of the individual quantities. For example, we might want to find the heat required to convert one pound of water at 70°F to vapor at the boiling point. The sensible heat is the heat capacity of water times the temperature difference between 70 and the boiling point, or $(212 - 70)$ Btu. It is known that the latent heat of vaporization at 212°F is 970 Btu/lb_m. The total heat is therefore 152 + 970, or 1122 Btu. Calculations of this type are frequently simplified by using the thermodynamic property, enthalpy, which was defined in the preceding chapter. It was also shown there that the heat associated with a constant pressure process for a fixed mass of material is equal to the change in enthalpy, with no restriction as to sensible or latent heats. If the data for a substance were available, it would therefore be possible to obtain the heat for any constant pressure process merely by taking a difference in enthalpies. Such data are available for many substances. One way by which these data are originally obtained is from the relation of enthalpies to heat capacities and latent heats. In the numerical calculation above, for example, the difference in enthalpy between saturated water vapor at 212°F and liquid at 70°F is 1122 Btu/lb_m. Since we are interested only in changes in enthalpy and never with an absolute value, we can arbitrarily set enthalpy equal to zero at some convenient reference state for purposes of tabulation. For water, the universally used reference state is saturated liquid at 32°F. Once a complete table of enthalpies has been built up, it then becomes unnecessary to refer back to the original heat capacity or latent heat information. As indicated in the previous chapter, enthalpy has applications to flow processes that go beyond simple heating and cooling processes.

TABLES AND CHARTS OF PROPERTIES

Data on pressure-volume-temperature relationships and thermal properties have been compiled for many substances in the form of tables or charts of thermodynamic properties. For water, the most complete and authoritative compilation is presented in the 1967 ASME Steam Tables, published by the American Society of Mechanical Engineers. Tables 4.3, 4.4, and 4.5 include excerpts from the ASME tables as reprinted by Combustion Engineering, Inc.

According to international agreement, the reference condition for these tables is established as zero internal energy and entropy of the liquid at the triple point. The triple point temperature is 32.018°F, slightly higher than the atmospheric freezing point. Older steam tables used a reference condition of zero enthalpy of saturated liquid at 32°F. The tables are arranged as follows:

Saturated Steam: Temperature Table

Table 4.4 includes properties of saturated vapor and liquid for temperatures ranging from 32°F to the critical temperature. The first set of columns following the temperatures lists equilibrium vapor pressures; a plot of these pressures versus temperature gives the vapor pressure curve represented by ac in Fig. 4.1. There are three columns under specific volume in the table: saturated liquid, saturated vapor, and the change in volume on evaporation. This latter quantity, v_{fg}, is equal to $v_g - v_f$, as explained previously. All volumes are given in ft^3/lb$_m$.

The columns under enthalpy correspond to those under volume. The difference between the saturated vapor and liquid enthalpies, h_{fg}, is the latent heat of vaporization. The reference condition stated above leads to a small negative value for the enthalpy of saturated liquid at 32°F. All enthalpies are expressed in Btu/lb$_m$ with respect to this reference state.

The last group of columns lists values of entropy, a property that is associated with the second law of thermodynamics. This subject lies beyond the scope of this text, and applications of entropy will not be discussed.

For properties at temperatures intermediate to those listed, it is customary to use linear interpolation. This practice is quite satisfactory for enthalpy since heat capacities are nearly constant over a small temperature range. The dependency of vapor pressure on temperature is more nearly logarithmic than linear, and linear interpolation for pressure can lead to some error.

Saturated Steam: Pressure Table

Table 4.5 presents the same information as the temperature table, but in terms of pressure as the independent variable rather than temperature. If it is desired to find properties at a specified pressure, it will usually be more convenient to interpolate in this table than to use the temperature table. It should be noted that specification of any of the properties listed permits either table to be used to determine the remaining properties. For example, if the enthalpy of saturated vapor is given, either Steam Table 4.4 or 4.5 can be used to determine the temperature and pressure.

Superheated Steam

In the saturation region, specification of any property fixes the state of the liquid and vapor and permits the remaining properties to be obtained. For superheated steam, as in any single phase region, it is necessary to specify two properties to fix the state. Any two properties can be specified, but it is customary to present tabulated data in terms of temperature and pressure. In Table 4.6, temperature appears across the top of the page and pressure is in the left hand column. At a point in the table corresponding to a temperature at the head of a column and a pressure at the left side of a row, a group of four properties appears. The first, designated Sh, or superheat, is the temperature minus the saturation temperature at the same pressure. The second property is specific volume, ft^3/lb$_m$; the third, enthalpy, Btu/lb$_m$; and the last, entropy. The number in parenthesis under each pressure in the left column is the corresponding saturation temperature. The next two columns include data for saturated liquid and vapor at the same pressure. These first three columns thus constitute a pressure

TABLE 4.4

SATURATED STEAM: TEMPERATURE TABLE

Temp Fahr t	Abs Press Lb per Sq In. p	Specific Volume			Enthalpy			Entropy			Temp Fahr t
		Sat. Liquid v_f	Evap v_{fg}	Sat. Vapor v_g	Sat. Liquid h_f	Evap h_{fg}	Sat. Vapor h_g	Sat. Liquid s_f	Evap s_{fg}	Sat. Vapor s_g	
32.0	0.08859	0.016022	3304.7	3304.7	0.0179	1075.5	1075.5	0.0000	2.1873	2.1873	32.0
34.0	0.09600	0.016021	3061.9	3061.9	1.996	1074.4	1076.4	0.0041	2.1762	2.1802	34.0
36.0	0.10395	0.016020	2839.0	2839.0	4.008	1073.2	1077.2	0.0081	2.1651	2.1732	36.0
38.0	0.11249	0.016019	2634.1	2634.2	6.018	1072.1	1078.1	0.0122	2.1541	2.1663	38.0
40.0	0.12163	0.016019	2445.8	2445.8	8.027	1071.0	1079.0	0.0162	2.1432	2.1594	40.0
42.0	0.13143	0.016019	2272.4	2272.4	10.035	1069.8	1079.9	0.0202	2.1325	2.1527	42.0
44.0	0.14192	0.016019	2112.8	2112.8	12.041	1068.7	1080.7	0.0242	2.1217	2.1459	44.0
46.0	0.15314	0.016020	1965.7	1965.7	14.047	1067.6	1081.6	0.0282	2.1111	2.1393	46.0
48.0	0.16514	0.016021	1830.0	1830.0	16.051	1066.4	1082.5	0.0321	2.1006	2.1327	48.0
50.0	0.17796	0.016023	1704.8	1704.8	18.054	1065.3	1083.4	0.0361	2.0901	2.1262	50.0
52.0	0.19165	0.016024	1589.2	1589.2	20.057	1064.2	1084.2	0.0400	2.0798	2.1197	52.0
54.0	0.20625	0.016026	1482.4	1482.4	22.058	1063.1	1085.1	0.0439	2.0695	2.1134	54.0
56.0	0.22183	0.016028	1383.6	1383.6	24.059	1061.9	1086.0	0.0478	2.0593	2.1070	56.0
58.0	0.23843	0.016031	1292.2	1292.2	26.060	1060.8	1086.9	0.0516	2.0491	2.1008	58.0
60.0	0.25611	0.016033	1207.6	1207.6	28.060	1059.7	1087.7	0.0555	2.0391	2.0946	60.0
62.0	0.27494	0.016036	1129.2	1129.2	30.059	1058.5	1088.6	0.0593	2.0291	2.0885	62.0
64.0	0.29497	0.016039	1056.5	1056.5	32.058	1057.4	1089.5	0.0632	2.0192	2.0824	64.0
66.0	0.31626	0.016043	989.0	989.1	34.056	1056.3	1090.4	0.0670	2.0094	2.0764	66.0
68.0	0.33889	0.016046	926.5	926.5	36.054	1055.2	1091.2	0.0708	1.9996	2.0704	68.0

TABLE 4.5

SATURATED STEAM: PRESSURE TABLE

Abs Press. Lb/Sq In. p	Temp Fahr t	Specific Volume			Enthalpy			Entropy			Abs Press. Lb/Sq In. p
		Sat. Liquid v_f	Evap v_{fg}	Sat. Vapor v_g	Sat. Liquid h_f	Evap h_{fg}	Sat. Vapor h_g	Sat. Liquid s_f	Evap s_{fg}	Sat. Vapor s_g	
0.08865	32.018	0.016022	3022.4	3022.4	0.0003	1075.5	1075.5	0.0000	2.1872	2.1872	0.08865
0.25	59.323	0.016032	1235.5	1235.5	27.382	1060.1	1087.4	0.0542	2.0425	2.0967	0.25
0.50	79.586	0.016071	641.5	641.5	47.623	1048.6	1096.3	0.0925	1.9446	2.0370	0.50
1.0	101.74	0.016136	333.59	333.60	69.73	1036.1	1105.8	0.1326	1.8455	1.9781	1.0
5.0	162.24	0.016407	73.515	73.532	130.20	1000.9	1131.1	0.2349	1.6094	1.8443	5.0
10.0	193.21	0.016592	38.404	38.420	161.26	982.1	1143.3	0.2836	1.5043	1.7879	10.0
14.696	212.00	0.016719	26.782	26.799	180.17	970.3	1150.5	0.3121	1.4447	1.7568	14.696
15.0	213.03	0.016726	26.274	26.290	181.21	969.7	1150.9	0.3137	1.4415	1.7552	15.0
20.0	227.96	0.016834	20.070	20.087	196.27	960.1	1156.3	0.3358	1.3962	1.7320	20.0
30.0	250.34	0.017009	13.7266	13.7436	218.9	945.2	1164.1	0.3682	1.3313	1.6995	30.0
40.0	267.25	0.017151	10.4794	10.4965	236.1	933.6	1169.8	0.3921	1.2844	1.6765	40.0
50.0	281.02	0.017274	8.4967	8.5140	250.2	923.9	1174.1	0.4112	1.2474	1.6586	50.0
60.0	292.71	0.017383	7.1562	7.1736	262.2	915.4	1177.6	0.4273	1.2167	1.6440	60.0
70.0	302.93	0.017482	6.1875	6.2050	272.7	907.8	1180.6	0.4411	1.1905	1.6316	70.0
80.0	312.04	0.017573	5.4536	5.4711	282.1	900.9	1183.1	0.4534	1.1675	1.6208	80.0
90.0	320.28	0.017659	4.8779	4.8953	290.7	894.6	1185.3	0.4643	1.1470	1.6113	90.0

TABLE 4.6

SUPERHEATED STEAM

Abs Press Lb/Sq In (Sat Temp)		Sat Water	Sat Steam	400	450	500	550	600	700	800	900	1000	1100	1200	1300	1400	1500
210 (385.91)	Sh	0.01844		14.09	64.09	114.09	164.09	214.09	314.09	414.09	514.09	614.09	714.09	814.09	914.09	1014.09	1114.09
	v		2.1822	2.2364	2.4181	2.5880	2.7504	2.9078	3.2137	3.5128	3.8080	4.1007	4.3915	4.6811	4.9695	5.2571	5.5440
	h	359.91	1199.0	1208.02	1239.2	1268.0	1295.3	1321.9	1373.7	1425.1	1476.7	1528.8	1581.6	1635.2	1689.6	1744.8	1800.8
	s	0.5490	1.5413	1.5522	1.5872	1.6180	1.6458	1.6715	1.7182	1.7607	1.8001	1.8371	1.8721	1.9054	1.9372	1.9677	1.9970
220 (389.88)	Sh	0.01850		10.12	60.12	110.12	160.12	210.12	310.12	410.12	510.12	610.12	710.12	810.12	910.12	1010.12	1110.12
	v		2.0863	2.1240	2.2999	2.4638	2.6199	2.7710	3.0642	3.3504	3.6327	3.9125	4.1905	4.4671	4.7426	5.0173	5.2913
	h	364.17	1199.6	1206.3	1237.8	1266.9	1294.5	1321.2	1373.2	1424.7	1476.3	1528.5	1581.4	1635.0	1689.4	1744.7	1800.6
	s	0.5540	1.5374	1.5453	1.5808	1.6120	1.6400	1.6658	1.7128	1.7553	1.7948	1.8318	1.8668	1.9002	1.9320	1.9625	1.9919
230 (393.70)	Sh	0.01855		6.30	56.30	106.30	156.30	206.30	306.30	406.30	506.30	606.30	706.30	806.30	906.30	1006.30	1106.30
	v		1.9985	2.0212	2.1919	2.3503	2.5008	2.6461	2.9276	3.2020	3.4776	3.7406	4.0068	4.2717	4.5355	4.7984	5.0606
	h	368.28	1200.1	1204.4	1236.3	1265.7	1293.6	1320.4	1372.7	1424.2	1476.0	1528.2	1581.1	1634.8	1689.3	1744.5	1800.5
	s	0.5588	1.5336	1.5385	1.5747	1.6062	1.6344	1.6604	1.7075	1.7502	1.7897	1.8268	1.8618	1.8952	1.9270	1.9576	1.9869
240 (397.39)	Sh	0.01860		2.61	52.61	102.61	152.61	202.61	302.61	402.61	502.61	602.61	702.61	802.61	902.61	1002.61	1102.61
	v		1.9177	1.9268	2.0928	2.2462	2.3915	2.5316	2.8024	3.0661	3.3259	3.5831	3.8385	4.0976	4.3456	4.5977	4.8492
	h	372.27	1200.6	1202.4	1234.9	1264.6	1292.7	1319.7	1372.1	1423.8	1475.6	1527.9	1580.9	1634.6	1689.1	1744.3	1800.4
	s	0.5634	1.5299	1.5320	1.5687	1.6006	1.6291	1.6552	1.7025	1.7452	1.7848	1.8219	1.8570	1.8904	1.9223	1.9528	1.9822
250 (400.97)	Sh	0.01865			49.03	99.03	149.03	199.03	299.03	399.03	499.03	599.03	699.03	799.03	899.03	999.03	1099.03
	v		1.8432		2.0016	2.1504	2.2909	2.4262	2.6872	2.9410	3.1909	3.4382	3.6837	3.9278	4.1709	4.4131	4.6546
	h	376.14	1201.1		1233.4	1263.5	1291.8	1319.0	1371.6	1423.4	1475.3	1527.6	1580.6	1634.4	1688.9	1744.2	1800.2
	s	0.5679	1.5264		1.5629	1.5951	1.6239	1.6502	1.6976	1.7405	1.7801	1.8173	1.8524	1.8858	1.9177	1.9482	1.9776

table for saturated steam that is somewhat more useful than Table 4.5 because data are given at smaller intervals of pressure.

In the usual situation, use of Table 4.6 requires interpolation. Since two variables are involved, it may be necessary to interpolate for both temperature and pressure. For example, a volume may be desired at temperature t between t_a and t_b and pressure P between P_a and P_b. One can first interpolate to find v at both t,P_a and t,P_b. The final volume is then found by interpolating between these two values for pressure P. It is equally satisfactory to interpolate first for pressure, then for temperature.

As with the saturated steam tables, properties other than pressure and temperature may be specified. For example, Table 4.6 can be used to find the temperature and pressure if volume and enthalpy are given. The principle is the same, but the interpolation is more inconvenient because volume and enthalpy do not appear in even intervals.

Example 5.—Obtain the specific volume of steam at 278 psia and 475°F from the steam tables and compare with the value calculated from the perfect-gas law.

A double interpolation is required in Table 4.6, for superheated steam. Specific volumes at adjacent temperatures and pressures are as follows:

	460°F	480°F
275 psia	1.8318	1.8879
280 psia	1.7957	1.8512

Interpolating for pressure,

at 460°F and 287 psia, $v = 1.8318 - (3/5)(1.8318 - 1.7957) =$
$$1.8101 \text{ ft}^3/\text{lb}_m$$

at 480°F and 278 psia, $v = 1.8879 - (3/5)(1.8879 - 1.8512) =$
$$1.8659 \text{ ft}^3/\text{lb}_m$$

Interpolating for temperature,

at 278 psia and 475°F, $v = 1.8101 + (15/20)(1.8659 - 1.8101) =$
$$1.8519 \text{ ft}^3/\text{lb}_m$$

It would have been equally satisfactory to interpolate first for temperature, then for pressure. By the perfect-gas law,

$$v = NRT/P = (1/18.02)(10.73)(460 + 475)/278 = 2.00 \text{ ft}^3/\text{lb}_m$$

Although the result from the perfect-gas law is reasonably close, the error is greater than we would desire for most engineering purposes.

Example 6.—0.2 lb_m of water is introduced into an evacuated container having a volume of 3 ft^3. If the container is kept at 190°F, how much liquid and vapor are present? The temperature is then raised to 300°F. Determine the final pressure and the enthalpies in the initial and final states.

The specific volume of the material in the container is 3.0/0.2, or 15 ft^3/lb_m. Since neither the container volume nor the mass changes, the specific volume remains constant throughout the entire process. From the steam tables at 190°F, $v_f = 0.01657$ and $v_g = 41.01$. Since the specific volume of the contents lies between these values, there is a mixture of liquid and vapor in the container, and the fraction of vapor can be calculated from Eq. 4-2.

$$x = \frac{v - v_f}{v_{fg}} = \frac{15.0 - 0.016}{41.0} = 0.365$$

$$m_{vap} = (0.365)(0.2) = 0.0730 \, lb_m$$

$$m_{liq} = 0.2 - 0.0730 = 0.127 \, lb_m$$

Since enthalpies of liquid and vapor are additive, just as volumes are, Eq. 4-2 applies to enthalpy as well as volume.

$$h = h_f + xh_{fg} = 158 + (0.365)(984.1) = 517 \, Btu/lb_m$$

The specific volume of saturated vapor at 300°F is much less than 15 ft^3/lb_m, so the final state is clearly in the superheated region. From Table 4.3, we obtain the following data at 300°F:

	25 psia	30 psia
v, ft^3/lb_m	17.84	14.82
h, Btu/lb_m	1190.2	1189.2

By interpolation, the pressure corresponding to a volume of 15.0 ft^3/lb_m is 29.7 psia, and the enthalpy at this pressure is 1189.3 Btu/lb_m. It should be noted that, since the heating process was at constant volume rather than constant pressure, the amount of heat required is not equal to the change in enthalpy.

Graphical Representation

Data on properties can be presented in graphical as well as tabular form. Such graphs or charts eliminate the need for numerical interpolation, but the data usually cannot be read to as many significant figures as in the tables. Earlier in this chapter, it was pointed out a plot of pressure versus volume, with lines of constant temperature, can provide complete pressure-volume-temperature data. For engineering purposes, coordinates other than pressure and volume are found to be more useful. One type of plot that is included with most steam tables is the so-called Mollier diagram, with coordinates of enthalpy and entropy. These diagrams will always include lines of constant pressure and constant temperature. For refrigeration calculations, charts with coordinates of pressure vs. enthalpy are convenient. Such charts, as well as tabulated data, are available for the common refrigerants.

PROBLEMS

1. Nitrogen gas from a cylinder is used at a rate of 0.25 ft^3/min to flush an apparatus. At a certain time, the pressure gage on the cylinder reads 100 psi. For how many minutes can the gas flow be maintained until the gage reading drops to 5 psi if the volume of the cylinder is 1.0 ft^3?

2. What is the density of air in lb$_m$/ft^3 at 1 atm. pressure and 75°F as calculated from the perfect gas law?

3. 1500 ft^3/min of air at 160°F and atmospheric pressure are required for a dehydrator operation. If the air is initially at 70°F, how many Btu/min are required to raise the temperature to 160°F?

4. (a) The heat for the air in Problem 3 is provided by burning natural gas, which may be considered to consist of methane. If the gas is burned with 25% more air than is theoretically required for complete combustion, calculate the composition in mole % of the total gas steam leaving the burner. Air may be considered to consist of 21 mole % O_2 and 79 mole % N_2. (b) If the heat requirement of Problem 3 is supplied by cooling this combustion gas from 2000°F to 160°F, how many ft^3 of methane fuel per minute are required? It may be assumed that there is no condensation of water vapor.

5. How much heat is required to raise the temperature of 5 lb$_m$ of H_2O from 0°F to 250°F at atmospheric pressure?

6. Compute the molecular weight of a mixture of gases at 25 psia, 250°F and a specific volume of 15 ft^3/lb$_m$. Use perfect gas law.

7. 500 lb$_m$/hr ambient 100°C air is to be heated to 300°F for a dryer. How much heat (Btu) is required per hour. Use the heat capacity data at constant pressure given in Table 4.2.

8. Find the following answers from the steam tables:
   (a) Vapor pressure at 417°F.
   (b) Temperature of saturated steam at 730 psi abs.
   (c) Latent heat of vaporization at 282°F.
   (d) Specific volume and density of steam at 22 psi abs. and 280°F. Compare with density calculated by the perfect gas law.
   (e) One lb$_m$ of water consisting of 65% vapor and 35% liquid is condensed at constant pressure of 40 psi *gage*. Find the amount of heat removed.
   (f) 0.2 lb$_m$ of water is introduced into an evacuated container having a volume of 3 ft^3. If the container is kept at 190°F, how much liquid and vapor are present?

9. Calculate the quantity of steam (in lb$_m$) required to heat 2000 lb$_m$ of milk (c_p = 0.93) from 60°F to 145°F. The heating efficiency is 0.85. Steam

is available at 105 psia with a 90% quality. The condensate is leaving at 160°F.

10. Determine the quantity and pressure of saturated steam at 259°F required to heat 20 lb_m of product (c_p = 0.5 Btu/lb_m°F) from 70°F to 250°F if condensate is released at 80°F.

SYMBOLS

Btu   British thermal unit = 778 ft-lb_f

°C   degrees Centigrade

c_p specific heat at constant pressure, Btu/lb_m °F or cal/gm °C

c_{pm} mean specific heat at constant pressure, Btu/lb_m °F or cal/gm °C

c_v specific heat at constant volume, Btu/lb_m °F or cal/gm °C

cal   calorie = 4.186 joules

F   friction work

[F]   dimensions of force

°F   degrees Fahrenheit

f   force, lb_f

ft   feet

G   mass flow rate for dry air, lb_m/hr

°K   degrees Kelvin (°K = °C + 273.2)

[L]   dimensions of length

lb_m pound mass

m   mass

M   molecular weight

[M]   dimensions of mass

N   moles

P   pressure, lb_f/in^2

Q   quantity of heat transferred, Btu

R   universal gas constant

°R   degrees Rankine (°R = °F + 459.7)

t   temperature (not absolute)

T   absolute temperature in °R or °K

[T]   dimension of time

v   specific volume, ft^3/lb_m

x   mole fraction or weight fraction

CHAPTER 5

Combined Mass and Energy Balance[1]

INTRODUCTION

Many times a simple mass balance will not provide sufficient information for solution of a problem, and energy relationships must be utilized. A combined mass and energy balance is simply an application of the first law of thermodynamics. Attention in this chapter will be directed to steady state or constant pressure batch processes involving only thermal energy effects. As shown in Chapter 3, any heat flowing in or out of such systems is equal to the change in enthalpy of the streams. Thus,

$$Q = \Delta H$$

In a constant-pressure batch process ΔH is the enthalpy of the contents of the batch at the end of the process less the enthalpy of the starting materials. In a steady-state process ΔH is the sum of the enthalpies of the streams leaving less the sum of the enthalpies of the entering streams. This simple enthalpy relationship will in general not be applicable to types of processes other than these two.

The procedure used in making enthalpy balances is the same as that described in Chapter 2 for mass balances. It is, of course, necessary to have information on enthalpies of the materials involved. For many substances, such as steam, tables of data are available. For other materials enthalpies may be calculated from heat capacity and latent heat data, as described in the chapter on thermodynamic properties. The enthalpies of simple mixtures and solutions can usually be broken down into the individual components. For example, the enthalpy of a wet food product is equal to the sum of the enthalpies of the water and the dry matter. If there are substantial heats of solution or heats of chemical reaction, this procedure will not be valid.

CALCULATION OF ENTHALPY BALANCE

In effect, the enthalpy balance provides one or more equations which are solved simultaneously with the mass balance equations for the unknown quantities. The following examples illustrate the procedure.

---

[1] Consult the list of symbols in Chapter 4.

Example 1

When tomatoes are broken or crushed for processing into liquid products such as juice, sauce, etc., they must be heated rapidly to inactivate pectic enzymes. One such hot break operation is conducted by passing steam directly into the tomato pulp. The condensate formed remains in the pulp and has a diluting effect. If the pulp initially has a concentration of 5.1% total solids and is heated from 70° to 190°F, calculate the concentration of total solids in the hot pulp leaving the operation. The process is conducted at atmospheric pressure. The solids portion of the pulp may be considered to have a specific heat of 0.5.

The process is represented in the sketch below, with a basis of 100 lb of tomato pulp.

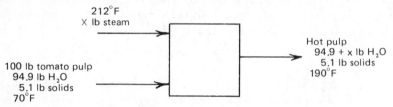

The enthalpies of the streams are as follows:

Tomato pulp:
 94.9 lb of water at 70°F, h = 38.0 Btu/lb (from steam tables)
 5.1 lb of solids at 70°F, $h = c_p(t - t_0) = 0.5(70 - 0) = 35.0$ Btu/lb
 (Note that a reference temperature of 0°F is used for convenience.)
Steam:
 x lb of saturated steam at 1 atm pressure, h = 1150.5 Btu/lb
Product:
 94.9 + x lb of water at 190°F, h = 158.0 Btu/lb
 5.1 lb of solids at 190°C, $h = 0.5(190 - 0) = 85$ Btu/lb
Enthalpy balance. Since there is no heat added, enthalpy in = enthalpy out.

$$38.0(94.9) + 35.0(5.1) + 1150.5 x = 158.0(94.9 + x) + 85(5.1)$$
$$x = 11.8 \text{ lb}$$

Total water in product = 94.9 + 11.8 = 106.7 lb
Solids concentration = 5.1(100/(106.7 + 5.1) = 4.56%

The enthalpy balance could be simplified by recognizing that the change in enthalpy of the tomato pulp must equal the change in enthalpy of the condensing steam. We can thus write

$$94.9(158.0 - 38.0) + 5.1(0.5)(190 - 70) = x(1150.5 - 158.0)$$

This equation is obviously the same as the previous one, but it saves the trouble of calculating individual enthalpies of the solids. Since we are always interested in enthalpy differences, it will frequently be simpler to set the equations up directly in terms of differences. In more complex problems where several streams are involved the proper enthalpy differences may be difficult to recognize. There may be less chance of error by evaluating the enthalpy of each steam individually.

BALANCE CALCULATIONS FOR EVAPORATORS

Many processes utilize enclosed steam heaters, in which steam condenses on one side of a jacketed or tubular surface to heat a product on the other side. The condensate is withdrawn separately and does not mix with the heated material. The steam condenses at constant pressure, and the condensate leaves at this pressure and corresponding equilibrium temperature. The condensate is not cooled to the temperature of the product on the other side of the surface. In a steam-heated evaporator the heat from the condensing steam boils water from a liquid that is being concentrated. The water vapor leaving the evaporator is simply steam that could be condensed to give up its latent heat. However, it is at a lower temperature and pressure than the original steam and can therefore be used to evaporate only a lower boiling temperature liquid. This necessary lower boiling temperature can be obtained by operating a second stage of evaporation at a lower pressure than the first, usually under a vacuum. A double-effect evaporator operates on this principle as shown in Fig. 5.1. The incoming feed is partially concentrated by steam in the first effect. The product stream passes to the second effect where concentration is completed utilizing the latent heat of the vapor from the first effect. When any solution is boiled, dissolved solids cause an elevation of the boiling point. Therefore, the condensation temperature of the vapor, which contains none of the solids, will be lower than the boiling point of the liquid. With most food processing applications the boiling point elevation is small enough to neglect, and the vapor can be considered to condense in the second effect at the same temperature as the boiling liquid in the first effect.

Vacuum evaporation is commonly employed with heat-sensitive food materials in order to obtain lower boiling temperatures. The second effect of a double-effect system, however, must always operate at a higher vacuum than the first effect in order to maintain the necessary difference in boiling temperatures between the two. These same principles can be extended to more than two effects. There are industrial applications where as many as five or six effects are used. Although the complete design of evaporator systems requires engineering principles beyond those discussed here, all such calculations involve simple heat and mass balances. The purpose of the above discussion is to provide a basis for making these heat and mass balances.

Example 2

Skim milk is being concentrated in a double-effect evaporator (Fig. 5.1).

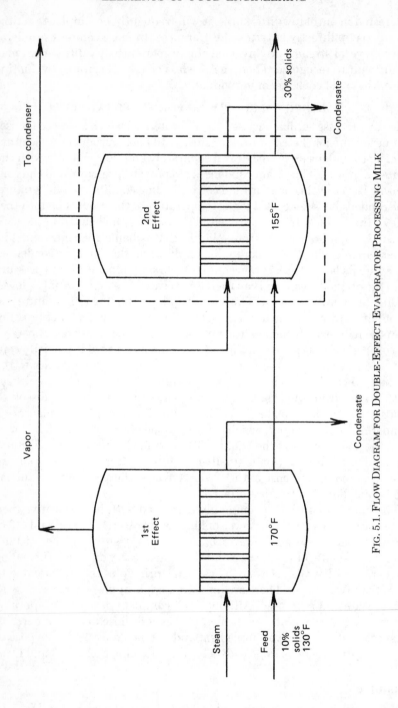

FIG. 5.1. FLOW DIAGRAM FOR DOUBLE-EFFECT EVAPORATOR PROCESSING MILK

On the basis of the figures given, calculate the solids content of the liquid leaving the first effect. The specific heat of the solids is 0.5. Using a basis of 100 lb of feed, there are 10 lb of solids and 90 lb of water entering. Ten lb of solids leave the second effect and, at 30% concentration, the water leaving in the product is $10(70/30) = 23.3$ lb. The total water evaporated is therefore $90 - 23.3 = 66.7$ lb. Let x be the amount evaporated in the first effect and y the amount evaporated in the second. An overall water balance then gives

$$x + y = 66.7$$

We will now make an enthalpy balance around the second effect.

Water entering: $(90 - x)$ lb at 170°F, $h = 138$ Btu/lb
Solids entering: 10 lb at 170°F, $h = c_p(t - t_0) = 0.5(170) = 85$ Btu/lb
Steam entering: x lb saturated at 170°F, $h = 1134.0$ Btu/lb
Water leaving: 23.3 lb at 155°F, $h = 123$ Btu/lb
Solids leaving: 10 lb at 155°F, $h = 0.5 (155) = 77.5$ Btu/lb
Vapor leaving: y lb saturated at 155°F, $h = 1127.9$ Btu/lb
Condensate leaving: x lb saturated liquid at 170°F, $h = 138$ Btu/lb

Total enthalpy in = total enthalpy out

$$138(90 - x) + 10(85) + 1134.0x$$
$$= 123(23.3) + 10(77.5) + 1127.9y + 138x$$

Collecting terms

$$1127.9y - 858x = 9645$$

The above equation, combined with the material balance equation, $x + y = 66.7$, gives the following results

$x = 33.0$ lb evaporated in first effect
$y = 33.7$ lb evaporated in second effect
water leaving first effect $= 90 - x = 57.0$ lb
solids conc. leaving first effect $= 10(100)/(10 + 57) = 14.9\%$

PROBLEMS

1. In an experimental study, peach puree is being concentrated in a continuous vacuum evaporator at a rate of 144 lb/hr. The feed material has a temperature of 60°F and a total solids content of 10.9%. A product of 40.1% total solids is withdrawn at a temperature of 105°F, and condensate leaves the condenser at 100°F.

(a) Calculate the flow rates of the product and condensate streams.
(b) If steam condensing at 250°F is used to supply the heat of evaporation, calculate the steam consumption in lb/hr. The specific heat of the solid material is 0.5.
(c) Cooling water enters the condenser at 70°F and leaves at 85°F. Calculate the cooling water flow rate.

2. A liquid food with a solids weight fraction of 0.1 is being heated by steam injection from an initial temperature of 181°F. The heating occurs at 50 psia and product has specific heat of 0.8 Btu/lb$_m$°F. The steam used for heating is at 90 psia with 85.5% quality. Compute steam requirements for product feed rate of 100 lb$_m$/min and determine total solids content of product leaving heating system.

3. A hot break operation on tomatoes is conducted by passing steam directly into the tomato pulp. In such an operation, the condensate formed remains in the tomato pulp. If the pulp initially has a concentration of 5.1% total solids and is heated from 70° to 190°F, calculate the concentration of total solids in the hot pulp leaving the operation. The process is conducted at atmospheric pressure.

4. In an experimental study, peach puree is being concentrated in a continuous vacuum evaporator at a rate of 144 lb/hr. The feed material has a temperature of 60°F and a total solids content of 10.9%. A product of 40.1% total solids is withdrawn at a temperature of 105°F, and condensate leaves the condenser at 100°F.

(a) Calculate the flow rates of the product and condensate streams.
(b) If steam condensing at 250°F is used to supply the heat of evaporation, calculate the steam consumption in lb/hr. The specific heat of the solid material is 0.5.
(c) Cooling water enters the condenser at 70°F and leaves at 86°F. Calculate the cooling water flow rate.

5. The evaporator of Example 2 in this chapter is operating with forward feed. That is, the feed enters the high temperature effect and the final product is withdrawn from the low temperature effect. A double-effect evaporator can also be operating with reverse feed, where the feed enters the low temperature effect and the product leaves the high temperature effect. Repeat Example 2 on the basis of reverse feed, with all other conditions remaining unchanged. The steam entering the first effect may be assumed to have a temperature of 212°F.

CHAPTER 6

Fluid Handling

INTRODUCTION

Before taking up details of the nature of fluids and the principles of fluid flow, it will be advantageous to gain some background about the types of equipment used in handling fluids. In this section, we will be concerned with mechanical equipment utilizing moving parts, such as pumps, fans and compressors. There are, of course, other ways in which fluids can be moved, for example, steam or water ejectors, gravity flow, and natural convection. It will be convenient to consider liquids and gases separately, although much the same types of equipment are used for both. Furthermore, it may be useful to make a distinction as to whether the primary objective is to transport the fluid from one point to another or simply to increase its pressure. For example, the objective in a milk homogenization pump is to develop a very high pressure in order to accomplish the homogenization, not to transport the milk. The purpose of an air compressor is to provide a supply of high pressure air.

Most moving equipment for fluid handling can be put into one of three categories: centrifugal, positive displacement, or propeller. The following discussion is not intended to be exhaustive, but rather to survey some of the more common types of equipment.

PUMPS FOR LIQUIDS

Centrifugal Pumps

Figure 6.1 is a cut-away view of a typical process pump. The essential components are the case and the enclosed rotating impeller. The centrifugal force created by the impeller produces the desired increase in pressure of the fluid, which enters at the center and leaves at the periphery. The gradually diverging discharge section of the pump in Fig. 6.1 is designed to recover the kinetic energy of the high velocity fluid and transform it into a pressure increase in addition to that provided by the centrifugal force alone. Many simple sanitary pumps used in food processing do not have this feature. Centrifugal pumps have their primary application for low viscosity fluids under conditions of relatively high throughput and moderate pressure increase. For higher pressures, multistage pumps are available with several impellers cased individually on a single shaft so that the fluid

Courtesy Buffalo Forge Co.

FIG. 6.1.   CENTRIFUGAL PUMP

flows from one impeller to the next in series. Such pump units are available with capacities of many thousands of gallons per minute at pressures up to a few thousand psi.

Although the capacity of centrifugal pumps depends on the speed of rotation, they are operated with constant-speed drives. For process purposes, flow rate is controlled by a valve on the discharge line. This type of control is much less expensive than providing a variable-speed drive and is a major advantage of centrifugal over positive displacement pumps. A centrifugal pump is not damaged by operation with the discharge valve completely closed, but the pump energy is dissipated as friction and causes an increase in temperature of the fluid. Any pump operating at a fixed speed and with a specified liquid will have a characteristic performance curve of pressure increase as a function of flow rate. The condition of maximum flow and minimum pressure is obtained with an unrestricted discharge. The maximum pressure is developed at or near zero flow by closing the discharge valve.

Both the centrifugal force and kinetic energy contributions to the pressure increase are proportional to the fluid density. Because gases have such low densities compared to liquids, they cannot be moved by centrifugal pumps. If a gas is admitted to the suction, the pump will fail to develop a pressure head, and liquid flow will stop. This behavior is in contrast to that of positive displacement pumps, which can effectively pump mixtures of liquids and gases. A particular problem with centrifugal pumps is that of cavitation. If the liquid is near its boiling point, a slight drop in pressure on the suction side may cause some vapor to form and interrupt the pumping. Operation under cavitation conditions can be very damaging to the pump. For this reason, it is important to maintain an adequate liquid head on the suction side when there is a possibility of cavitation.

Centrifugal pumps are not suitable for high viscosity fluids because fluid friction effects prevent attainment of the necessary fluid velocities inside the pump. Various types of impeller design are available for liquids with suspended solids. It is possible, for example, to pump such suspensions as whole peaches in water without damaging the peaches. Figure 6.2 shows cutaway views of some different types of impellers. On the left is a 4-vane enclosed impeller for normal pumping of liquid streams which do not contain large particles. In the middle is a 2-vane impeller with the inlet ends of the vanes rounded so that trash or fibrous solids will not hang up. On the right is an open impeller that will handle large particulate matter. The efficiency of such an impeller is much lower than that of the close-clearance enclosed types.

Positive Displacement Pumps

A centrifugal pump creates pressure from a high fluid velocity. A positive displacement pump, on the other hand, applies a direct force to a confined volume of fluid to push it up to a higher pressure. Because of this direct force, it is not possible to control the flow rate with a valve on the discharge line. If these pumps are operated with a closed discharge, extremely high pressures can be developed that would result in damage to the pump or piping. The direct force, however, makes it possible to develop much higher pressures than with centrifugal pumps and to handle liquids of very high viscosity. Because of the low fluid velocities, the energy lost in fluid friction is not a serious problem.

In operation, a positive displacement pump handles the fluid in discrete portions or slugs. A slug of fluid is drawn into the pump cavity and is then forced out the discharge. The flow rate is determined by the number of slugs delivered per unit time, which is proportional to the speed at which the pump is driven. Theoretically, the volumetric flow rate thus depends only on the pump speed regardless of whether the fluid is a liquid or gas. Actually, there is always some leakage of fluid or "slippage", so that strict proportionality will not be observed. Because the liquid is delivered in slugs, the discharge is intermittent or pulsating to some degree. Under some conditions, these pulsations can lead to undesirable variations in flow rate or excessive vibrations. It is possible to combine the output from two or

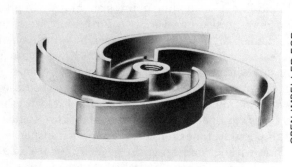

OPEN IMPELLER FOR
LARGE SOLIDS
Courtesy Nagle Pumps

2-VANE TRASH IMPELLER

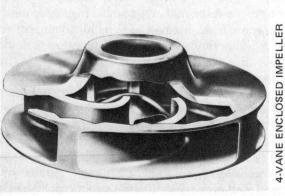

4-VANE ENCLOSED IMPELLER

FIG. 6.2.   CENTRIFUGAL PUMP IMPELLERS

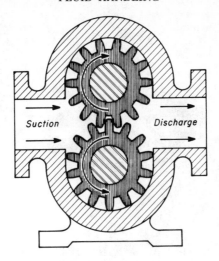

FIG. 6.3.   GEAR PUMP

more pumps so as to minimize or eliminate the pulsations. Positive displacement pumps may generally be classified as reciprocating, rotary or axial flow, as described below.

Reciprocating Pumps.—These devices consist essentially of a piston moving inside a cylinder. Fluid is drawn into the cylinder on the backward stroke and is forced out the discharge on the forward stroke. A discharge valve prevents the high pressure liquid from flowing back into the piston on the backward stroke, and an intake valve prevents liquid from flowing out the intake line on the forward stroke. These are usually spring-loaded self acting valves, whose action would be impaired by liquids in the higher viscosity ranges. Reciprocating pumps can easily develop pressures of several thousand pounds per square inch. Their primary application is for liquids of lower viscosities with requirements of relatively high pressures and low volumetric throughput.

Rotary Pumps.—These pumps are available in a wide variety of designs. In operation, a pocket of fluid is entrapped between a rotating member and a stationary housing, or stator. The pocket of fluid is carried forward from the intake to the discharge by the rotation, and the rotor picks up another quantity of fluid on the next revolution. There may be several pulses or slugs per revolution. The rotor turns continuously in one direction and always maintains a seal against the stator. There is thus no need for valves, and the intake and discharge ports can be full line size with no flow restrictions. The direction of flow can be reversed simply by reversing the direction of

Courtesy Viking Pumps

FIG. 6.4.   INTERNAL GEAR PUMP WITH FIXED CRESCENT

Courtesy Waukesha Foundry Co.

FIG. 6.5.   2-LOBE PUMP

rotation. Speeds of rotation are a few hundred rpm at most, much lower than for centrifugal pumps. Variable-speed drives must be provided for control of flow rate.

In some rotary pumps, either the stator or the rotor is constructed of a resilient material so that the rotor can actually maintain a rubbing contact to provide a tight seal. In other pumps, all parts are of metal, and it is necessary to provide a small clearance. The pumps must be constructed to very close tolerances; excessive clearance permits back-leakage of fluid, and too

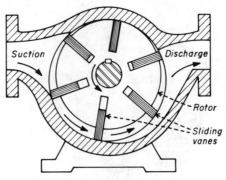

FIG. 6.6.   SLIDING-VANE PUMP

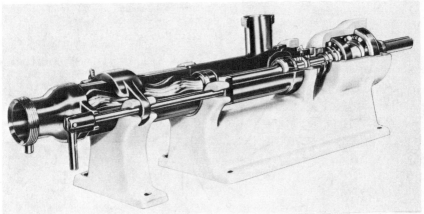

Courtesy Moyno Pumps

FIG. 6.7.   SCREW PUMP

much contact pressure results in high friction and pump wear. The wear problem makes rotary pumps unsatisfactory for fluids containing suspended abrasive solids.

Some of the more common types of rotary pumps are illustrated in the accompanying figures. Perhaps the most common is the simple gear pump of Fig. 6.3. External drive is applied to only one gear, which in turn drives the other. A modification of this type is the internal gear pump with fixed crescent of Fig. 6.4. An example of a lobe pump is shown in Fig. 6.5. There may be up to four lobes on each rotor. Lobes are of various configurations, but are always designed so that they maintain essential contact throughout a revolution. One rotor will not drive the other, and it is necessary to provide an external drive to both shafts. Another common type is the sliding-vane

Courtesy American Standard

FIG. 6.8.   VANEAXIAL FAN

FORWARD CURVED   BACKWARD INCLINED   RADIAL

FIG. 6.9.   CENTRIFUGAL FAN WHEELS

pump of Fig. 6.6. The vanes may be spring loaded or they may be held against the stator by centrifugal force.

Axial Flow Pumps.—These devices are screw type pumps in which the fluid moves parallel to the axis of rotation rather than perpendicular to it. One such pump very commonly used in the food industry is shown in Fig. 6.7. The rotor is a steel shaft formed into a single helix, and the rubber stator has a double helix. The space between the rotor and stator forms a series of sealed cavities that progress along the axis and carry the fluid with them.

FIG. 6.10.   FORWARD-CURVED FAN

Propeller Pumps

Propeller devices are widely used in liquid mixing applications. In pumps, they find application where there is a requirement for moving a very large volume with a low head. Handling storm drainage would be a typical example. A use in the food industry is handling cannery waste water.

PUMPS FOR GASES

Almost all of the types of equipment described above are used for gases with, of course, modifications of design. With gases, there are many more applications than with liquids for moving large volumes at low pressure differentials. Consequently, propeller and centrifugal equipment predominate over positive displacement.

Propeller Fans

Propeller fans are available in sizes from small household appliances to large industrial models. The commonest example is in automobile engine cooling. It should be noted that propeller equipment is always axial flow. For various applications, many modifications can be made in the design and number of blades. Effectiveness in delivering air against higher resistances is improved if the fan is enclosed in a tubular housing. The discharge from a fan has a rotary motion imparted by the rotating fan blades. In the tube-type equipment, a set of stationary guide vanes following the fan may be provided to redirect the rotary velocity into axial velocity and thereby improve the efficiency. The vaneaxial fan in Fig. 6.8 shows the guide vanes behind the four-bladed fan. An axial-flow compressor is an extension of the tubeaxial fan. These are constructed with shorter blades in proportion to the rotor diameter and there are several times as many blades as in a fan. A number of stages of rotor blades and stationary stator blades are mounted along the axis of a machine. A common use of axial flow compressors is in aircraft jet engines.

Centrifugal Fans

As the required delivery pressure increases, centrifugal fans become more efficient than propeller equipment. The blades in the wheels of centrifugal fans are of three general types as shown in Fig. 6.9: forward curved, backward inclined, and radial. The forward curved type, shown in Fig. 6.10 is frequently called a squirrel cage fan. It runs at lower speeds and is relatively more quiet and lower in cost than the other types. It is available in sizes ranging from very small (wheel diameters of a few inches) up to large industrial models. A very common application is in residential and commercial hot air heating and air conditioning systems.

As with centrifugal pumps, fans have characteristic curves of developed pressure and power requirement as a function of volumetric throughput. As the pressure against which the fan operates decreases, the volumetric capacity increases. Forward curved fans have the disadvantage that the power requirement also increases along with the increased throughput. Thus, a fan motor selected for some specific operating condition could become overloaded if the resistance encountered by the fan were to decrease. The power curve of a backward inclined fan goes through a maximum and then declines with further increase in throughput. If the fan is selected to operate near the peak of its power curve, it is impossible to overload the motor by either increasing or decreasing the resistance against which it operates. Backward inclined fans are also capable of higher efficiencies than forward inclined. Radial bladed fans are used for gases containing particulate matter such as dust or exhaust from wood or metal working machines.

For higher pressures than fans will supply, centrifugal compressors are available. Essentially, they differ from backward inclined fans only in dimensions and speed of rotation, and they are quite similar to centrifugal pumps in appearance. Multistage centrifugal compressors can develop pressures of several hundred psi. These are high capacity machines, and they are not competitive with positive displacement compressors in small sizes.

Positive Displacement Compressors

All of the general types of positive displacement equipment used for liquids are also designed for gases. Reciprocating compressors are used in a very wide range of sizes and are the only type suitable for very high pressures, i.e., upwards of 1000 psi. Lobe type and screw-type axial flow blowers are useful in bridging the range of pressures and volumes between centrifugal fans and centrifugal compressors. Positive displacement equipment of all types has particular application in vacuum operations, where centrifugal equipment is ineffective because of the very low gas densities. Most laboratory vacuum pumps are the sliding vane type as shown in Fig. 6.6.

CHAPTER 7

Fluid Flow[1]

CHARACTERISTICS OF FLUIDS

A fluid may exist as either a liquid or a gas. From the standpoint of fluid flow, it is more convenient to think in terms of incompressible or compressible fluids. An incompressible fluid is one whose volume (or density) is independent of pressure, whereas the density of a compressible fluid varies directly with pressure. Strictly speaking, there is no such thing as an incompressible fluid; the density of all substances will be affected to some degree by pressure. From a practical point of view in dealing with fluid flow, however, liquids can be considered to be incompressible. If pressure changes are small enough, even gases can be treated as though they are incompressible. Although the fundamental relationships that are to be developed are applicable to both compressible and incompressible fluids, certain simplifications are possible if the density can be considered to be constant. Most of the fluid flow problems in food processing are concerned with liquids, and the following sections will therefore be primarily directed toward incompressible fluids.

Both density and viscosity of fluids are dependent on temperature, and a variation in temperature over the path of a flow process will therefore affect the fluid behavior. The following discussion does not include the effect of changes in fluid properties caused by non-constant temperatures, although there is a brief discussion of the nature of the effects.

For flow to take place, there must be some unbalanced force or pressure. In the absence of such a condition, the fluid will remain at rest. For example, the pressure at the bottom of a bucket of water is higher than the pressure at the top surface. This higher pressure, however, is exactly balanced by the restraining force of the bottom of the bucket, and the water remains at rest. If a hole is made in the bucket, the restraining force is removed, and water will flow because of the difference in pressure. Because of the direct connection of fluid flow to applied pressures or forces, it will be helpful to consider some definitions of these quantities.

Force is a fundamental quantity in the subject of mechanics, along with mass, length, and time. This subject was treated previously in Chapter 1. Pressure is defined as force per unit area. The most commonly used unit

[1] Symbols used in this chapter are listed and defined at the end of the chapter.

of pressure in the English system is the pound force per square inch, or lb_f/in^2. A more general term for force per unit area is stress. Just as the direction of a force must be given in order to specify it completely, so must the direction of a stress. A normal stress is one that is directed normal, or perpendicular, to a surface. Pressure is always a normal stress. A fluid at rest can exert a force only perpendicular to the walls of a confining surface. Thus, water in a bucket will exert a vertical force on the bottom and a horizontal force on the sides. A stress that acts in a direction parallel to a surface or a plane in a fluid is called a shear stress. It can be seen that a shear stress will tend to "shear" off layers of a fluid. For example, the skis of a water skier will exert a shear stress (as well as a normal stress) on the water.

The existence of a pressure, or normal stress, does not, in itself, cause fluid flow. Gas can be contained inside a cylinder at an extremely high pressure, but it does not flow. On the other hand, a shear stress is necessary for fluid flow, and a true fluid will always flow on application of a shear stress. This action under a shear stress serves to define the difference between fluids and solids. A true fluid will deform or flow continuously as long as a shear stress is applied. When the stress is removed, flow will stop, but there is no tendency for the fluid to recover or return to its original state. A shear stress will cause an elastic solid to undergo a fixed deformation. If the elastic limit is not exceeded, the solid will return to its original state when the stress is removed. Plastic materials are intermediate in that they deform continuously but also show some elastic recovery. Food gels are in this category.

When a fluid is flowing in the vicinity of a confining surface, such as a pipe wall, it is a general finding that the fluid directly in contact with the wall has zero velocity. In other words, the fluid does not slip along the wall as one solid can slip past another. The velocity will thus increase from zero at the wall up to some maximum value in the main stream. Although it is a difference in pressure between the ends of the pipe that provides the driving mechanism for flow, the retarding force or friction along the pipe wall converts the pressure difference into a shear stress across the liquid. In order to visualize this shearing mechanism, it is helpful to imagine that the flowing fluid is made up of a series of concentric shells or tubes. The shear stress causes one shell to slip past the one immediately surrounding it, and the velocity of the shells will thus decrease continuously from a maximum at the pipe center to zero at the wall. The friction between the adjacent shells is what causes the resistance to flow.

Viewed as a molecular phenomenon, this frictional resistance is caused by the random motion of molecules across the imaginary boundary from one shell to another. Let us consider a situation in which one shell or layer of fluid is moving past another with a definite difference in velocity. In

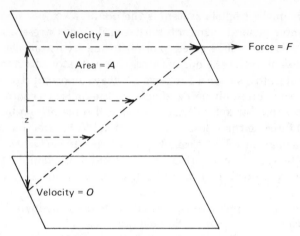

FIG. 7.1. FLUID VELOCITY PROFILE BETWEEN A STATIONARY PLATE AND A PLATE
MOVING PARALLEL TO IT

addition to the forward velocity of the two layers in the direction of flow,
there is random molecular motion in all directions. When molecules from
the slow layer move by this random motion into the fast layer, they create
a retarding force and tend to slow the fast layer down. On the other hand,
molecules moving from the fast into the slow layer create a forward force
on the slow layer. In order to maintain flow, a continuous driving force must
be provided, as by a pressure difference. The energy that this force supplies
is ·dissipated throughout the fluid by this friction between layers and
eventually appears as a rise in temperature.

The viscosity of a fluid is the property that is a measure of this frictional
resistance to shear. Consider the situation illustrated in Fig. 7.1, in which
a fluid is confined between two parallel plates. The lower plate is stationary,
and the upper plate moves in a parallel direction with a velocity V. The
velocity of the fluid between the plates will vary uniformly from zero at the
bottom plate to V at the top plate. The motion of the upper plate obviously
creates a shear stress on the fluid. This shear stress, or force per unit area,
must be applied to the top plate to keep it in motion. Newton proposed that
this force per unit area is proportional to the difference in velocities of the
two plates divided by the distance between them, or $F/A \propto V/z$. In order
to develop a more general expression, let us replace the two plates by two
imaginary planes in the fluid and let these planes be separated by an infinitesimal distance. The distance can then be represented by the differential dz, and the difference in velocity by dV. Newton's law can then be
represented by the expression

$$F/A = \tau = \mu(dV/dz) \qquad \text{Eq. 7-1}$$

In this expression, τ is a symbol used to represent shear stress and the
proportionality constant μ is called the coefficient of viscosity, or simply

the viscosity. The symbol η is also frequently used for this quantity. In the above expression, the ratio, or derivative, dV/dz is called the velocity gradient or rate of shear. It is a measure of how rapidly the velocity is changing with distance at right angles to the direction of flow. If a plot is made of velocity against distance in a flowing fluid, the velocity gradient at any point is simply given by the slope of a tangent to the curve. In the above case of a fluid between two parallel plates, the velocity curve is a straight line and the velocity gradient is constant.

Solving the above expression for viscosity, we obtain

$$\mu = \frac{F/A}{dV/dz} = \left(\frac{F}{A}\right)\left(\frac{dz}{dV}\right)$$

In dimensional symbols,

$$\mu = \frac{[F]}{[L^2]} \cdot \frac{[L]}{[L]/[\theta]} = \frac{[F][\theta]}{[L^2]}$$

In the CGS system, shear stress is commonly expressed in dyne/cm^2, and the corresponding unit of viscosity is (dyne)(sec)/(cm^2), which is called the poise. Viscosities of common liquids and gases expressed in poise are usually rather small numbers, and the centipoise (0.01 poise) is the unit customarily used. The viscosity of water is about one centipoise at ordinary temperatures.

Since one dyne is equivalent to one (gm)(cm)/(sec^2), a substitution shows that one poise can also be expressed as one (gm)/(cm)(sec). In English engineering units, the corresponding units of viscosity are the (lb$_f$)(sec)/(ft^2) and the (lb$_m$)/(ft)(sec). There is no other common name for these English units. It must be noted that since one lb$_f$ is equivalent to 32.2 (lb$_m$)(ft)/ (sec^2), one (lb$_f$)(sec)/(ft^2) is equal to 32.2 (lb$_m$)(ft)/(sec). In the CGS system, since mass and force units of viscosity are the same size, the viscosity of a fluid has the same numerical value whichever set is used. In the English system, the force units represent a larger quantity than the mass units, so the viscosity expressed in force units will be a smaller number than in mass units. All of the above units are used throughout the literature on fluid flow, and it is essential that the above relationships be kept clearly in mind.

A Newtonian fluid is one that obeys Newton's viscosity law. For such fluids, viscosity is a property of the material. Its value depends on the state of the material, primarily the temperature, but not on the conditions of flow. The viscosity of gases increases with increases in temperature, and the viscosity of liquids decreases, usually very markedly, with increases in temperature. All gases obey Newton's viscosity law, and by kinetic theory it is possible to develop the relationship of viscosity to other molecular parameters. It is found experimentally that pure liquids and simple solutions are also Newtonian. In general, mixtures or solutions of very high molecular weight substances and concentrated suspensions of particles do not obey the law. For these materials, there is not a simple proportionality between shear stress and velocity gradient and, accordingly, there is not a unique value of viscosity. In other words, the apparent viscosity depends on the conditions of flow as well as the properties of the fluid. Such materials are called non-Newtonian fluids. Most liquids of biological origin, such as solutions or suspensions of proteins or polysaccharides fall into this category. Naturally occurring or synthetic polymers of high molecular weight, either in the liquid state or dissolved, are non-Newtonian. Fruit and vegetable purees, particularly where substantial amounts of insoluble particulate matter are present, are highly non-Newtonian. Outside of the food area, materials such as petroleum asphalts, oil well drilling mud, plastic melts, rubber latex, and paint are non-Newtonian. Although the greatest volume of fluids handled in the process industries is Newtonian (all gases, water and most aqueous solutions, most petroleum liquids, etc.), by far the greatest number of different fluids encountered are non-Newtonian. Most of the discussion that follows is devoted to the subject of Newtonian fluids, both because such applications are of primary importance in themselves and because an understanding of the behavior of Newtonian fluids is an essential background for any study of non-Newtonian fluids.

THE NATURE OF FLUID FLOW

In the preceding paragraphs, viscosity was described as a measure of the frictional resistance of a fluid to flow or to a shear stress. This resistance was seen to arise from the random motion of molecules passing back and forth between adjacent layers of fluid of different velocity. Actually, of course, the velocity in a flowing fluid varies continuously from one point to another; there is no sharply defined boundary of any layer except at a solid surface. The hypothetical layers, which are considered to be infinitesimal in thickness, are useful as an aid in visualizing the physical process that takes place. Flow that is accurately described by this mechanism of layers, or lamina, sliding past each other, and in which all resistance arises from random molecular motion, is called laminar flow. In such flow, there is no bulk mixing, and the different layers maintain their identities. This process can be easily demonstrated as was first described by the Englishman, Reynolds, in the latter part of the last century. In this experiment, fluid flows at a controlled rate through a clear glass or plastic tube. At a point in the tube, some of the same fluid with a coloring agent added is injected from a hypodermic needle in the direction of flow. This injected fluid forms a colored filament that maintains its identity and position down the length of the tube. Because of molecular diffusion, this filament will eventually become fuzzy and blend in with the main stream, but there will be no bulk mixing or disruption of the filament. The line that this filament forms down the tube is called a streamline. Regardless of where the colored fluid is injected across the diameter of the tube, the streamlines will maintain their identities, and the term streamline flow is used as a synonym for laminar flow. Fluids of high viscosity, such as concentrated sugar solutions, lubricating oils, etc., usually flow by this mechanism, and viscous flow is a third descriptive term that is frequently used. The three terms, *streamline, laminar,* and *viscous* flow all have the same meaning and are used interchangeably.

If the fluid velocity in the Reynolds experiment is gradually increased, a point is reached at which the colored filament is no longer a straight line but becomes wavy. As the velocity is further increased, the waviness will increase, until eventually the filament breaks up and the segments mix individually with the surrounding fluid. At sufficiently high velocities, the injected fluid will be mixed almost immediately throughout the main stream, and no separate filament will be observed. What is happening as the velocity is increased in this experiment is a change from streamline to turbulent flow. In turbulent flow, small whorls or eddies are formed that move across the flow path and bring about bulk mixing. These eddies are continuously forming and dying out throughout the entire volume of flowing fluid. Although the eddies are small, they are still very large compared to molecular dimensions. They therefore have a much greater effect than molecular motion in mixing a fluid stream. Recalling the explanation given above of the origin of the frictional resistance to fluid flow, it is to be expected that this much larger amount of material carried between faster and slower moving parts of the stream by turbulent eddies would create a much greater frictional resistance than exists in streamline flow. The experiment described above shows that the change from streamline to turbulent flow is not sharp but takes place over a range of velocity. This change will be discussed in more detail below.

STEADY FLOW IN PIPES

A steady state process is one in which there is no change with respect to time. Steady flow in a pipe or conduit means, first of all, that the mass flow rate (not velocity) past any cross section is the same at every point from the entrance to the exit. Variables such as pressure, temperature, velocity, elevation, etc. may change from point to point along the flow path, but all variables remain constant at any particular position. There is, of course, no requirement that the diameter of the pipe be constant. The mass flow rate, in lb_m/sec, for example, divided by the density gives the volumetric flow rate in ft^3/sec. The volumetric flow rate, in turn, divided by the cross sectional area gives the average velocity in ft/sec at that point. These relationships may be expressed in the form of the following extremely important equation:

$$\dot{m} = VS_\rho = \text{constant} \qquad\qquad \text{Eq. 7-2}$$

where $\dot{m}$ is mass per unit time and S is cross-sectional area. It must be emphasized that velocity, represented by the symbol V, is always expressed in units of length divided by time. The general term, flow rate, has no specific definition and might refer to mass per unit time, volume per unit time, or even to velocity.

Velocity Distribution

As discussed previously, the velocity of a fluid flowing in a pipe varies from zero at the wall to a maximum at the center. The average velocity, which appears in Eq. 7-2, is the velocity that would exist if the fluid at the same mass rate were to flow as a plug, with constant velocity over the entire cross section. With instruments described in a later section, it is possible to measure the velocity at any point across the diameter of the pipe and thus to make a plot of velocity vs. diameter, or velocity profile. The average velocity can be obtained by graphical integration of the velocity profile information. A Newtonian fluid in isothermal streamline flow has a constant viscosity, and Eq. 7-1 applies at every point across the diameter. For this case, it can be shown that the velocity profile is a parabola. The maximum velocity, at the pipe center, is exactly twice the average velocity. For turbulent flow, there is no exact relationship such as Eq. 7-1, and a similar derivation cannot be made. Experimentally, it is found that the velocity profile is flatter for turbulent than for streamline flow. The maximum velocity will therefore be something less than twice the average. The ratio is not a constant, but varies according to flow parameters.

Characterization of Flow

From the foregoing, it can be seen that there is a need for some general way to characterize the flow in a pipe. In particular, it is important to have some means of predicting whether flow would be streamline or turbulent in a given situation. To be useful, any such method would have to be valid for all types of Newtonian fluids, for all flow rates, and for all pipe sizes. It is not difficult to predict what variables would be important in establishing a suitable flow parameter. The only fluid properties affecting flow conditions are viscosity and density. Velocity is obviously directly involved. Pipe diameter is certainly of importance, and the nature of the pipe surface might also be expected to be a factor. If the flowing fluid is a single phase, either liquid or gas, the material of which the pipe is made does not in itself affect the flow. Whether the material is metal, plastic, ceramic, or any other, the velocity is zero at the surface, and it is only at the surface that the material could have any effect. If a mixture of gas and liquid were flowing, the degree of wetting of the surface by the liquid phase would have to be considered. The texture of the pipe surface, however, cannot be disregarded. One might very well expect a rough pipe surface to affect the flow differently than a smooth surface. In order to simplify the problem, we will limit our consideration for the present to smooth pipes such as glass, extruded plastic, or drawn metal.

Close to the inlet of a pipe, the flow has not yet had time to reach a fully developed pattern, and the pipe length would be important in this region. We shall consider here only the flow characteristics at distances far enough from the entrance that flow patterns are fully established. With this restriction, pipe length can be eliminated as a factor.

The problem, then, is resolved into finding some way to use the four variables viscosity, density, velocity, and diameter to characterize the flow. It would be possible, of course, to prepare extensive tables, based on experimental observations, that would cover the entire range of possible values of these variables and that would show, for example, whether flow would be streamline or turbulent for any desired combination. Such a method would be difficult to establish and inconvenient to use. It would provide no understanding of or general approach to the problem, and each situation would have to be considered as a specific case. A much more desirable approach would be to combine the numerical values of the above variables in some way to give a number or parameter that characterizes the flow. If such a parameter is to have general application, its value clearly must not depend on the particular units in which the individual variables are expressed. For example, whether the pipe diameter is given in feet or inches or centimeters, the parameter should come out with the same numerical value. The only way to get a parameter that does not depend on the units of the individual factors is to have it in the form of a dimensionless ratio. If the arrangement of the factors is such that all the dimensions (or units) cancel, the parameter is a pure number. For example, a parameter that is important for flow in short pipes is the ratio of length to diameter. This ratio is a pure number whose value is independent of the unit of length used. Obviously, the same unit must be used for both length and diameter.

The dimensions of the four variables involved in the desired flow parameter are as follows:

velocity (V)	$[L]/[\theta]$
density (ρ)	$[M]/[L^3]$
diameter (D)	$[L]$
viscosity (μ)	$[M]/[L\theta]$

It is seen that mass appears only in the two variables ρ and μ. Clearly, the only way that mass can be eliminated from the final parameter is to have ρ and μ appear as a ratio. If viscosity were given in force instead of mass units, it would be necessary to convert it to mass units by the factor g_c. The ratio ρ/μ has the net dimensions $[\theta]/[L^2]$. The factor θ is eliminated if this latter ratio is multiplied by V, leaving a dimension of $1/[L]$. The removal of this last length dimension is accomplished by using D as a factor. The resulting dimensionless ratio is called the Reynolds number after the investigator mentioned previously and is represented by the symbol

$$Re = DV\rho/\mu \qquad \text{Eq. 7-3}$$

The above procedure illustrates one method that may be used to obtain dimensionless ratios describing physical processes. Such a derivation does not necessarily prove that the ratio obtained has significance, but it does provide a basis for experimental configuration. There are other more rigorous theoretical methods by which the significance of the Reynolds number as a flow parameter can be justified. It has been shown, both theoretically and by thousands of experiments, that the Reynolds number does indeed serve to characterize flow in a pipe. In other words, two flow situations having the same Reynolds number are "similar," or correspond to each other, regardless of the range of the values of the individual variables involved. With respect to type of flow, it is found that flow is always streamline if Re is less than about 2100. In careful experiments, streamline flow can be maintained up to substantially higher values of Re, but 2100 can be taken as a lower limit for the existence of turbulent flow, for rough as well as smooth pipes. At Reynolds numbers immediately above 2100, there is a transition region between streamline and turbulent flow. The width of this region depends on the individual case and cannot be predicted accurately. Turbulence will usually be well established above Re of about 4000. The utility of the Reynolds number is not limited to flow in round pipes. In different flow situations, however, a length variable other than diameter may have to be used, and the value of 2100 will no longer serve to define the limit of streamline flow.

It is frequently convenient to express Re in terms of mass flow rate instead of velocity. If Eq. 7-2 is used to eliminate velocity and the cross-sectional area is set equal to $\pi D^2/4$, we obtain

$$Re = 4\dot{m}/\pi D\mu \qquad \text{Eq. 7-4}$$

MECHANICAL ENERGY BALANCE

Equation 3-10 (Chap. 3) is frequently called the mechanical energy equation. This is an exact equation that applies regardless of whether or not temperature is constant or heat is transferred to or from the system. We shall now consider the application of this equation to the steady flow of constant density fluids in round pipes. Carrying out the indicated integration with the restriction of constant density, we obtain

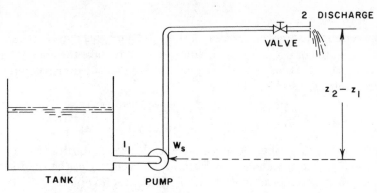

FIG. 7.2.   A FLOW SYSTEM BOUNDED AT POINTS 1 AND 2

$$-W_s = \Delta P/\rho + \Delta KE + \Delta PE + F \qquad \text{Eq. 7-5}$$

All the terms in Eq. 7-5 represent energy per unit mass of fluid flowing, given as ft-lb$_f$/lb$_m$ in the usual engineering units. Although we are dealing with a flow process, we are applying the equation to a system of unit mass. This procedure is legitimate because, in a steady state flow process, the mass flow rate is a constant and each unit of mass undergoes exactly the same treatment as every other unit. If energy per unit time, or power, is desired, it is merely necessary to multiply each of the terms by the mass flow rate. Evaluation of the individual terms in Eq. 7-5 will be discussed with respect to a typical flow arrangement as shown in Fig. 7.2. Here, liquid is pumped from a tank and discharged from a pipe at a higher elevation. The inlet and outlet of the system to be considered are indicated by the dotted lines numbered 1 and 2.

Shaft Work

The shaft work, W_s, is simply the work per pound of fluid that is put into the pump shaft. It is to be emphasized again that if there is no shaft, there is no shaft work. If the inlet section had been taken on the other side of the pump, the pump would not be in the system and the shaft work would be zero.

Pressure Effect

ΔP in the pressure term is the difference in pressure between points 2 and 1, or $P_2 - P_1$. The symbol Δ always means the final value minus the initial value of a quantity. The difference in pressures might be obtained from pressure gage readings or from a differential manometer. In Fig. 7.2, the pressure at section 2 is 1 atmosphere, since the fluid discharges into the atmosphere at that point. If pressure is expressed in units of lb$_f$/ft^2 and density in lb$_m$/ft^3, the ratio $\Delta P/\rho$ has the desired units of ft lb$_f$/lb$_m$.

Kinetic Energy

The common expression for kinetic energy of a moving mass is $(1/2)mV^2$, leading to units of $(lb_m)(ft^2)/sec^2$. Since we wish to have the energy terms in force rather than mass units, we must divide by the dimensional conversion factor g_c as shown below.

$$KE = \left(\frac{mV^2}{2}\frac{(lb_m)(ft^2)}{(sec^2)}\right)\left(\frac{1}{g_c}\frac{(lb_f)(sec^2)}{(lb_m)(ft)}\right) = \frac{mV^2}{2g_c}\text{ ft-lb}_f$$

If we let $m = 1\ lb_m$, kinetic energy becomes $V^2/2g_c$ ft-lb$_f$/lb$_m$.

The velocity in the above expression is the velocity of the fluid at the desired point. If the fluid moved as a plug, like a solid object, there would be no question as to the correct velocity. The fluid velocity varies across the diameter, however, and the average velocity in the above expression will not give the correct kinetic energy. For example, suppose that $\frac{1}{2}\ lb_m$ of a fluid has a velocity of 2 ft/sec and $\frac{1}{2}\ lb_m$ a velocity of 4 ft/sec:

$$KE = (1/2g_c)(1/2)(2^2) + (1/2g_c)(1/2)(4^2) = 5/g_c$$

If we use the average velocity of 3 ft/sec, for the entire pound, we obtain

$$KE = (1/2g_c)(1)(3^2) = 4.5/g_c$$

It is therefore necessary to include a factor in the kinetic energy expression to allow for the velocity distribution across the pipe, as follows

$$KE = V^2/2\alpha g_c$$

For the parabolic velocity distribution of isothermal streamline flow, it can be shown that the factor α is exactly 0.5. The kinetic energy is higher than if the average velocity were used, just as in the example above. With turbulent flow, the factor will depend on the Reynolds number. Velocity profiles are much flatter than with streamline flow, however, and it is usually a satisfactory approximation to set $\alpha = 1.0$. Accordingly, for the complete kinetic energy term, we can write

$$\Delta KE = (V_2{}^2 - V_1{}^2)/2\alpha g_c \qquad \text{Eq. 7-6}$$

where $\alpha = 0.5$ for Re less than 2100 and 1.0 for Re greater than 2100.

If the pipe diameter is constant with a constant density fluid, the velocity is also constant, and the kinetic energy term is equal to zero. If the pipe diameter changes, as indicated in Fig. 7-2, we obtain from Eq. 7-2

$$V_1S_1 = V_2S_2 = \dot{m}/\rho = \text{constant}$$

and

$$V_2/V_1 = S_1/S_2 = D_1{}^2/D_2{}^2 \qquad \text{Eq. 7-7}$$

Potential Energy

The general expression for potential energy resulting from a change in elevation is mgz, which gives units of $(lb_m)(ft^2)/sec^2$ in the English system. As in the case of kinetic energy, we must divide by g_c in order to obtain the desired units. Accordingly,

$$\Delta PE = (z_2 - z_1)g/g_c \text{ ft lb}_f/lb_m \qquad \text{Eq. 7-8}$$

We are obviously concerned here only with a change in elevation, so that the reference level above which the individual elevations are measured can be arbitrary.

Before proceeding with a discussion of fluid friction, it will be helpful to summarize the results of the preceding paragraphs. Equation 7-5 may now be written as

$$-W_s = (P_2 - P_1)/\rho + (V_2^2 - V_1^2)/2\alpha g_c + (z_2 - z_1)g/g_c + F \qquad \text{Eq. 7-9}$$

As has been noted, the units of each term in the English system are ft-lb_f/lb_m. It will be recalled that, by definition, g_c is numerically equal to the standard gravitational acceleration, or 32.17. Although the value of g varies with location, for all practical industrial engineering purposes it can also be considered constant at 32.17. The ratio g/g_c is therefore numerically equal to unity. The units of this ratio do not cancel, but are as follows:

$$\left(g \frac{ft}{sec^2}\right) \left(\frac{1}{g_c} \frac{(lb_f)(sec^2)}{(lb_m)(ft)}\right) = \frac{g}{g_c} \frac{lb_f}{lb_m}$$

The ratio thus has the units of lb_f/lb_m. Both sides of Eq. 7-9 can be multiplied by the ratio g_c/g without affecting its validity or changing the numerical value of any terms. If this is done, the ratio g/g_c will drop out of the potential energy term, g will take the place of g_c in the kinetic energy term, and the units of each term will simply be ft. It is this equivalence that permits us to observe a pressure difference as the height of a column of liquid and to use pressure units such as cm of mercury or in. of water. Accordingly, it is a common practice to refer to the various energy terms of Eq. 7-9 as "feet" or "feet of head." For example, if a pump handling water at a given flow rate will put up 30 ft of head, this means that the pump will do enough work to supply the potential energy of lifting the water a height of 30 ft, and the quantity of work is 30 ft-lb_f/lb_m. Because all the terms are numerically the same whichever set of units is used, some lack of consistency in terminology will not ordinarily lead to errors. If one were designing a hydraulic system to be used on the moon, the situation would be entirely different.

It is of interest to note that Eq. 7-9 can be used to establish the relationship between pressure and liquid height in a manometer. In a static system such as a column of liquid balanced by a pressure, velocity is zero and there is no work or friction. Accordingly, Eq. 7-9 reduces to

$$(P_1 - P_2)/\rho = (z_2 - z_1)g/g_c$$

Since the ratio g/g_c is numerically equal to unity, the difference in pressure between the bottom and top of the liquid column divided by the density is numerically equal to the height of the column. Thus, a column of water 10 ft high corresponds to 10 ft-lb_f/lb_m, and the pressure difference is $(10)(62.4) = 624 \ lb_f/ft^2$. A similar calculation shows that the atmospheric pressure of 14.7 lb_f/in^2 is equivalent to 33.9 ft of water.

FLUID FRICTION

The derivation of Eq. 7-9 by energy balance principles tells nothing about the nature of the friction term. This term merely represents the difference between ideal and actual energy quantities for a process. If we experimentally measure all the other quantities of Eq. 7-9 for a particular system, we can obtain the friction by difference. In most cases, however, we want to be able to predict the friction in advance. Such predictions are possible with the aid of correlations that are based on a very large number of experimental measurements made by many investigators.

Friction for Flow in Straight Pipes

In applying Eq. 7-9 to this situation, the system will be taken to consist of a horizontal length of pipe with a constant diameter. No pump or other mechanical device is present, so $W_s = 0$. For constant diameter and constant density, there is no change in velocity, and the kinetic energy term drops out. A horizontal pipe means that there is no change in potential energy. Accordingly, the equation reduces to

$$F = -(P_2 - P_1)/\rho \qquad \text{Eq. 7-10}$$

Experimentally, then, all that is necessary is to measure the pressure drop along a known length of pipe. Many such measurements have been made, covering wide ranges of velocity, density, viscosity, and pipe diameter. The effect of surface roughness has also been studied extensively.

Just as the velocity profile for streamline flow can be derived from theory, so can an expression for pressure drop. The result, known as Poiseuille's Law, can be written

$$F = -(P_2 - P_1)/\rho = \frac{32\mu VL}{g_c D^2 \rho} \qquad \text{Eq. 7-11}$$

Whenever the Reynolds number is less than 2100, Eq. 7-11 can be used to calculate the pressure drop, whether the pipe is smooth or rough. Equation 7-11 has received extensive experimental confirmation.

No exact mathematical derivation can be made for pressure drop in turbulent flow, and it is necessary to resort to an empirical correlation among the pertinent variables. For flow in smooth pipes, these variables are ΔP, ρ, V, D, L, and μ. If a correlation is to have general applicability, these variables must be grouped in dimensionless ratios, as was discussed in obtaining the expression for Reynolds number. It is found that three dimensionless ratios will satisfy the requirements. The Reynolds number is an obvious choice and will take care of the viscosity effect. The ratio L/D is the simplest way to handle the pipe length. For the remaining variables, we note that Eq. 7-9 shows $\Delta P/\rho$ to have the same dimensions as kinetic energy. The ratio of these two terms will give a dimensionless ratio that includes the effects of ΔP and V. In taking this ratio, we are concerned with the actual value of kinetic energy, not a change. Furthermore, the effect of velocity distribution is included in the Reynolds number, so that α can be omitted. Accordingly, the third dimensionless ratio becomes

$$\frac{\Delta P/\rho}{V^2/2g_c} = \frac{2g_c \Delta P}{\rho V^2}$$

According to our theory, there must be some functional relationship among these three dimensionless ratios. Since we desire to obtain an expression for pressure drop, we can write

$$\frac{2g_c \Delta P}{\rho V^2} = \phi \left(\frac{L}{D}, \frac{DV\rho}{\mu} \right)$$

Both by intuition and by experiment, we know that pressure drop is directly proportional to length. We can therefore factor the L/D ratio out of the above function and write

$$\frac{2g_c \Delta P}{\rho V^2} = \frac{L}{D} \phi \left(\frac{DV\rho}{\mu} \right)$$

Dimensional analysis tells us nothing about the nature of the function of the Reynolds number that appears above, and we must turn to an experimental determination. It is customary to designate this dimensionless function by the symbol f, which is called the friction factor. Furthermore, a factor of 4 is frequently inserted on the right hand side of the equation. Making these substitutions, we obtain $2g_c \Delta P/\rho V^2 = 4f(L/D)$, or

$$-\frac{\Delta P}{\rho} = F = \frac{2fV^2L}{g_c D} \qquad \text{Eq. 7-12}$$

Equation 7-12 is known as the Fanning equation. If the factor of 4 is not included, the result is the same except the number 2 appears in the denominator instead of the numerator of the right hand side, thus giving a friction factor 4 times as large. In this form, it is usually known as the Darcy equation. According to the development, f is a function only of Reynolds number, at least for smooth pipes.

By combining Eq. 7-11 and 7-12, we obtain for streamline flow

$$f = 16(\mu/DV\rho) = 16/Re \qquad \text{Eq. 7-13}$$

Because streamline flow always prevails at Reynolds numbers less than 2100, regardless of whether the pipe is rough or smooth, Eq. 7-13 is always valid in this region. Values of f for turbulent flow can be determined experimentally as explained above from pressure drop measurements in straight pipes.

Figure 7.3 represents the results of a very large number of friction factor measurements covering a wide range of variables and including both liquids and gases. The straight line on the left hand side is for streamline flow as given by Eq. 7-13. The bottom line on the right hand side represents turbulent flow in smooth pipes. To take care of rough pipes, it is necessary to introduce an additional dimensionless ratio, ϵ/D, where ϵ is the equivalent height of a rough projection above the smooth surface. The lines for various values of ϵ/D shown on Fig. 7.3 are based on experimental work in which grains of sand were glued onto smooth pipe surfaces. Included in Fig. 7.3 is a table of equivalent roughness heights for various types of commercial pipe. These values of ϵ were obtained, not by direct measurement, but by plotting experimental friction factor results and determining which of the roughness lines they correspond to. In the critical range shown on the figure between Re of 2100 and 4000, the flow can be either streamline or turbulent, and there is no way to make a positive prediction for a specific situation. As explained previously, turbulent eddies in a stream will create a much greater frictional resistance to flow than molecular motion, and it is to be expected that friction factors for streamline flow will be less than for turbulent flow at the same Reynolds number. If Re falls in the critical range, the usual practice is to read f from the turbulent flow line. If the streamline flow line were used, a lower frictional resistance would be predicted, and a situation could arise in which a pump selected for the system would be too small if the flow actually turned out to be turbulent.

Friction factor plots appear in many textbooks and handbooks. In using any such plot, it is important to note whether f is defined as in Eq. 7-12 or as some multiple of this quantity.

Assuming that the fluid properties and pipe roughness are known, four variables remain to be specified: $\Delta P, V, D$, and L. Equation 7-12, together with the friction factor plot, provides a relationship among these variables so that, if three are specified, the fourth can be calculated. If V, D, and L are given and ΔP is desired, the problem is simple. Re is calculated, f is read from Fig. 7.3, and ΔP calculated directly by substituting the known quantities into Eq. 7-12. Sometimes, there may be a need to obtain V for

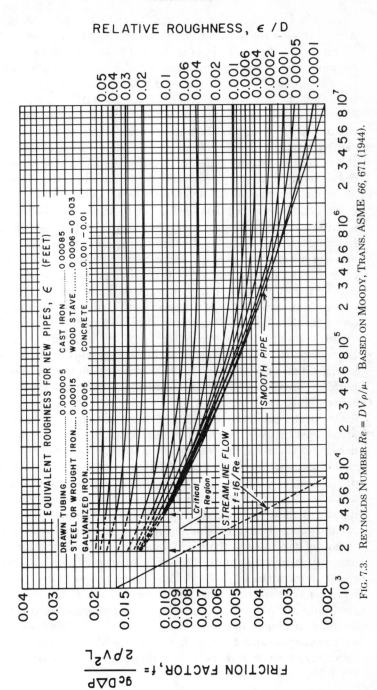

RELATIVE ROUGHNESS, ∈ /D

FRICTION FACTOR, $f = \dfrac{g_c D \Delta P}{2 \rho V^2 L}$

EQUIVALENT ROUGHNESS FOR NEW PIPES, ∈ (FEET)

DRAWN TUBING..............0.000005   CAST IRON...........0.00085
STEEL OR WROUGHT IRON.....0.00015   WOOD STAVE.......0.0006 – 0 003
GALVANIZED IRON...........0.0005   CONCRETE...........0.001 – 0.01

Critical
Region

STREAMLINE FLOW
f = 16/Re

SMOOTH PIPE

FIG. 7.3. REYNOLDS NUMBER $Re = DV\rho/\mu$. BASED ON MOODY, TRANS. ASME 66, 671 (1944).

given ΔP, D, and L. The problem becomes complicated because Re is needed to obtain f from the chart, but a value of V is necessary for calculation of Re. The most direct method of handling this problem is to use a trial and error procedure. Assume a value of V and calculate ΔP in the normal manner. If the calculated ΔP agrees with the given value, the assumption of V was correct. If the two values of ΔP disagree, assume a new V and repeat the calculation. There are various techniques of plotting that can be used to minimize the number of calculations that must be made to get the desired agreement. It is also possible to plot the friction factor data shown in Fig. 7.3 with a different arrangement of variables so as to eliminate the necessity of trial and error calculations when ΔP is given instead of V. Such plots may be found in various references dealing with fluid flow.

It should be realized that the friction factor plot in the turbulent region is empirical and an appreciable error may arise in a specific application. In particular, the roughness factors constitute an uncertainty, as there can be substantial differences in roughness from one lot to another of the same type of commercial pipe. Many times, however, one is interested in estimating the effect of a change in some variable on the performance of a system, and the accuracy of the chart on a relative basis is much better than on an absolute basis. For example, the effect of doubling the flow rate on the pressure drop through a system might be desired. If the pressure drop is known at the original flow rate, the new pressure drop can be predicted with good accuracy. In effect, what we are doing here is to use the actual performance data on a system to provide a correction factor to the generalized chart.

One postulate in the preceding development is that fluid properties remain constant over the entire length of pipe. If there is a change in either density or viscosity, the relationships strictly apply only on a differential basis. One would thus calculate a differential pressure drop, dP, for a length, dL, instead of ΔP over a finite length. To handle this problem exactly, it would be necessary to write Eq. 7-12 as a differential equation and integrate it so as to allow for the changing properties. The most common example of this type is the decrease in density that accompanies the pressure drop in flow of gases. If the change in density is not more than about 10%, satisfactory results are obtained by using an average density and treating the gas as an incompressible fluid. For larger changes in density, a proper integration of the equation should be carried out. Calculations of this type are important in applications such as gas transmission pipelines, but are of minor concern in food processing operations. An additional complication with a compressible fluid is that a change in density causes a change in velocity. Accordingly, there is a kinetic energy change that is not accounted for in Eq. 7-12.

The viscosity of a liquid or gas will change if the temperature changes, and the Reynolds number will be affected accordingly. Here, again, an improved calculation can be made by integrating the equation to allow for the viscosity effect, but the use of an average viscosity will be satisfactory for most purposes. If a fluid flowing in a pipe is rapidly heated or cooled, there will be a temperature gradient and an accompanying variation in viscosity across the diameter. This non-uniform viscosity will produce a different velocity profile, and the theoretical basis for the preceding development for both streamline and turbulent flow will be changed. This effect can be important with liquids of high viscosity, but its treatment is beyond the scope of this discussion.

Another postulate of this development is that the flow under consideration is far enough from the pipe entrance that the velocity profile has achieved its equilibrium shape. The length of entrance section necessary to establish a fully developed velocity profile may vary from about 25 up to 100 pipe diameters, with the longer lengths required for streamline flow. The pressure drop in the entrance region will always be greater than for the same length of pipe with fully-developed flow.

Friction Caused by Sudden Contraction

The frictional effects discussed in the preceding section are those resulting from fully-developed flow in straight pipes. Any sudden change in diameter, a restriction of a valve or fitting, or a sharp bend will create a flow disturbance and cause friction in addition to that of straight pipe flow. One of the most common effects is a sudden contraction, as with a reduction in pipe size or with a pipe leading from a tank. These losses can be estimated by the equation

$$F_c = K_c V_2^2 / 2\alpha g_c \qquad \text{Eq. 7-14}$$

where V_2 is the downstream, or higher, velocity and K_c is a constant that depends on the ratio of the cross-sectional areas (or velocities). Values of K_c are given in Table 7.1.

Friction Caused by Sudden Enlargement

The frictional energy loss resulting from a sudden increase in pipe diameter can be estimated from the equation

$$F_e = (V_1 - V_2)^2 / 2\alpha g_c \qquad \text{Eq. 7-15}$$

where V_1 is the upstream and V_2 the downstream velocity. Note that this loss is not the same as the difference in kinetic energies, which would be given by the difference in the squares of the velocities. The quantity here

TABLE 7.1

FACTORS FOR CALCULATING CONTRACTION LOSSES

S_2/S_1	K_c	S_2/S_1	K_c
0	0.5	0.5	0.30
0.1	0.46	0.6	0.26
0.2	0.42	0.7	0.22
0.3	0.38	0.8	0.15
0.4	0.34	0.9	0.075

TABLE 7.2

VALUES FOR L_e/D FOR PIPE FITTINGS

Screwed fittings	
90° elbow	32
45° elbow	15
Tee, straight through	20
Tee, through side outlet	70
Couplings, unions	negligible
Smooth fittings (soldered, welded, sanitary, etc.)	
Long radius elbow	3
Short radius elbow	10
Square elbow	50
Valves	
Globe valve, open	300
Gate valve, open	7
Gate valve, half-open	200

is the square of the difference in velocities. If the pipe discharges into a tank, so that V_2 is zero, the entire kinetic energy is lost as friction.

Friction Caused by Pipe Fittings

Frictional energy losses resulting from flow through fittings such as elbows, tees, and valves is conveniently expressed in terms of equivalent lengths of straight pipe. That is, for each fitting, a fictitious or equivalent length, L_e, is added to the straight pipe length in Eq. 7-12. It is found that the ratio of L_e to pipe diameter for a particular type of fitting is the same for all diameters. Table 7.2 lists values of L_e/D for several common types of fittings.

General Considerations of Frictional Effects

The relationships presented in the preceding sections for evaluating special frictional effects are strictly applicable only to turbulent flow, and the validity of using them for streamline flow is questionable. Even for turbulent flow, the calculations are only approximate as no actual instal-

TABLE 7.3

STEEL PIPE DIMENSIONS

(All Dimensions in Inches)

Nominal Size	Outside Diam	Schedule 40		Schedule 80	
		Inside Diam	Wall Thickness	Inside Diam	Wall Thickness
$1/8$	0.405	0.269	0.068	0.215	0.095
$1/4$	0.540	0.364	0.088	0.302	0.119
$3/8$	0.675	0.493	0.091	0.423	0.126
$1/2$	0.840	0.622	0.109	0.546	0.147
$3/4$	1.050	0.824	0.113	0.742	0.154
1	1.315	1.049	0.133	0.957	0.179
$1^1/4$	1.660	1.380	0.140	1.278	0.191
$1^1/2$	1.900	1.610	0.145	1.500	0.200
2	2.375	2.067	0.154	1.939	0.218
$2^1/2$	2.875	2.469	0.203	2.323	0.276
3	3.500	3.068	0.216	2.900	0.300
$3^1/2$	4.000	3.548	0.226	3.364	0.318
4	4.500	4.026	0.237	3.826	0.337
5	5.563	5.047	0.258	4.813	0.375
6	6.625	6.065	0.280	5.761	0.432

lation will ever conform in all its details to a standard model. Small variations in details of dimensions, roughnesses, etc., can have a pronounced effect on friction losses. In most cases, however, friction losses from enlargements, contractions, and fittings are a small part of the total, so that these uncertainties are not a source of serious error. It should also be noted that the frictional resistance of a piping system can change with time. Corrosion or scale deposits can increase the surface roughness, thus causing increased friction loss. Over a long period of time, scale build-up can appreciably reduce the cross-sectional area for flow, resulting in either an increased pressure drop or a reduced flow rate.

PIPE AND TUBING DIMENSIONS

Many different types of materials are used for fluid conduits: metal, plastic, glass, ceramic, concrete, wood. In processing plants, metal is by far the most common piping material, although the use of plastics and glass in selected applications is increasing. Metal conduit is usually in the form of welded steel pipe or seamless tubing of various metals and alloys. Welded steel pipe may be either galvanized or plain. Seamless tubing has a smooth surface, and friction factors fall close to the line for smooth pipe in Fig. 7.3. Pipe and tubing are available in a wide range of diameters and wall thicknesses. Since pipe fittings must match the outside diameter, different thicknesses are obtained by keeping the outside diameter constant and varying the inside diameter.

TABLE 7.4

PARTIAL LIST OF TUBING GAGES

Tubing is Available in These Gages in Multiples of $\frac{1}{8}$-in. Outside Diameter; All Dimensions Given in Inches

Gage No.	Wall Thickness
8	0.165
10	0.134
12	0.109
14	0.083
16	0.065
18	0.049
20	0.035

Sanitary Stainless Steel Tubing Dimensions

Outside Diam	Gage	Wall Thickness	Inside Diam
1	18	0.049	0.902
$1\frac{1}{2}$	18	0.049	1.402
2	16	0.065	1.870
$2\frac{1}{2}$	16	0.065	2.370
3	16	0.065	2.870
4	14	0.083	3.834

TABLE 7.5

COPPER WATER TUBE DIMENSIONS

(All Dimensions in Inches)

Nominal Size	Outside Diam	Type K Inside Diam	Type K Wall Thickness	Type L Inside Diam	Type L Wall Thickness
$\frac{1}{4}$	0.375	0.305	0.035	0.315	0.030
$\frac{3}{8}$	0.500	0.402	0.049	0.430	0.035
$\frac{1}{2}$	0.625	0.527	0.049	0.545	0.040
$\frac{5}{8}$	0.750	0.652	0.049	0.666	0.042
$\frac{3}{4}$	0.875	0.745	0.065	0.785	0.045
1	1.125	0.995	0.065	1.025	0.050
$1\frac{1}{4}$	1.375	1.245	0.065	1.265	0.055
$1\frac{1}{2}$	1.625	1.481	0.072	1.505	0.060
2	2.125	1.959	0.083	1.985	0.070
$2\frac{1}{2}$	2.625	2.435	0.095	2.465	0.080
3	3.125	2.907	0.109	2.945	0.090
$3\frac{1}{2}$	3.625	3.385	0.120	3.425	0.100
4	4.125	3.857	0.134	3.905	0.110
5	5.125	4.805	0.160	4.875	0.125
6	6.125	5.741	0.192	5.845	0.140

Standard steel pipe is made in a series of nominal diameters, as shown in Table 7.3. In this Table, dimensions are given for Schedule 40 and Schedule 80 pipe. Schedule 40 is the size that is commonly available and is used in all ordinary applications. High pressure applications that would require the use of a heavy wall pipe such as Schedule 80 are infrequent in food processing plants. Table 7.3 shows that, except for 2.5-in. pipes, Schedule 40, and pipe greater than 1.5 in., Schedule 80, the actual inside diameter is greater than the nominal size. Welded steel pipe is not a precision-made product, and some variation in dimensions can be expected.

Seamless tubing is specified in terms of outside diameter and wall thickness, or gage. Table 7.4 includes a partial list of wall thicknesses corresponding to gage number. Tubing is ordinarily available in increments of $\frac{1}{8}$ in. outside diameter in these as well as other thicknesses. Table 7.4 also includes dimensions of stainless steel tubing commonly used in food process operations. Standard sanitary fittings are available only for these outside diameters.

Copper tubing, either hard or annealed, with soldered fittings is widely used for ordinary plumbing applications. Dimensions of this tubing, which is commonly referred to as copper pipe, are listed in Table 7.5.

EXAMPLES

Example 1

In a food plant, a 20° Brix sucrose solution at 70°F is being pumped from a large open tank at a rate of 16 gal. per min through a 1-in. galvanized iron pipe to an upper level. The pipe is 100 ft long and includes three 90° elbows. The liquid level in the tank is 10 ft above the ground and the pipe discharge is 40 ft above the ground. The pressure at the discharge is 5 psi gage. Calculate the work in ft-lb$_f$ per pound of solution and the power requirement in horsepower. The efficiency of the pump and motor may be taken as 50%.

The first step in a flow problem is to draw a diagram of the system, as shown in Fig. 7.4.

The Reynolds number and the velocity will obviously be needed. For these calculations, the density and viscosity of the sucrose solution are required; 20° Brix is 20 wt %, and from handbook data we find that at 70°F

specific gravity = 1.081

$\rho = (1.081)(62.4) = 67.4 \ lb_m/ft^3$

$\mu = (1.9 \ cP) \left(0.000672 \ \frac{lb_m/(ft)(sec)}{cP} \right) = 0.00128 \ lb_m/(ft)(sec)$

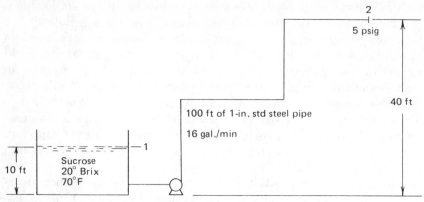

FIG. 7.4.   THE FLOW SYSTEM FOR EXAMPLE 1

Inside diameter of 1 in. standard pipe = 1.049 in.

$$S = (\pi/4)D^2 = (\pi/4)(1.049/12)^2 = 0.00598 \text{ ft}^2$$

$$V = \left(16 \frac{\text{gal.}}{\text{min}}\right) \left(\frac{1}{7.48} \frac{\text{ft}^3}{\text{gal.}}\right) \left(\frac{1}{0.00598 \text{ ft}^2}\right) \left(\frac{1}{60} \frac{\text{min}}{\text{sec}}\right) = 5.96 \text{ ft/sec}$$

$$Re = DV\rho/\mu = \left(\frac{1.049}{12} \text{ft}\right) \left(5.96 \frac{\text{ft}}{\text{sec}}\right) \left(67.4 \frac{\text{lb}_m}{\text{ft}^3}\right)$$

$$\left(\frac{1}{0.00128} \frac{(\text{ft})(\text{sec})}{\text{lb}_m}\right) = 27400$$

The next step is to calculate the work by Eq. 7.9

$$-W_s = (P_2 - P_1)/\rho + (V_2^2 - V_1^2)/2\alpha g_c + (z_2 - z_1)g/g_c + F$$

Pressure drop.—P_1 is 1 atm and P_2 is 5 psi gage, or 5 psi above atm pressure.

$$(P_2 - P_1)/\rho = \left(\frac{5 \text{ lb}_f}{\text{in.}^2}\right) \left(144 \frac{\text{in.}^2}{\text{ft}^2}\right) \left(\frac{1}{67.4} \frac{\text{ft}^3}{\text{lb}_m}\right) = 10.7 \text{ (ft)(lb}_f)/\text{lb}_m$$

Kinetic energy.—V_1 is the velocity in the tank and can be taken as zero. V_2 is the velocity in the 1 in. pipe. Flow is turbulent, so $\alpha = 1$.

$$\frac{V_2^2 - V_1^2}{2\alpha g_c} = \left((5.96)^2 \frac{\text{ft}^2}{\text{sec}^2} - 0\right) \frac{1}{2(32.2)} \frac{(\text{lb}_f)(\text{sec}^2)}{(\text{lb}_m)(\text{ft})} = 0.6 \text{ (ft)(lb}_f)/\text{lb}_m$$

Potential energy.

$$(z_2 - z_1)g/g_c = (40 - 10) \text{ ft} \left(\frac{g}{g_c} \frac{\text{lb}_f}{\text{lb}_m}\right) = 30 \text{ (ft)(lb}_f)/\text{lb}_m$$

Friction.—Pipe friction is given by Eq. 7-12, with the equivalent length of fittings included.

$$F = \frac{2fV^2}{g_c}\left(\frac{L + L_e}{D}\right) \qquad\qquad \text{Eq. 7-12a}$$

The total length is 100 ft, and there are 3 elbows. From Table 7.2, L_e/D for an elbow is 32.

$$\frac{L}{D} + \frac{L_e}{D} = \frac{(100)(12)}{1.049} + 3(32) = 1144 + 96 = 1240$$

From Fig. 7.3 for galvanized iron,

$\epsilon = 0.0005$ ft

$\epsilon/D = 12(0.0005)/1.049 = 0.006$

$f = 0.0088$

Then,

$$F = \frac{2(0.0088)(5.96)^2(1240)}{32.2} = 24.0 \text{ (ft)(lb}_f)/\text{lb}_m$$

There is no expansion loss since section 2 is taken inside the 1-in. pipe. There is a contraction loss where the fluid enters the pipe from the tank. Since the pipe:tank cross-sectional area ratio is essentially zero, the value of K_c to be used in Eq. 7-14 is 0.5. As before, $\alpha = 1$.

$$F_c = K_c V^2/2\alpha g_c = \frac{0.5(5.96)^2}{2(32.2)} = 0.3 \text{ (ft)(lb}_f)/\text{lb}_m$$

$$\Sigma F = F + F_c = 24.0 + 0.3 = 24.3 \text{ (ft)(lb}_f)/\text{lb}_m$$

The work required is the sum of the above energy terms

$$-W_s = 10.7 + 0.6 + 30.0 + 24.3 = 65.6 \text{ (ft)(lb}_f)/\text{lb}_m$$

$$\dot{m} = \left(16\,\frac{\text{gal.}}{\text{min}}\right)\left(\frac{1}{7.48}\,\frac{\text{ft}^3}{\text{gal.}}\right)\left(67.4\,\frac{\text{lb}_m}{\text{ft}^3}\right)\left(\frac{1}{60}\,\frac{\text{min}}{\text{sec}}\right) = 2.4\ \text{lb}_m/\text{sec}$$

$$\text{power} = \dot{m}(-W_s) = \left(2.4\,\frac{\text{lb}_m}{\text{sec}}\right)\left(65.6\,\frac{\text{(ft)(lb}_f)}{\text{lb}_m}\right)\left(\frac{1}{550}\,\frac{\text{(hp)(sec)}}{\text{(ft)(lb}_f)}\right)$$

$$= 0.286 \text{ horsepower}$$

The above figure is the theoretical horsepower. To get the actual horsepower requirement, we must divide by the efficiency:

$$\text{actual power} = 0.286/0.50 = 0.57 \text{ horsepower}$$

A ¾ horsepower motor, which is the next largest standard size, would be satisfactory for this service.

Example 2

There is frequently a need to determine the effect of a change in operating conditions on the performance of a flow system. Here, information on the original operation is used as a basis of comparison for the new operation.

Water at 70°F for a cooler in a processing plant is flowing at a rate of 20 gal./min through a horizontal length of ¾-in. standard galvanized pipe. The pressure drop is found to be 100 psi. In order to reduce the pressure drop, it is proposed that the pipe be replaced with 1-in. standard pipe. If the same length of 1-in. pipe is used, what will the pressure drop be with the water flow rate remaining constant at 20 gal./min?

In this problem, the system is simply a straight length of horizontal pipe, and it is not really necessary to draw a diagram. It should be noted that there are actually two systems: the original pipe and the new pipe. Equation 7-9 must be applied to each one separately. There is no shaft work and no change in elevation in the system. In either the original or the new system, the pipe diameter is constant, so there is no change in velocity. Equation 7-9 therefore reduces to Eq. 7-12. The length of original pipe is not stated in the problem, but the diameter, velocity, and pressure drop are known. A length could therefore be calculated from Eq. 7-12, and this length used with the new diameter to calculate the new pressure drop. A more direct approach is to write Eq. 7-12 for each case and to take the ratio of the pressure drops. In this way, the common factors will cancel, and the calculations will be greatly simplified.

$$\frac{\Delta P_a/\rho}{\Delta P_b/\rho} = \frac{2f_a V_a^2/g_c D_a}{2f_b V_b^2/g_c D_b}$$

Canceling common factors,

$$\frac{\Delta P_a}{\Delta P_b} = \frac{f_a V_a^2 D_b}{f_b V_b^2 D_a}$$

For the same volumetric or mass flow rate, Eq. 7-2 shows that

$$\frac{V_a}{V_b} = \frac{S_b}{S_a} = \left(\frac{D_b}{D_a}\right)^2$$

Substituting,

$$\frac{\Delta P_a}{\Delta P_b} = \frac{f_a}{f_b}\left(\frac{D_b}{D_a}\right)^5$$

If subscript b refers to the 1-in. pipe and a to the ¾-in. pipe, we find from the pipe dimension Table 7.3 that

$$D_b/D_a = 1.049/0.824 = 1.273$$

In order to evaluate the friction factor ratio, we must calculate the Reynolds numbers. It will be convenient to use Eq. 7-4 for Re.

$$\dot{m} = \left(20\,\frac{\text{gal.}}{\text{min}}\right)\left(\frac{1}{7.48}\,\frac{\text{ft}^3}{\text{gal.}}\right)\left(62.4\,\frac{\text{lb}_m}{\text{ft}^3}\right)\left(60\,\frac{\text{min}}{\text{hr}}\right) = 10000\ \text{lb}_m/\text{hr}$$

$$\mu = (0.98\ \text{cP})\left(2.42\,\frac{\text{lb}_m/(\text{ft})(\text{hr})}{\text{cP}}\right) = 2.37\ \text{lb}_m/(\text{ft})(\text{hr})$$

$$Re_a = 4\dot{m}/\pi\,D\mu = 4(10000)/\pi(0.824/12)(2.37) = 78000$$

$$Re_b = Re_a(D_a/D_b) = 78000(0.824/1.049) = 61000$$

$$(\epsilon/D)_a = 0.0005(0.824/12) = 0.0073$$

$$(\epsilon/D)_b = 0.0005/(1.049/12) = 0.0057$$

$$f_a = 0.0086$$

$$f_b = 0.0083$$

$$\Delta P_a/\Delta P_b = (0.0086/0.0083)(1.273)^5 = 3.48$$

$$\Delta P_b = 100/3.48 = 28.8\ \text{lb}_f/\text{in.}^2$$

It is obvious that a considerable saving in calculation has been made by setting the problem up in terms of ratios. This procedure has the further advantage that the effect of variables is more easily visualized. For example, we see here that for a constant mass flow rate in the turbulent region, the pressure drop varies inversely approximately as the fifth power of the diameter. A small change in diameter can have a major effect on a system.

Example 3

Concentrated skim milk is to be pumped from an evaporator at ground level to a spray dryer on an upper floor of a dairy processing plant. The evaporator body from which the milk is pumped operates at an absolute pressure of 1.4 in. Hg, and the line discharges into a tank at atmospheric pressure with a net gain in elevation of 25 ft. The line is made up of 125 ft of 1.5-in. stainless steel sanitary tubing with 4 short radius elbows. A centrifugal pump with a 1 horsepower motor is available for this service. The milk has a specific gravity of 1.2 and a viscosity of 2.0 cP. If the efficiency of the pump-motor combination is 55%, estimate the milk flow rate in gallons per minute.

This problem is similar to Example 1 except that here the power available is given, and we are asked to estimate the flow rate. Consequently, since a velocity is not given to obtain a Reynolds number, a trial and error calculation for the friction loss will be necessary. A direct approach would be to assume a flow rate and then calculate the power requirement as in Ex-

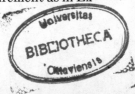

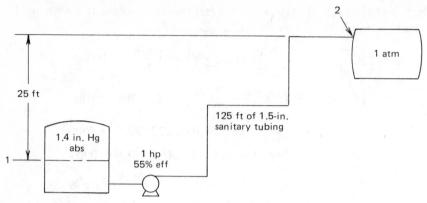

FIG. 7.5.   THE EVAPORATOR-SPRAY-DRYER SETUP FOR EXAMPLE 3

ample 1. If the calculated power is equal to the 1 horsepower available, the assumed flow rate is correct. Otherwise, a new flow rate is assumed and the calculation repeated. A problem of this type may require several repeated calculations, and it will be convenient to set the work up in a form to facilitate this process. A diagram of the system is shown in Fig. 7.5. The inlet, or section 1, is taken in the evaporator body where the pressure is known and the velocity is essentially zero. Section 2 is taken just inside the end of the pipe where is discharges into the tank. The pressure at the end of the pipe is atmospheric, either just inside or just outside the end. The velocity at section 2 is that which prevails throughout the length of the pipe.

In applying Eq. 7-9, the pressure drop and potential energy terms do not depend on the velocity and can be calculated directly:

$$P_1 = 1.4 \text{ in. Hg} = 0.7 \text{ psi absolute}$$

$$P_2 = 1 \text{ atm} = 14.7 \text{ psi absolute}$$

$$(P_2 - P_1)/\rho = \frac{(14.7 - 0.7)144}{1.2(62.4)} = 26.9 \text{ (ft)(lb}_f)/\text{lb}_m$$

$$(z_2 - z_1)g/g_c = 25 \text{ (ft)(lb}_f)/\text{lb}_m$$

In order to make a preliminary estimate of the flow rate, we might assume that the total friction will be 20 $(ft)(lb_f)/lb_m$. The kinetic energy term will be small enough to be unimportant. With this assumption:

$$-W_s = \Delta P/\rho + \Delta z(g/g_c) + \Sigma F = 26.9 + 25 + 20 = 72 \text{ (ft)(lb}_f)/\text{lb}_m$$

For a 1 horsepower motor and an overall efficiency of 55%, the available theoretical power is 0.55 horsepower

$$\dot{m}(-W_s) = 0.55 \text{ hp} \left(550 \frac{(\text{ft})(\text{lb}_f)}{(\text{hp})(\text{sec})}\right) = 302 \text{ (ft)}(\text{lb}_f)/\text{sec}$$

$$\dot{m} = \left(302 \frac{(\text{ft})(\text{lb}_f)}{\text{sec}}\right) \left(\frac{1}{72} \frac{\text{lb}_m}{(\text{ft})(\text{lb}_f)}\right) = 4.2 \text{ lb}_m/\text{sec}$$

For the first trial, we will use a flow rate rounded off to 4 lb_m/sec:

$$\rho = 1.2(62.4) = 75 \text{ lb}_m/\text{ft}^3$$

$$\mu = 2.0(0.000672) = 0.00134 \text{ lb}_m/(\text{ft})(\text{sec})$$

Inside diameter of 1.5-in. sanitary tubing = $1.5 - 2(0.049) = 1.402$ in.

$$S = (\pi/4)(1.402/12)^2 = 0.0107 \text{ ft}^2$$

$$V = \left(4 \frac{\text{lb}_m}{\text{sec}}\right) \left(\frac{1}{75} \frac{\text{ft}^3}{\text{lb}_m}\right) \left(\frac{1}{0.0107 \text{ ft}^2}\right) = 5.0 \text{ ft/sec}$$

$$Re = DV\rho/\mu = (1.402/12)(5.0)(75)/0.00134 = 32700$$

Kinetic Energy

$$V_2{}^2/2g_c = (5.0)^2/2(32.2) = 0.4 \text{ (ft)}(\text{lb}_f)\text{lb}_m$$

Friction

$$L/D + L_e/D = 125(12/1.402) + 4(10) = 1070 + 40 = 1110$$

The smooth pipe curve in Fig. 7.3 applies to sanitary tubing of Re at 32,700.

$$f = 0.0057$$

$$F = 2(0.0057)(5.0)^2(1110)/32.2 = 9.8 \text{ (ft)}(\text{lb}_f)\text{lb}_m$$

There is a contraction loss at the pipe entrance, but no expansion loss

$$K_c = 0.5$$

$$F_c = 0.5(5.0)^2/2(32.2) = 0.2 \text{ (ft)}(\text{lb}_f)/\text{lb}_m$$

$$\Sigma F = 9.8 + 0.2 = 10.0 \text{ (ft)}(\text{lb}_f)/\text{lb}_m$$

We see that the calculated friction is smaller than the value assumed for the preliminary calculation. Using the previous pressure drop and potential energy terms,

$$-W_s = 26.9 + 25 + 0.4 + 10.0 = 62.3 \text{ (ft)}(\text{lb}_f)/\text{lb}_m$$

As before,

$$\dot{m} = 302/(-W_s) = 302/62.3 = 4.85 \text{ lb}_m/\text{sec}$$

We can see that the original flow rate assumption was not too far off, but it will be necessary to make at least one more calculation. Repeating with a larger value of $\dot{m}$ will give a higher friction loss than calculated above and therefore a lower calculated $\dot{m}$ than 4.85. The correct value will lie somewhere between 4.0 and 4.85, undoubtedly closer to the latter. As a second trial, we will use a flow rate of 4.6 lb_m/sec. We can simplify many of the previous calculations by using a ratio of the flow rates.

Kinetic energy = $0.4(4.6/4.0)^2 = 0.5$ (ft)(lb_f)/lb_m

$$Re = 32700(4.6/4.0) = 37700$$

$$f = 0.0056$$

$$F = 9.8(0.0056/0.0057)(4.6/4.0)^2 = 12.7 \text{ (ft)}lb_f/lb_m$$

$$F_c = 0.2(4.6/4.0)^2 = 0.3 \text{ (ft)}(lb_f)/lb_m$$

$$-W_s = 26.9 + 25 + 0.5 + 12.7 + 0.3 = 65.4 \text{ (ft)}(lb_f)/lb_m$$

$$\dot{m} = 302/65.4 = 4.62 \ lb_m/sec$$

Within the limits of accuracy of the calculation, the value of $\dot{m}$ obtained is equal to the assumed value, so no further trials are necessary.

$$\text{Flow rate} = \left(4.6 \frac{lb_m}{sec}\right) \left(\frac{1}{75} \frac{ft^3}{lb_m}\right) \left(7.48 \frac{gal.}{ft^3}\right) \left(60 \frac{sec}{min}\right) = 27.5 \text{ gal./min}$$

In this problem, the correct answer was obtained on the second trial. Many times, calculations such as this will not converge rapidly and more trials will be necessary. We were helped here by an initial assumption that was not too far off and by a judicious choice of the value for the second trial. For example, if $\dot{m}$ of 4.85 had been assumed instead of 4.6, the calculated value would have been 4.5. Since this is significantly different from the assumption, a third trial would have been desirable.

Success in solving material and energy balance problems frequently depends on a proper choice of system boundaries. In order to apply Eq. 7-9, for example, it is necessary to select boundaries where sufficient information is available as to pressure, velocity, and elevation. In Examples 1 and 3, the kinetic energy and contraction loss terms could have been eliminated by taking section 1 in the line just ahead of the pump, but we would not have been able to evaluate the pressure drop term. In Example 3, on the other hand, we could have taken section 2 just beyond the end of the pipe, where the pressure is still 1 atm. Since the velocity in the tank is zero, there would no longer be a kinetic energy term, but an enlargement loss would take its place. Equation 7-15 shows that this enlargement loss is exactly the same as the kinetic energy term that was eliminated.

VELOCITY MEASUREMENT

The primary variable in the preceding development of fluid flow relationships is velocity. Measurement of velocity or flow rate is obviously an

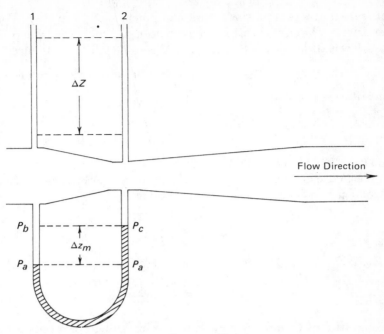

FIG. 7.6. VENTURI METER

essential part of any experimental study or actual operation concerned with fluid flow. The simplest way of measuring liquid flow rate is to collect the liquid in a container at the pipe discharge and weigh the amount collected over a measured time interval. This principle can be applied to gases by measuring the total volume discharged into a so-called floating roof container. Although useful for experimental purposes, this method becomes impractical or impossible for large flow rates and for most commercial operations. Consequently, there are a number of commercial flow rate instruments based on various operating principles.

The most widely used class of instruments gives a measurement of velocity rather than mass or volumetric flow rate. Because these instruments are so widely used and because they can usually be constructed inexpensively, it is important to have an understanding of the principles of their operation. These principles are derived directly from the relationships developed in the preceding sections. In effect, they take advantage of the change in pressure that accompanies a change in velocity of a flowing fluid.

Venturi Meter

Consider a liquid flowing through a section of pipe-line that has a converging and diverging section as shown in Fig. 7.6. In applying Eq. 7-9 to this system, there is no shaft work and no change in elevation. For the present, we will consider that friction can be neglected. We will also consider that flow is turbulent, so that $\alpha = 1.0$. Accordingly, Eq. 7-9 reduces to:

$$(P_1 - P_2)/\rho = (V_2^2 - V_1^2)/2g_c = (V_1^2/2g_c)(V_2^2/V_1^2 - 1)$$

Substituting from Eq. 7-7,

$$(P_1 - P_2)/\rho = (V_1^2/2g_c)(S_1^2/S_2^2 - 1)$$
$$= (V_1^2/2g_c)(D_1^4/D_2^4 - 1) \quad \text{Eq. 7-16}$$

Equation 7-16 is based on the assumptions of no friction and flat velocity profiles. We can solve for velocity and account for both of these effects by introducing an empirical coefficient as follows:

$$V_1 = C \sqrt{\frac{2g_c(P_1 - P_2)/\rho}{D_1^4/D_2^4 - 1}} \qquad \text{Eq. 7-17}$$

If Eq. 7-17 is used to eliminate V_1 instead of V_2, we obtain

$$V_2 = C \sqrt{\frac{2g_c(P_1 - P_2)/\rho}{1 - D_2^4/D_1^4}} \qquad \text{Eq. 7-18}$$

The coefficient C must be determined empirically. For a well-designed venturi meter, the coefficient is given with sufficient accuracy by the expression

$$C = 1 - \frac{1.1}{Re_2^{1/3}} \qquad \text{Eq. 7-19}$$

where Re_2 is the Reynolds number at the throat.

If the vertical tubes in Fig. 7.6 are open so that the pressure at the top of the liquid is the same for both, the discussion in the previous section on potential energy effects shows that we can express the pressure difference in terms of the difference in liquid height as follows:

$$(P_1 - P_2)/\rho = \Delta z g/g_c$$

or,

$$g_c(P_1 - P_2)/\rho = g \Delta z \qquad \text{Eq. 7-20}$$

and Eq. 7-17 can be written

$$V_1 = C \sqrt{\frac{2g \Delta z}{D_1^4/D_2^4 - 1}} \qquad \text{Eq. 7-17a}$$

The height difference Δz is referred to as the meter head and, in the usual units, is expressed as feet of fluid. In actual practice, a closed U-tube manometer would be used rather than the two open tubes of Fig. 7.6. Obviously, the manometer fluid must have a higher density than the flowing fluid and be immiscible with it. If the flowing fluid is a gas, water would be a satisfactory manometer fluid. With flow of liquids, mercury is most frequently used in the manometer.

It must be remembered that the meter head is in feet of flowing fluid, not in feet of manometer fluid. It is also necessary to consider the effect of the fluid in the manometer legs above the manometer fluid. In the simple arrangement shown in Fig. 7.6, this space is filled by the flowing fluid. The desired pressure difference $(P_1 - P_2)$ for the flow calculations is the same as the pressure difference $(P_b - P_c)$ measured at the upper level of the manometer liquid. The pressure P_a at the lower manometer level is the same in both legs. Therefore,

$$\Delta z_m g/g_c = (P_a - P_c)/\rho_m = (P_a - P_b)/\rho$$

where ρ_m is the density of the manometer fluid. Eliminating P_a,

$$P_b - P_c = (\rho_m - \rho)\Delta z_m g/g_c$$

and

$$(P_b - P_c)/\rho = (\rho_m/\rho - 1)\Delta z_m g/g_c$$

The correct fluid head to be substituted into Eq. 7-17a is therefore given by the expression

$$\Delta z = \Delta z_m(\rho_m/\rho - 1) \qquad \text{Eq. 7-21}$$

If there were no friction, the pressure downstream of the meter, where the velocity has regained its original value, would be the same as the upstream pressure. Friction cannot be completely eliminated, but it can be minimized by proper design. An entrance cone angle of about 21° and an exit cone angle of about 7°, as shown in Fig. 7.6, corresponds to standard practice. The gradual velocity decrease in the diverging section is particulary important in minimizing the friction loss. In a well-constructed meter, the total loss may be about 10% of meter pressure drop.

Venturi meters have advantages in applications in which it is important to have a low permanent pressure loss. They are, however, relatively expensive to construct, and the small angles of the entrance and exit cones require a long section of the piping system. If a higher permanent pressure loss can be tolerated, the orifice meter is a simpler and less costly solution.

Orifice Meter

The orifice meter essentially consists of a flat plate with a round hole placed between flanges in a pipe, as shown in Fig 7.7. The meter operates on the same principle as the venturi. The velocity of the fluid increases as

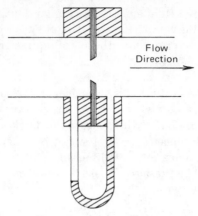

FIG. 7.7.   ORIFICE METER

it passes through the plate, and the pressure decreases. The fluid stream continues to converge after passing through the orifice, and the point of maximum velocity is not at the orifice, but a short distance downstream. This point of maximum velocity is known as the vena contracta. In contrast with the venturi, there is no direct way of knowing the point of maximum velocity or the effect diameter of the stream at this point. The position of the throat and the throat diameter are fixed for a venturi, whereas the corresponding quantities for an orifice depend on the velocity.

Although any restriction in a pipe can serve as a flow measuring device, best results are obtained if the orifice is carefully constructed to conform to a standardized design. In particular, the hole must be centered and must have a sharp edge on the upstream side. Ideally, the downstream pressure tap would be located at the vena contracta and the upstream tap far enough ahead of the orifice to avoid any disturbing influences. Locating the taps in this manner is inconvenient in practice, and they are usually positioned in the flanges that hold the plate.

All the equations derived above for the venturi meter are applicable to the orifice. In this case, V_2 and D_2 refer to the orifice, not the point of maximum velocity. The fact that P_2 is not measured at this position in the pipe is taken into account in the coefficient of discharge C. In general, the value of the coefficient depends on the position of the pressure taps, the Reynolds number, and the orifice-pipe diameter ratio. For Reynolds numbers at the orifice greater than 30,000, C has an average value of about 0.61. At lower Re, particularly in the streamline region, C varies widely with Re and the diameter ratio. For dependability, an orifice meter should be calibrated in place. For purposes of estimation or approximate measurements, the value of C of 0.61 can be used at Re greater than 30,000.

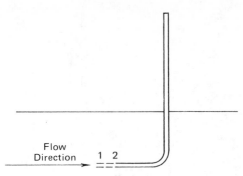

FIG. 7.8.   PRINCIPLE OF THE PITOT TUBE

The orifice obviously creates a flow disturbance that results in a much greater friction loss than a venturi. The gradually diverging outlet of the venturi meter allows the velocity to decrease slowly to its original value, and essentially all of the kinetic energy is recovered as increased pressure. In the orifice meter, the fluid jets into a more slowly moving stream, and this excess kinetic energy is essentially all lost to friction.

In using the equations derived here for either the venturi or orifice, it should be remembered that they are based on Eq. 7-9, which is strictly valid only for constant density fluids. They can be applied to gas flow with negligible error if the meter pressure drop is not more than a few percent of the absolute pressure.

Pitot Tube

The term, pressure, that has been used up to this point should more accurately be called static pressure. With a fluid at rest, there is no problem of definition. A pressure gage indicates the static pressure at the point at which it is placed. In a moving fluid, however, special care must be taken in pressure measurement. It is an everyday experience to observe that a fluid stream exerts a force or pressure against objects which it strikes. For this excess pressure to exist, the velocity of the stream must be directed to some degree against the surface. If flow is parallel to a surface, as with fully-developed flow in a straight pipe, the velocity has no direct effect on the pressure against the surface. The static pressure of a fluid flowing in a pipe is most simply measured by making a pressure gage connection to a small opening in the pipe wall. If the opening is smooth on the inside and there are no projections extending into the pipe that could disturb the flow in the vicinity, a manometer or pressure gage will accurately indicate the static pressure.

Consider now the arrangement shown in Fig. 7.8. A small diameter tube with a 90° bend near one end is placed so that the short end faces upstream

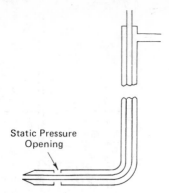

FIG. 7.9.   DOUBLE TUBE ARRANGEMENT FOR PRESSURE SENSING (PITOT TUBE)

parallel to the axis of the pipe and the long end extends out through the pipe wall. The outer end of this bent tube is closed so that there is no flow through it. The dashed lines extending from the short end define the boundary of a hypothetical flow tube. The velocity at section 1 of this hypothetical tube is simply the velocity that prevails at this point in the main stream, whether the small tube is present or not. Since there is no flow through the small tube, the end of the tube acts as though it were a flat plate, and the velocity at section 2 is zero. In the application of Eq. 7-9 to the hypothetical flow tube, there is obviously no shaft work or change in elevation. Even though there may be a substantial velocity gradient in the main stream, the diameter of the small tube is so small that velocity can be considered constant over its cross-section, and $\alpha = 1$. The effect of any friction or velocity disturbance at the end of the bent tube will be included by applying a coefficient to the final result, as with the venturi and orifice meters. Accordingly, Eq. 7-9 reduces to

$$(P_2 - P_1)/\rho = V_1{}^2/2g_c$$

The pressure difference, $P_2 - P_1$, is called the velocity pressure. It is simply the pressure created if all the kinetic energy of a stream is converted into pressure head. P_1 is the static pressure, and P_2 is therefore the sum of the static and velocity pressures. This sum is called the impact pressure. Solving the above expression for velocity, and introducing a coefficient C, we obtain

$$V_1 = C \sqrt{2g_c(P_2 - P_1)/\rho} \qquad \text{Eq. 7-22}$$

As explained above, the simplest way of measuring the static pressure P_1 is through a pressure tap in the wall of the pipe. A manometer connected between such a pressure tap and the end of the small tube that extends through the pipe will indicate the pressure difference $(P_2 - P_1)$. With a

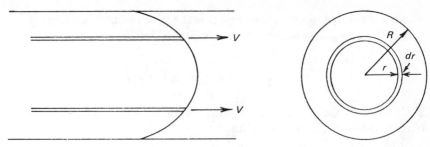

FIG. 7.10.   VELOCITY PROFILE AND INTEGRATION RING OF THICKNESS dr AT RADIAL
DISTANCE r

knowledge of the coefficient C, the corresponding velocity can be calculated
from Eq. 7-22. Correlations are available in the literature for estimating
the value of C. For practical engineering purposes, it can be considered to
be 1.0. If a separate tap for static pressure is not convenient, the double-tube
arrangement shown in Fig. 7-9 can be used. Here, the inside tube senses
the impact pressure as before. The outer tube, which is sealed to the inner
tube at both ends, has holes drilled around its circumference near the impact end. Since these holes are in a surface that is parallel to the flow direction, they respond to the static pressure.

This velocity measuring device is called a pitot tube. A pitot tube measures the velocity at a point in the stream, whereas venturi and orifice
meters give an average velocity for the entire stream. By arranging a pitot
tube so that it can be moved across the diameter, a velocity profile can be
obtained. These velocity profiles can be integrated graphically to give the
total volumetric flow rate and thus be used to calibrate other types of flow
meters. Since flow rates cannot be measured for gases as for liquids simply
by collecting the stream in a container and weighing it, pitot tubes are
particularly useful for gas flow meter calibration.

Integration of a velocity profile to obtain the average velocity is approached by considering the flowing stream to be made up of a set of hypothetical annular rings, one of which is represented in Fig. 7.10. We will
let the width of each ring decrease to the infinitesimal dr. The ring at any
distance r from the center has a length $2\pi r$ and corresponds to a velocity
V. The volumetric flow rate through each ring is equal to the product of
the velocity and cross-sectional area, or $V(2\pi r dr)$. The total volumetric
flow rate for the pipe is the sum of the flows through the individual rings
or, in the limit, the integral of these flows from the center to the wall of the
pipe. Accordingly,

$$\dot{v} = \int_O^R 2V\pi r dr$$

where $\dot{v}$ is volume per unit time and R is the pipe radius. The average velocity is equal to the volumetric flow rate divided by the cross-sectional area, or

$$V_{av} = \dot{v}/\pi R^2 = (2/R^2) \int_O^R Vr\,dr \qquad \text{Eq. 7-23}$$

Equation 7-23 can be put in an alternate form by noting that $2r\,dr = d(r^2)$. Making this substitution, we obtain

$$V_{av} = (1/R^2) \int_O^R V\,d(r^2) = \int_O^R V\,d(r/R)^2$$

If we let the ratio $r/R = y$, at the upper limit of $r = R$, $y = 1$, and

$$V_{av} = \int_0^1 V\,d(y^2) \qquad \text{Eq. 7-24}$$

Equation 7-24 is the most convenient form for a graphical integration. From experimental results of velocity vs radius, we can make a plot of V vs y^2. In this plot, y will vary from zero at the center to 1.0 at the wall, while V will vary from a maximum to zero. By definition, the value of the integral is equal to the area under the curve. The student should refer to other references for various methods of performing graphical integrations.

Example 4.—Water at 70°F is flowing through a 2-in. standard steel pipe at a rate of 50 gal./min. An orifice meter is to be installed to measure the flow rate. A manometer to be used with the meter has a maximum reading of 10 in. Hg. What orifice diameter will be required to give this pressure drop in 50 gal./min?

Inside diameter of 2-in. pipe = 2.067 in.

$$S_1 = (\pi/4)(2.067/12)^2 = 0.0233 \text{ ft}^2$$

$$V_1 = \left(50\,\frac{\text{gal.}}{\text{min}}\right) \left(\frac{1 \text{ ft}^3}{7.48 \text{ gal.}}\right) \left(\frac{1 \text{ min}}{60 \text{ sec}}\right) \left(\frac{1}{0.0233 \text{ ft}^2}\right) = 4.77 \text{ ft/sec}$$

$$Re_1 = \frac{(2.067/12)(4.77)(62.4)}{(0.98)(0.000672)} = 78,000$$

The Reynolds number in the orifice will be even higher, so we can use an orifice coefficient of 0.61. For a manometer reading of 10 in. Hg, Eq. 7-21 gives

$$\Delta z = (10/12)(13.6 - 1) = 10.5 \text{ ft H}_2\text{O}$$

By Eq. 7-17a:

$$4.77 = 0.61 \sqrt{\frac{2(32.2)(10.5)}{(2.067/D_o)^4 - 1}}$$

$$D_o = 1.16 \text{ in.}$$

Example 5.—The velocity of an air stream at 70°F and atmospheric pressure is to be measured with a pitot tube. The pitot tube is used with a water manometer that can be read to the nearest 0.001 in. If the uncertainty in the manometer reading is to cause an error in velocity of no more than 5%, what is the lowest velocity that can be measured?

If the manometer can be read to the nearest 0.001 in., the maximum error is 0.0005 in. According to the problem statement, then, a difference in the manometer reading of 0.0005 in. is to cause a 5% change in velocity.

$$V = C\sqrt{2g\,\Delta z}$$

By Eq. 7-21,

$$\Delta z = (\Delta z_w/12)(\rho_w/\rho_a - 1) = (\Delta z_w/12)(\rho_w/\rho_a)$$

$$V = C\sqrt{(2g/12)(\rho_w/\rho_a)(\Delta z_w)}$$

$$1.05V = C\sqrt{(2g/12)(\rho_w/\rho_a)(\Delta z_w + 0.0005)}$$

Taking the ratio of the two previous equations,

$$1.05 = \sqrt{(\Delta z_w + 0.0005)/\Delta z_w}$$

$\Delta z_w = 0.005$ in. H_2O, the minimum permissible manometer height

By the perfect gas law,

$$\rho_a = M_a P/RT = (29.0)(14.7)/(10.73)(530) = 0.075\ \text{lb}_m/\text{ft}^3$$

$$\Delta z = (0.005/12)(62.4/0.075) = 0.347\ \text{ft of air}$$

Assuming a pitot coefficient of 1.0,

$$V = \sqrt{2(32.2)(0.347)} = 4.7\ \text{ft/sec}$$

NON-NEWTONIAN FLUIDS

Earlier in this chapter, the statement was made that the majority of actual food liquids do not obey Newton's viscosity law, Eq. 7-1. The behavior of these liquids is relevant to both product quality and performance of processing equipment, and some understanding of the characteristics of non-Newtonian fluids is important for anyone concerned with food processing.

Non-Newtonian characteristics can be most easily described in terms of the relationship between shear stress and rate of shear. Equation 7-1 shows that these two quantities are proportional for Newtonian fluids, with viscosity as a proportionality constant. This proportionality does not exist for non-Newtonian fluids, and a more complex equation is needed to describe the behavior. The shear-stress shear-rate relationship can be measured in principle by placing the fluid between two parallel plates as represented in Fig. 7.1. A parallel-plate viscometer is not a practical device,

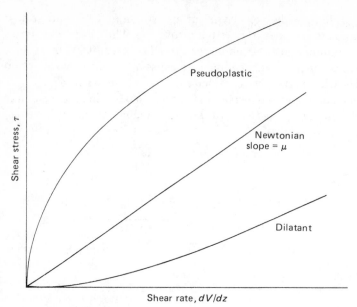

FIG. 7.11.   THE EFFECT OF VISCOSITY ON SHEAR STRESS AND RATE

and a coaxial-cylinder viscometer is used instead. In this instrument, a sample of the fluid is placed in the annular space between two concentric cylinders and one cylinder is rotated to provide the shearing action. The shear rate is proportional to the rotational speed, and the shear stress is obtained by measuring the rotational force (torque) on one of the cylinders. With the rotational speed varied over a wide range, the instrument provides the information necessary to construct plots of shear-stress vs shear-rate for the fluid being tested.

On such a plot, as shown in Fig. 7.11, a Newtonian fluid is represented by a straight line whose slope is the viscosity, μ. The most common type of non-Newtonian behavior corresponds to the top line labeled "pseudo-plastic." At low shear rates, the shear stress rises steeply, corresponding to a high viscosity. At higher shear rates, the shear stress increase is more gradual, and the fluid has a lower apparent viscosity. This type of behavior is typical of tomato catsup, for example. If a bottle is tipped up, the catsup will run out slowly. If the bottle is shaken vigorously, however, the catsup becomes more fluid and runs out easily. This behavior can be explained in terms of a structure that is set up in the fluid by very large molecules and solid particulate matter. When this structure is well established, it resists shearing and creates a high apparent viscosity when subjected to low shearing forces. Higher shearing forces progressively break the structure down and thus cause a decrease in viscosity. These changes are reversible, and the structure reforms when the fluid is allowed to remain at rest. It is quite common for fluids of this type to have a yield stress that must be exceeded before any flow will take place. An open can of tomato paste, for example, might lie on its side indefinitely without having the contents run out under the force of gravity. A greater force, as might be applied by a spoon, is needed to get the material to flow. This behavior is distinctly different from that of a viscous syrup, which might flow very slowly but continuously with even a small force.

The breakdown or buildup of fluid structure requires some definite length of time. In many cases, this time is too short to be measured easily, and a viscometer reading will always correspond to an equilibrium value. With some fluids, the changes may take place over an extended period of time, perhaps ½ hr or longer. In this case, the viscometer reading depends on the length of time used in making a measurement. A fluid exhibiting a reversible time dependency is said to be thixotropic. One problem that arises is that many fluids will undergo an irreversible, or permanent breakdown while being sheared in the viscometer (or in actual flow). It is difficult to separate the effects of reversible and irreversible breakdown.

Another type of fluid behavior that is observed less frequently is called dilatancy and is represented by the bottom line in Fig. 7.11. A dilatant liquid has a relatively low viscosity when at rest or at low shear rates. As the shear rate increases, the fluid thickens and the apparent viscosity increases. Quick-sand is a good example of a dilatant fluid. Some starch pastes behave in this manner.

Yield stress and time-dependency effects, together with certain other aspects of non-Newtonian behavior, create uncertainties in representing fluid characteristics on a quantitative basis. However, a simple pseudo-plastic model is adequate for handling the majority of flow problems. If experimental shear-stress shear-rate data are plotted on logarithmic coordinates, it is found that they tend to fall on straight lines. This purely empirical result can be expressed in the form of an equation as

$$\tau = K(dV/dz)^n \qquad \text{Eq. 7-25}$$

Equation 7-25 is known as the power law equation. Instead of a single viscosity, fluid behavior is represented by the two constants K and n. In the limiting case of a Newtonian fluid, the exponent n is 1.0, and K becomes the viscosity. The exponent n is thus an indication of the degree of non-Newtonian behavior. It is less than 1.0 for pseudoplastic fluids and greater than 1.0 for dilatant fluids. Fruit and vegetable purées and concentrates may have values of n ranging from about 0.2 to 0.5.

Non-Newtonian fluids can exhibit both streamline and turbulent flow in pipes. Most fluids with marked non-Newtonian behavior, however, have such high consistencies that turbulent flow is difficult to attain. For practical reasons in food processing operations, such fluids will always be in streamline flow. In pipe flow, the velocity varies from zero at the wall to a maximum at the center of the pipe. At the center, the velocity gradient is flat, that is, a tangent to the curve of velocity vs radius has zero slope. Since dV/dr is zero, the fluid at the center is not being sheared, and consequently there is no shear stress. The shear stress thus varied from zero at the center to a maximum at the wall. A psuedoplastic fluid will therefore show a higher apparent viscosity near the center and a lower apparent viscosity near the wall. The velocity profile will be flatter than the parabolic profile of a Newtonian fluid and will perhaps more closely resemble turbulent velocity profiles of Newtonian fluids. In the extreme case of very high consistency, the fluid may move as a plug, with a completely flat velocity profile except for a thin layer next to the wall.

Equation 7-25 can be used just as Eq. 7-1 to derive expressions for velocity profiles and pressure drops in streamline flow. The pressure drop expression can be written

$$\frac{D\Delta P}{4L} = \frac{K}{g_c}\left(\frac{1+3n}{4n}\right)^n\left(\frac{8V}{D}\right)^n \qquad \text{Eq. 7-26}$$

For n equal to 1.0, Eq. 7-26 reduces to Eq. 7-11, Poiseuille's law for Newtonian fluids. Equation 7-26 shows that for n less than 1.0, pressure drop increases less rapidly with velocity than for Newtonian fluids. On a physical basis, the flatter velocity profile means less shearing in the central region of the pipe and therefore less dissipation of energy as friction.

The foregoing is intended only as a brief introduction to the subject of non-Newtonian fluids. In a broader sense, this is a part of the field of rheology, which is concerned with the deformation and flow of fluids and solids. There is a very large literature on rheology, ranging from the practical to the highly theoretical. In general, the properties of food materials are so complex that they must be handled empirically, and accordingly there are a large number of arbitrary consistency and other rheological measurements in use. The relationships discussed above have only limited application in handling quantitative problems that may arise in food processing.

PROBLEMS

No. 1. Derive factors to convert viscosity in centipoise to $lb_m/(ft)(sec)$ and $lb_m/(ft)(hr)$.

No. 2. Water at 70°F is flowing at a rate of 5.0 gal./min through a 2.0-in. diameter tube. The viscosity at this temperature is 0.98 cP. What is the value of the Reynolds number?

No. 3. If the tube diameter for the flow conditions in Problem No. 2 is narrowed to 1.0 in., what is the Reynolds number? If friction can be neglected, what is the difference in pressure between the two sections of the tube?

No. 4. At the end of the 1-in. tube of Problem No. 3, the water discharges to the atmosphere. A piece of very small diameter tubing with a right angle bend near one end is held so that the short end is in the discharging water stream facing the direction of flow and the long end is vertical. To what height will the water rise in the vertical tube above the right angle bend? Neglect any effects of friction. Note that there is no flow through the small tube, that is, the velocity at the entrance is zero. The water rises to a height just sufficient to balance the pressure at the entrance.

No. 5. A sugar solution (60 wt%, μ = 60 cP, ρ = 80 lb$_m$/ft^3) flows out of a pressurized tank through a short piece of ¼-in. (inside diameter) tubing. What is the volumetric flow rate out of the tank at a time when the fluid height above the outlet is 6 ft? Assume no friction losses. The pressure at the top of the fluid is 10 psig and the sugar solution is discharging into the air.

No. 6. Calculate the horsepower necessary to pump water from a reservoir up 50 ft to a tank at a rate of 50 gal./min. Assume pipe diameter (inside) = 0.10 ft; viscosity = 1 cP; density = 62.4 lb$_m$/ft^3; the water velocity is zero in the reservoir and in the tank; neglect friction; the pressure is 1 atm in the reservoir and in the tank; the pump efficiency is 60%.

No. 7. An oil is in laminar flow in a 0.6-in. horizontal tube at 14.4 ft/sec. A pressure drop measurement between two locations which are 10 ft apart indicates a loss due to friction of 1 lb$_f$/in.^{2} Use this information to compute the viscosity of the fluid.

No. 8. What is the pressure drop caused by friction of cream flowing in a pipe at 600 cm/sec (19.6 ft/sec)? The pipe is 1½-in. outside diameter sanitary stainless steel tubing (hydraulically smooth) 100 meters long. The specific gravity of cream is 1.00, the viscosity of cream is 12 cP and g_c = 32.2 (lb$_m$)(ft)/(lb$_f$)(sec^2).

No. 9. Soya bean oil is pumped through a ½-in., Schedule 40 steel pipe at a rate of 2 gal./min. What is the pressure drop from one end of the pipe to the other? The length of the pipe is 90 ft, the viscosity of the oil is 40 cP, and the density is 57.4 lb$_m$/ft^3.

No. 10. A fruit juice flows at a Reynolds number of 64,200 in a ¾-in. diameter standard galvanized pipe. The velocity is 15.1 ft/sec.

A. What is the actual inside diameter of the pipe?

B. Calculate the friction loss for 60 ft of pipe.

No. 11. Water for a hydraulic conveyor is pumped at 2.30 ft/sec through a 4.0-in. inside diameter pipe into the bottom of a very large tank. Assume that the pipe is hydraulically smooth, there are 4 threaded elbows, the velocity in the tank is zero, the total pipe length is 80 ft (including the 4 elbows), the surface of the water in the tank is 40.0 ft above the pump, the water density is 62.4 lb_m/ft^3 and the Reynolds number is 7.11×10^4. The gage at the inlet to the pump reads 10.0 psi absolute and atmospheric pressure at the surface of the water in the tank is 15.0 psi absolute. Calculate the water horsepower output of the pump.

No. 12. What is the pressure in psig on the floor of a tank filled to a depth of 5 ft with a liquid of density 75 lb_m/ft^3? The pressure on the top surface is 5 psig.

No. 13. Find the friction factor for a waste product flowing in a 10-in. id cast iron pipe at a Reynolds number of 60,000.

No. 14. The pressure increase across a pump is 10 psi when milk is being pumped at a flow rate of 1000 lb_m/min. The density of the milk is 64.3 lb_m/ft^3. Estimate the work done by the pump and the necessary horsepower rating of the pump assuming 80% efficiency.

No. 15. For the conditions of Example 2 in this Chapter, a decision was made to install a 1-in. standard steel pipe in parallel with the existing $\frac{3}{4}$-in. pipe. The pipes are connected together at both ends in such a way that there is no friction loss from fittings, enlargements, or contractions. If the total flow rate is still 20 gal./min, determine the flow rate through each of the pipes.

No. 16. Wine is pumped from a storage tank to a brandy still through a 2-in. id smooth copper pipe. The total length of pipe is 200 ft, and there are 3 elbows. The liquid level in the tank is 10 ft above the ground, and the pipe enters the distillation column at an elevation of 20 ft. The centrifugal pump is located immediately adjacent to the storage tank, and the flow rate is controlled by a valve near the still. If wine is flowing at a rate of 30 gal./min, estimate the gage pressure at the pump discharge. Both the storage tank and the still are at atmospheric pressure. It is known that the pressure drop across the valve with this flow rate is 12 psi. The wine has a specific gravity of 0.985 and a viscosity of 1.5 cP.

No. 17. A fruit juice evaporation is to be conducted at such a high vacuum that chilled water must be supplied to the condenser. In the proposed operation, water at 40°F will be circulated from a tank, through the condenser, and back to the tank at a rate of 25 gal./min. At this rate, there is a pressure drop of 5 psi across the condenser. The characteristics of the centrifugal pump available for circulating the water are such that it will provide a head of 75 ft of water at this flow rate. What is the smallest size of standard galvanized steel pipe that can be used in this service? A total length of 60 ft of pipe with four 90° elbows will be used. The chilled water tank is at atmospheric pressure.

No. 18. A manometer is used to measure the pressure drop across an orifice as in Fig. 7.7. The fluid flowing is water and the manometer oil has a specific gravity of 1.30. What is the pressure drop in psi if the manometer reading is 10 in.?

No. 19. Refer to Fig. 7.6 of the text for a diagram of a Venturi meter. Calculate the mass flow rate (lb_m/sec) of steam which enters section 1 of the meter at 65.3 psig gage pressure and at a temperature of 400°F. The differential manometer shows a reading of 4 in. of mercury (specific gravity = 13.6, density of water = 62.4 lb_m/ft^3). The diameter of the throat of the meter is 2 in., that of the pipe is 4 in. The coefficient C for this case is known to be 0.95.

No. 20. What is the inside diameter of 1½-in. Schedule 40 steel pipe?

No. 21. Air flows through a 6-in. pipe line which is fitted with a Venturi meter with a 3-in. throat. The gage pressure at the entrance to the meter (section 1 in Fig. 7.6, is 20 lb_f/in.^{2} and the temperature is 60°F. The differential manometer shows a reading of 6 in. of mercury. Barometric pressure is 14.70 lb_f/in.^{2} and C can be taken as 0.93. Find the mass flow rate of air in lb_m/sec.

No. 22. A pitot tube is installed at the center of a 12-in. water line and connected to one end of a U tube manometer containing carbon tetrachloride (sp gr 1.59). The other end of the manometer is connected to the pipe wall. If water fills the manometer tubes above the carbon tetrachloride and the manometer reads 10 in., what is the velocity at the center of the pipe?

No. 23. Water at 70°F is flowing through a 2-in. standard steel pipe at a rate of 50 gal./min. An orifice meter is to be installed to measure the flow rate. A manometer will be used with the meter with a maximum reading of 10 in. Hg. What orifice diameter will be required to give this pressure drop at 50 gal./min?

No. 24. Saturated steam at a pressure of 100 psi gage is flowing through a 2-in. standard steel pipe (Schedule 40). The pipe is fitted with an orifice having a diameter of 1.5 in. The orifice pressure drop is found with a manometer to be 4 in. of mercury. What is the steam flow rate in pounds per hour?

SYMBOLS

A	area
C	empirical friction-velocity coefficient for a converging pipe section or venturi meter, dimensionless
D	pipe diameter
F	force and friction work per unit of fluid mass
$[F]$	dimension of force
f	Fanning friction factor, dimensionless
F_e	friction caused by a sudden enlargement in pipe diameter
g	gravitational acceleration
g_c	reciprocal of constant of proportionality (K) in Newton's second law, 32.17 lb_m ft/lb_f sec^2 or 980 gm-mass cm/gm-force sec^2

K	empirical constant for shear stress in non-Newtonian fluids
K_c	friction constant given in Table 7.1
KE	kinetic energy, ft-lb$_f$
L	length
$[L]$	dimension of length
L_e	length of pipe which causes friction equal to a given pipe fitting
$[M]$	dimension of mass
m	mass, lb$_m$
$\dot{m}$	mass flow rate, lb$_m$/sec
n	empirical power constant for shear stress in non-Newtonian fluids
PE	potential energy, ft-lb$_f$
R	pipe radius to inside pipe wall
r	pipe radius, distance from center of pipe
Re	Reynolds number, dimensionless
S	cross-sectional area of pipe or conduit, ft^2 or in.^{2}
V	velocity, ft/sec
V_{av}	average velocity, ft/sec
$\dot{v}$	flow volume per unit time, ft^3/sec
dV/dz	velocity gradient, shear rate
W_s	shaft work, ft-lb$_f$
z	distance in z direction, especially vertical height
α	factor which accounts for velocity distribution in KE term in mechanical energy balance, dimensionless
ΔKE	change in kinetic energy, ft-lb$_f$/lb$_m$
ΔP	pressure drop in pipe, $P_2 - P_1$, lb$_f$/in.^{2}
ΔPE	change in potential energy, ft-lb$_f$/lb$_m$
Δz	potential energy head difference, ft
Δz_m	manometer fluid head difference, ft or in.
Δz_w	water manometer fluid head difference, ft or in.
ϵ	equivalent height of pipe roughness, ft
θ	time, sec, min, or hr
$[\theta]$	dimension of time
μ	coefficient of viscosity, lb$_f$ sec/ft^2 or lb$_m$/ft sec
π	3.1416
ρ	fluid density, lb$_m$
ρ_m	manometer of fluid density, lb$_m$
ΣF	sum of friction losses, ft
τ	shear stress in fluids, lb$_f$/ft^2

CHAPTER 8

Heat Transfer[1]

INTRODUCTION

Quantity of heat was defined in the chapter on thermodynamics as energy that is transferred as a result of a temperature difference. The thermodynamic treatment of heat was concerned with relationships among this energy quantity and the equilibrium or steady-state properties of systems. Nothing was said about the mechanism of the heat transfer process or the rate at which a given quantity of energy can be transferred over a temperature difference.

We know, of course, that physical processes do not occur instantaneously. In a study of equilibrium properties, it is assumed that there is no limit on the length of time available for changes to take place. The solution of many engineering problems requires nothing more than the application of equilibrium thermodynamic relationships. In those instances in which simple energy and material balances are insufficient to provide solutions, it is necessary to bring in additional information concerning the mechanism of processes. The estimation of friction by the use of friction factors in fluid flow problems is an example of this type that is related to work effects or mechanical energy. In dealing with thermal energy, we are faced with the problems of how and at what rate does the heat get from one point to another.

Thermal energy in a substance is manifested through the random motions of molecules, atoms, and sub-atomic particles. The temperature is merely a measure of the level of such motions. For example, the temperature of a perfect gas can be completely expressed in terms of the kinetic energy of the molecules. Transfer of heat therefore consists of transferring some of this molecular or atomic motion from one region to another. There are three broad mechanisms by which such transfer can occur: conduction, convection, and radiation. In conduction, the energy is transmitted from particle to particle by a process of direct contact or random collisions, with no bulk movement of material. Transfer of heat by convection involves bulk mixing of fluids of different temperatures. Radiation is the transfer of energy from a radiating source through space which may or may not be occupied by matter. It is by radiation that we receive all our energy from the

---

[1] Symbols used in this chapter are listed and defined at the end of the chapter.

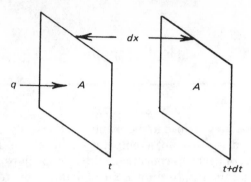

FIG. 8.1.   CONDUCTIVE HEAT FLOW CONVENTIONS

sun. Each of these three mechanisms will be considered in detail in the following sections.

CONDUCTION

As discussed, temperature is the driving force for flow of heat. The larger the temperature difference over a region, the greater will be the rate of heat flow. Heat flow rate is also proportional to the area perpendicular to the direction of flow. If heat is flowing at a certain rate through an area of 1 ft^2, the flow rate through an area of 2 ft^2 will obviously be twice as great. Finally, heat flow rate decreases as the length of path for a given temperature difference increases. These conditions are illustrated in Fig. 8.1, which represents a differential section of a material through which heat is flowing. The two planes of area A are separated by the distance dx. Over this distance, the temperature changes by an amount dt. The rate of heat flow is accordingly given by the expression

$$q = -kAdt/dx \qquad\qquad \text{Eq. 8-1}$$

In the usual engineering units, q is expressed in Btu/hr, A in ft^2, x in ft, and t in °F. The factor k is a proportionality constant that is called the thermal conductivity, with consistent units of Btu/(hr)(ft)(°F). The minus sign is included as a convention to give a positive value of q. In order for heat to flow in the direction of the arrow in Fig. 8.1, the temperature must decrease in this direction, and dt is therefore a negative quantity.

Equation 8-1 is known as Fourier's law and dates from the year 1822. It applies to heat conduction in solids, liquids, or gases. In treating conduction in fluids, care must be taken to exclude any effects of convection. Experimentally, this result may be difficult to achieve. The Fourier law equation is seen to be very similar in form to Newton's viscosity law developed in the chapter on fluid flow. Both laws were developed empirically, but both can be derived theoretically for gases by kinetic theory relationships.

Thermal conductivity, like viscosity, is a property of a substance, and tables of thermal conductivities are widely available in the literature. It is within everyone's experience that metals have high thermal conductivities. This characteristic is related to the number of free electrons in a metal available for transferring energy and is parallel to the electrical conductivity. Gases have the lowest thermal conductivities, which may be lower than those for metals by a factor of 10^4 or more. As with most properties, thermal conductivity depends on the temperature of the material. A complete vacuum, of course, has zero thermal conductivity, and evacuated jackets are commonly used insulating devices. Most commonly used thermal insulating materials obtain their low conductivities by having a porous structure that entraps a quantity of air or other gas. The effective thermal conductivity therefore approaches that of the gas rather than the actual solid substance. A thick layer of gas would in principle have the same low thermal conductivity, but it would be impossible to eliminate convection currents.

Equation 8-1 applies to conduction of heat in the x direction at a point within a volume of some substance. For a complete mathematical description, we would need to write similar equations for the other two directions in a three-dimensional system and integrate over the entire volume. Most of our processing applications are concerned with heat conduction only in one direction, and we do not have to be concerned with a general mathematical solution. Furthermore, we are primarily interested in steady-state heat conduction, which means that q is constant. In this respect, heat can be considered analogous to the fluid in a fluid flow system. Just as the mass flow rate of fluid is constant throughout a steady-state system, so must the heat flow rate be constant at every point in steady-state heat conduction. Keeping these restrictions in mind, we can rearrange Eq. 8-1 as follows:

$$(q/A)dx = -kdt \qquad \text{Eq. 8-2}$$

If the area A is constant over the length of the heat flow path and the thermal conductivity can be considered constant, Eq. 8-2 integrates to give

$$(q/A)\Delta x = k(t_1 - t_2) \qquad \text{Eq. 8-3}$$

Equation 8-3 is the usual integrated form of Fourier's law for uni-directional steady-state heat conduction over a path of constant cross-sectional area. A numerical calculation is shown in the following example.

Example 1

A steel rod having a 1-in. diameter is placed with one end in boiling water at 212°F and the other end in an ice bath. The rod is insulated so that there

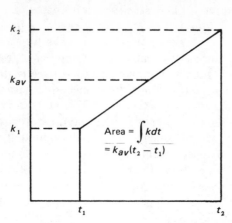

Area = $\int k dt$

= $k_{av}(t_2 - t_1)$

FIG. 8.2.   GRAPH OF THERMAL CONDUCTIVITY k VERSUS TEMPERATURE t

is no heat lost or gained through the outer surface of the rod between the two water baths. If the net length of the rod is 30 in., how much heat flows through the rod from the hot to the cold bath? The thermal conductivity of steel is 26 Btu/(hr)(ft)(°F). From Eq. 8-3,

$$q = (kA/\Delta x)(t_1 - t_2)$$

$$A = \pi D^2/4 = (\pi/4)(1/144) = 0.00545 \text{ ft}^2$$

$$\Delta x = 30 \text{ in.} = 2.5 \text{ ft}$$

$$q = (26)(0.00545)(1/2.5)(212 - 32) = 10.2 \text{ Btu/hr}$$

Equation 8-2 was integrated above on the basis of a constant thermal conductivity. If the temperature difference is very large, the variation of k with temperature may be important. Conductivities of gases always increase with increased temperature. With liquids and solids, conductivities may either increase or decrease with increase in temperature, depending on the material. Although there are some general rules, in practice one must refer to experimentally determined data. A generally valid approximation is to represent a plot of conductivity versus temperature as a straight line. If values of conductivity are known at two temperatures, a straight line drawn through these points will give the conductivity at any other temperature. It should be remembered that this is an empirical rule, and extrapolations of data should be kept within reasonable limits. With this straight line variation of conductivity, it is easy to show that the correct average value of k in Eq. 8-3 is the arithmetic average of k at the two terminal temperatures or, what is equivalent, the value of k at the arithmetic average temperature. Consider the straight line plot of k versus t in Fig.

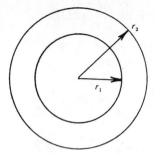

FIG. 8.3.   CYLINDRICAL CROSS SECTION

8.2. Graphically, the integral of the right-hand side of Eq. 8-2 is simply the area under the curve of k versus t between the limits of t_1 and t_2. Because the curve is a straight line, the desired result is the area of a trapezoid, or the product of the width and the average height. The width is the temperature difference and the average height is value of k at the midpoint. We can thus write,

$$\int_{t_1}^{t_2} k\,dt = k_{\mathrm{av}}(t_2 - t_1) \qquad\qquad \text{Eq. 8-4}$$

where k_{av} is the arithmetic average conductivity. It should be noted that this result depends only on the relationship between conductivity and temperature and is entirely independent of the shape of the material or the rate of heat flow. All factors relating to dimensions or heat rate appear on the opposite side of Eq. 8-2 and do not enter into the integration.

Conduction Through Cylindrical Surface

Another consideration in the integration of Eq. 8-2 arises when the area of the heat flow path varies along its length. Such a situation exists in conduction through the wall of a hollow cylinder as, for example, a cylindrical layer of insulation around the outside of a pipe. Figure 8-3 represents the cross-section of such a cylinder of length L. In this case, all heat flow is in a radial direction, and the area through which the heat flows is the cylindrical surface. This cylindrical area increases from the inner to the outer radius and is given by the expression

$$A = 2\pi r L$$

Substituting into Eq. 8-2, and letting r replace x as the distance measure,

$$q\,dr/2\pi r L = -k\,dt$$

Integrating between the limits of r_1 and r_2,

$$(q/2\pi L)\ln(r_2/r_1) = k_{av}(t_1 - t_2)$$

or

$$q = \frac{2\pi L k_{av}(t_1 - t_2)}{\ln(r_2/r_1)} \qquad \text{Eq. 8-4}$$

By a little algebraic manipulation, we can find an expression for a mean area which, if substituted into Eq. 8-3, will give the correct heat flow rate. We will rearrange Eq. 8-3 as

$$q = A_m k_{av}(t_1 - t_2)/(r_2 - r_1) \qquad \text{Eq. 8-3a}$$

where $r_2 - r_1$ represents the length of path Δx. Comparing Eqs. 8-3a and 8-4, we can write

$$A_m/(r_2 - r_1) = 2\pi L/\ln(r_2/r_1)$$

or

$$A_m = 2\pi L(r_2 - r_1)/\ln(r_2/r_1) = (A_2 - A_1)/\ln(A_2/A_1) \qquad \text{Eq. 8-5}$$

where $A_1 = 2\pi r_1 L$ and $A_2 = 2\pi r_2 L$.

The expression on the right side of Eq. 8-5 is called a logarithmic mean. Just as the arithmetic mean of two numbers a and b is given by $(a + b)/2$, so the logarithmic mean is given by $(a - b)/\ln(a/b)$. The logarithmic mean of two numbers is always smaller than the arithmetic mean. For a ratio of the two numbers of 2:1, the logarithmic mean is about 4% lower. As the two numbers come closer together, these two mean values also approach more closely. In a large number of calculations, it is therefore a satisfactory approximation to use an arithmetic mean value as a substitute for a logarithmic mean. Summarizing the problem of heat conduction through a cylindrical surface, Eq. 8-3 will give the correct answer if the area is taken as the logarithmic mean of the inner and outer areas. As noted previously, this result and the result for average conductivity are independent and do not affect each other.

Example 2.—A 2-in. standard steel pipe is carrying steam at a temperature of 250°F. The pipe is covered with a 1-in. thickness of magnesia insulation [$k = 0.05$ Btu/(hr)(ft)(°F)]. If the outer temperature of the insulation is 115°F, what is the heat loss per foot of length?

The inside radius of the insulation is the same as the outside pipe radius, or 2.375/2 in. The logarithmic mean area is most directly obtained from the logarithmic mean radius.

$$r_1 = 2.375/(2)(12) = 0.099 \text{ ft.}$$

$$r_2 = r_1 + 1/12 = 0.099 + 0.083 = 0.182 \text{ ft.}$$

$$r_m = (r_2 - r_1)/\ln(r_2/r_1) = 0.083/\ln(0.182/0.099) = 0.136 \text{ ft.}$$

$$A_m = 2\pi r_m L = 2\pi(0.136)(1) = 0.856 \text{ ft}^2$$

$$q = A_m k_{av}(t_1 - t_2)/(r_2 - r_1) = (0.856)(0.050)(250 - 115)/(1/12)$$

$$= 69.4 \text{ Btu/hr}$$

Concept of Resistance

In the study of natural phenomena, there are many instances in which some kind of driving force or potential difference results in a flow of some quantity. For example, fluids flow as a result of a pressure driving force. Electricity, or electric charge, flows under the action of an electrical potential, or voltage, difference. In the present case, we have heat flowing from a temperature driving force. In each of these cases, the driving force is an intensive property of the system. Whatever it is that is flowing is an extensive quantity, that is, it behaves like a quantity of some substance that can be collected and measured. Obviously, heat cannot be measured as fluids can by collecting a quantity in a bucket and weighing it. However, heat flowing through a system must be accounted for in total quantity just as a fluid. We make a heat balance around a system in the same manner that we make a material balance.

In a very large number of applications of the type of flow systems just discussed, whether heat, fluid, or electricity, we find that the rate of flow is proportional to the driving force. It is common practice to express the proportionality constant as a resistance. The most familiar example is that of electrical resistance, where we say that the flow of electric current is equal to the voltage difference divided by the resistance. This relationship is known as Ohm's law, and electrical resistances are expressed in ohms. A slight rearrangement will put Eq. 8-3, the integrated form of Fourier's law, into this form:

$$q = \frac{(t_1 - t_2)}{\Delta x/kA} = \frac{(t_1 - t_2)}{R} \qquad \text{Eq. 8-3b}$$

where the thermal resistance, R, is equal to $\Delta x/kA$. This form of Fourier's law provides no new information, but it does simplify many calculations. Since it is mathematically identical to Ohm's law for electric current flow, we can use directly many results that have already been obtained for electrical applications. This analogy between flow of heat and electricity provides a very powerful experimental tool. We can set up an apparatus consisting of equivalent electrical components, make electrical measurements,

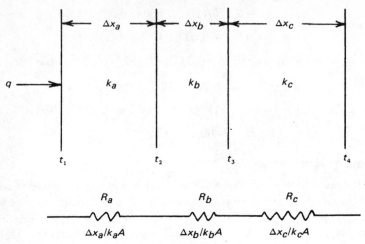

FIG. 8.4. WALL SECTION OF THREE DIFFERENT THERMAL CONDUCTIVITIES WITH
EQUIVALENT ELECTRICAL RESISTANCES

and convert the results over to heat flow quantities. Electrical measurements can be made much more easily and with much greater accuracy than thermal measurements.

Resistances in Series and Parallel

A very common application in practice is that of heat conduction through a wall made up of layers of several different materials. For example, a furnace wall might have layers of different kinds of brick to provide high temperature resistance, thermal insulation, and structural support. Figure 8.4 illustrates a section of plane wall composed of three layers, each with a different thickness and conductivity. Under steady state conditions, the heat flow rate, q, must be the same through each of the layers. From Eq. 8-3b, we can write

$$q = \frac{(t_1 - t_2)}{R_a} = \frac{(t_2 - t_3)}{R_b} = \frac{(t_3 - t_4)}{R_c} = \frac{(t_1 - t_4)}{R_t} \qquad \text{Eq. 8-6}$$

where $R_a = \Delta x_a/k_a A$; $R_b = \Delta x_b/k_b A$; $R_c = \Delta x_c/k_c A$; and R_t is an overall or total resistance. Solving for the temperature differences in the above equation,

$$t_1 - t_2 = qR_a$$

$$t_2 - t_3 = qR_b$$

$$t_3 - t_4 = qR_c$$

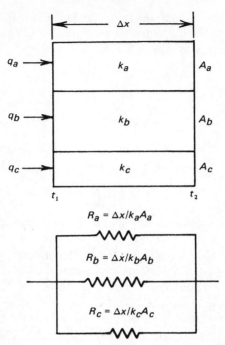

FIG. 8.5. PARALLEL HEAT FLOW THROUGH THREE DIFFERENT THERMAL CONDUC-
TIVITIES

Adding these three expressions,

$$t_1 - t_4 = q(R_a + R_b + R_c) = qR_t \qquad \text{Eq. 8-7}$$

We thus see that for resistances in series, the total resistance is simply the
sum of the individual resistances. This is, of course, the familiar Ohm's law
result for electrical resistances. The equalities of Eq. 8-6 can be used to
obtain the intermediate temperatures between the layers if these are desired. If the conductivity of a layer varies with temperature, the value
corresponding to the average temperature of the particular layer should
be used. The above expressions are applicable to conduction through a
series of concentric cylindrical layers if the resistance of each layer is calculated from a mean area as given by Eq. 8-5. In the lower part of Fig. 8-4,
a diagram is represented in the usual manner of electrical resistances. Such
an equivalent electrical diagram is frequently more illustrative and simpler
to draw than one that attempts to portray the actual physical situation.

Figure 8.5 illustrates the problem of heat flow through several resistances
in parallel. In the previous case of series resistances, the overall temperature
difference is the sum of the individual temperature differences and the same
q flows through all the resistances. With resistances in parallel, the total

q is the sum of the q's through the individual resistances, and the temperature differences for the individual resistances are all the same and equal to the overall temperature difference. We can write

$$q_a = (t_1 - t_2)/R_a$$
$$q_b = (t_1 - t_2)/R_b$$
$$q_c = (t_1 - t_2)/R_c$$

Adding,

$$q = q_a + q_b + q_c = (t_1 - t_2)(1/R_a + 1/R_b + 1/R_c) = (t_1 - t_2)(1/R_t)$$

$$1/R_t = 1/R_a + 1/R_b + 1/R_c \qquad \text{Eq. 8-8}$$

Various combinations of resistances in series and parallel can be treated in a similar manner.

Example 3.—The walls of a frozen food warehouse are made up of a 4-in. concrete slab lined with a 3-in. layer of foamed plastic insulation. The thermal conductivities of the concrete and plastic are 0.50 and 0.03 Btu/ (hr)(ft)(°F), respectively. If the inside surface temperature of the plastic insulation is 0°F and the outer surface of the concrete wall is at 78°F, calculate the heat flow per square foot of area through the wall and the temperature at the boundary between the concrete and the insulation.

$$R_c = x_c/k_cA = (4/12)/(0.50)(1.0) = 0.667 \ (°F)(hr)/(Btu)$$

$$R_i = x_i/k_iA = (3/12)/(0.03)(1.0) = 8.333 \ (°F)(hr)/(Btu)$$

$$R_t = R_c + R_i = 0.667 + 8.333 = 9.00 \ (°F)(hr)/(Btu)$$

$$q = (t_1 - t_2)/R_t = (78 - 0)/9.0 = 8.67 \ \text{Btu/hr}$$

By Eq. 8-6, if t' represents the intermediate temperature,

$$(t_1 - t')/R_c = (t' - t_2)/R_i$$

$$(78 - t')/(t' - 0) = 0.667/8.333 = 0.080$$

$$t' = 72.2°F$$

CONVECTION

Convective heat transfer occurs as a result of bulk movement in a fluid stream in which a temperature gradient exists. In any convective heat transfer situation, conduction must obviously be proceeding simultaneously. Such conduction is ordinarily completely overshadowed by the convection and, except in a few special cases, no attempt is made to evaluate the effects of conduction separately. Results obtained for convection therefore automatically include the associated conduction contribution.

We recognize two general categories of convection: natural, or free, convection and forced convection. In natural convection, movement of the fluid arises from density gradients that in turn result from temperature variations. The coefficient of thermal expansion of a fluid is obviously an important property affecting natural convection. If there were no thermal expansion, there could be no natural convection. Natural convection proceeds in any large fluid-filled space, whether it is desired or not. One of the major problems in thermal insulation is elimination of natural convection. Natural convection effects are particularly important with gases because their low viscosity provides little resistance to movement. Any source of heat or cold, such as a hot or cold water line, an exposed window, an electric light, etc. can create the necessary density variation.

In forced convection, some positive means of moving the fluid is provided, such as a pump or fan. Processing applications of convective heat transfer generally are concerned with forced convection. Here we have direct control over the fluid movement and can therefore more easily design systems to meet desired specifications. Furthermore, it is possible to obtain much higher velocities in forced than in natural convection, and therefore greater heat transfer rates. In forced convection, it is usually necessary to make the further distinction of streamline or turbulent flow.

Film Coefficient of Heat Transfer

Most processing applications of convection are concerned with steady-state heat transfer between a fluid and a solid surface. In order to develop the basic convection relationships, we will consider the situation represented in Fig. 8.6, in which a fluid at temperature t is moving past a surface at a higher temperature t_s. The flow may be either natural or forced convection, streamline or turbulent. The curve of temperature versus distance in Fig. 8.6 represents the temperature profile corresponding to a given position on the surface. Under steady-state conditions, this profile does not change with time, but it may vary from one position to another along the surface.

From the fluid flow chapter, it will be recalled that the velocity is always zero at a surface. Immediately adjacent to the surface, there is a thin layer in which the velocity is low enough that flow is streamline, regardless of the nature of flow in the main stream. Heat transferred across this thin, essentially stagnant layer must be by conduction. There is no sharply defined thickness of this layer, and we cannot calculate the heat transfer by a simple application of the conduction equations. Moving farther away from the surface, the velocity increases, and consequently the resistance to heat transfer decreases. The temperature profile of Fig. 8.6 accordingly shows a sharp drop across the stagnant streamline layer, where the thermal resistance is high. Farther from the surface, where convection is more effective

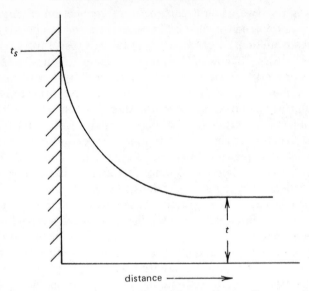

distance ──────────►

FIG. 8.6.   TEMPERATURE PROFILE IN A FLUID MOVING PAST A SURFACE AT TEMPERA-
TURE t_s

and the thermal resistance is lower, the change in temperature is less rapid.
For a fluid temperature higher than the surface temperature, the profile
would have the same shape but be reversed. The temperature profile is seen
to be very similar to the velocity profile, which also changes rapidly near
the surface and more gradually farther out in the stream.

Newton's law of cooling (or heating) states that the rate of heat flow per
unit surface area is proportional to the difference between the surface and
fluid temperatures, or

$$q = hA(t_s - t) \qquad \text{Eq. 8-9}$$

The proportionality constant h in Eq. 8-9 represents a thermal conductance
of the fluid film across which the temperature change (and velocity change)
takes place. It is commonly called the film coefficient of heat transfer, or
simply the heat transfer coefficient. In streamline flow, there are no eddies
that bring about bulk mixing of portions of the fluid at different temperatures, and all heat flow results from molecular motion. Just as it is possible
to derive an exact expression for friction factors in streamline flow, relationships for heat transfer coefficients can be derived by combining the
basic fluid flow and heat conduction equations. In general, however, an
exact derivation is not possible, and Eq. 8-9 must be considered to represent
an empirical law with values of h based on experimental measurements.

Comparison of Eqs. 8-3 and 8-9 shows that h has the units of k divided by distance, or Btu/(hr)(ft^2)($^\circ$F). As in the case of conduction, it is frequently convenient to express convective heat transfer in terms of a temperature difference driving force divided by a resistance, $1/hA$. Some physical insight as to the nature of this resistance may be obtained by considering a fluid in turbulent flow to consist of a stagnant surface layer which contains all the resistance to heat transfer and a turbulent core in ,which the mixing effect of the eddies result in negligible heat transfer resistance. The value of h is then given by the thermal conductivity of the fluid divided by the thickness of the hypothetical stagnant film. Conversely, the film thickness is given by the ratio of an experimentally determined h to the thermal conductivity. It should be emphasized that this stagnant film is purely hypothetical and that there is no definite boundary separating the surface layer from the turbulent core.

Figure 8.6 represents a situation in which the fluid temperature drops from a fixed value at the surface to the constant temperature of the main stream. Such a condition would exist if an unconfined fluid at a constant temperature were flowing over a heated flat surface. In the more usual situation, as in the case of flow through a pipe, the fluid temperature varies continuously across the diameter, going through a minimum (or maximum), and it does not come to any constant value. Just as friction factors for pipe flow are based on average velocities, so it is customary to base heat transfer coefficients on average temperatures. The average temperature is that which would be obtained if the fluid at that point were discharged into a bucket and the temperature allowed to equalize. Obviously, the average temperature is higher than the centerline in heating and lower in cooling. This situation is illustrated in the following section.

Overall Heat Transfer Coefficient

One of the most common process heat transfer applications consists of heat flow from a hot fluid, through a solid wall, to a cooler fluid on the other side. The solid wall may be a flat surface, but more commonly will be a cylindrical pipe. There may be a scale or dirt deposit that creates a heat transfer resistance on either the inside or outside surface of the pipe. The heat flowing from one fluid to the other must therefore pass through several resistances in series: the outside fluid film, the pipe wall, the scale deposit, and the inside fluid film. The temperature profile through this series of resistances is represented in Fig. 8.7. The temperature profile through the hot and cold fluid films is similar to that in Fig. 8.6, discussed above. The pipe wall and scale deposits are pure conduction resistances, and the temperature profile through each of them is a straight line. It should be remembered that a steep temperature gradient corresponds to a high thermal resistance and a flat temperature gradient to a low resistance. The

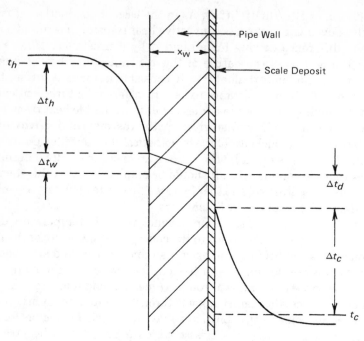

FIG. 8.7.   TEMPERATURE PROFILE FROM A HOT FLUID AT t_h INSIDE A PIPE TO A LOWER
FLUID TEMPERATURE AT t_c OUTSIDE THE PIPE

metal pipe wall of course has a low resistance. A scale deposit, although
usually quite thin, will always have a much higher resistance for a given
thickness than a metal pipe wall, and the temperature gradient through
it will be correspondingly steep. Neither the thickness nor the thermal
conductivity of a scale deposit will ordinarily be known, and its effect is
expressed in terms of an equivalent conductance, h_d, with the same units
as the film coefficient of heat transfer. Scale deposits are usually very thin,
so that their presence on a pipe wall does not appreciably change the heat
transfer area as would a thick layer of insulation.

The relationship previously derived for resistances in series is quite
general and applies regardless of the nature of the individual resistances.
Accordingly, we can write

$$R_t = R_h + R_w + R_d + R_c$$

or

$$1/UA = 1/h_h A_h + x_w/k_w \ A_w + 1/h_d A_d + 1/h_c A_c \qquad \text{Eq. 8-10}$$

where the areas are based on some unit length of pipe. The quantity U in
the above expression is known as the overall heat transfer coefficient. If

the individual resistances (or coefficients) are known, U is easily calculated. Conversely, experimental heat transfer studies frequently involve measuring values of U under controlled conditions and calculating individual coefficients from these. If the surface in Fig. 8.7 is flat, all the areas in Eq. 8-10 will have the same value and cancel. If the surface is a pipe wall with a thickness appreciable compared to the diameter, the areas of the hot and cold sides will be different, and a mean area calculated from Eq. 8-5 is used for A_w.

Equation 8-10 gives the value of the product UA. The values of U depends on the area that is used with it, which can be the inside, the outside, or the mean area, thus,

$$q = UA(t_h - t_c) = U_c A_c (t_h - t_c) = U_h A_h (t_h - t_c)$$
$$= U_w A_m (t_h - t_c) \quad \text{Eq. 8-11}$$

Although any of these combinations can be used, the customary practice is to base the overall coefficient and the heat transfer rate on the inside area. In calculating U, it is convenient to rearrange Eq. 8-10 so that the areas appear as ratios. Thus, if U is to be based on the cold side area,

$$\frac{1}{U_c} = \frac{1}{h_h A_h / A_c} + \frac{x_w}{k_w A_m / A_c} + \frac{1}{h_d} + \frac{1}{h_c} \quad \text{Eq. 8-12}$$

The scale deposit is considered to have negligible thickness, so that $A_d = A_c$. Since the ratio of the areas is equal to the ratios of the diameters, we can write

$$\frac{1}{U_c} = \frac{1}{h_h D_h / D_c} + \frac{x_w}{k_w D_m / D_c} + \frac{1}{h_d} + \frac{1}{h_c} \quad \text{Eq. 8-13}$$

The above development is based on the presence of four resistances, but any others can be included in the same manner. Thus, there might be a scale deposit or a layer of insulation on the outside of the pipe. It should be emphasized that Eq. 8-11 gives the heat transfer rate per unit area at a particular point along the pipe. Although the temperatures remain constant with time in steady state conditions, in general they will change from point to point. The method of calculating the total heat transfer rate over some specified length of pipe will be treated in the section on heat exchangers.

Example 4.—A 2-in. standard steel pipe carrying steam at 250°F is covered with a 1-in. layer of magnesia insulation. The heat transfer coefficient for the steam film in the inside is 1000 Btu/(hr)(ft^2)(°F), and the coefficient for natural convection to the air from the outside of the insulation is 3.0 Btu/(hr)(ft^2)(°F). The thermal conductivities of pipe wall and the magnesia insulation are 26 and 0.04 Btu/(hr)(ft)(°F), respectively. The room air temperature is 75°F. Calculate the overall heat transfer coefficient based on the inside area and the heat loss per foot of pipe.

pipe i.d. = 2.067 in.

pipe o.d. = 2.375 in.

x_w = (2.375 − 2.067)/2 = 0.154 in.

D_w (2.375 + 2.067)/2 = 2.22 in. (arithmetic mean can be used instead of logarithmic mean because the inside and outside diameters are close to each other)

magnesia i.d. = 2.375 in.

magnesia o.d. = 4.375 in.

x_m = 1.0 in.

$$D_m = \frac{4.375 - 2.375}{\ln(4.375/2.375)} = 3.28 \text{ in.}$$

By Eq. 8-13,

$$\frac{1}{U_i} = \frac{1}{h_i} + \frac{x_w}{k_w D_w/D_i} + \frac{x_m}{k_m D_m/D_i} + \frac{1}{h_o D_o/D_i}$$

$$= \frac{1}{1000} + \frac{0.154/12}{26(2.22/2.067)} + \frac{1/12}{0.04(3.28/2.067)} + \frac{1}{3(4.375/2.067)}$$

$$= 0.001 + 0.0005 + 1.32 + 0.16 = 1.48$$

$$U_i = 1/1.48 = 0.675 \text{ Btu/(hr)(ft}^2)(°F)$$

For a 1 ft. length of pipe,

$$A_i = \pi D_i L = \pi(2.067/12)(1.0) = 0.542 \text{ ft}^2$$

$$q = U_i A_i \Delta t = (0.675)(0.542)(250 - 75) = 64 \text{ Btu/hr}$$

It is seen that the resistances of the steam film and the pipe wall are negligible compared to those of the insulation and the natural convection to the air.

Example 5.—Milk flowing through a 1-in. sanitary stainless steel tube is being heated by steam on the outside of the tube. Initially, experimental measurements show that the overall heat transfer coefficient, based on the inside area, is 300 Btu/(hr)(ft²)(°F). After a period of time, formation of a deposit on the inside surface of the tube causes the overall coefficient to drop to 45 Btu/(hr)(ft²)(°F). What is the value of the heat transfer coefficient for the deposit?

TABLE 8.1

APPROXIMATE RANGE OF INDIVIDUAL HEAT TRANSFER COEFFICIENTS
$Btu/(hr)(ft^2)(°F)$

Gases—natural convection	0.5–5
Gases—forced convection	2–20
Viscous liquids—forced convection	10–100
Water—forced convection	100–1000
Boiling water	300–5000
Condensing steam	1000–20000

$$\frac{1}{U_1} = \frac{1}{h_i} + \frac{x_w}{k_w D_w/D_i} + \frac{1}{h_o D_o/D_i} = 1/300$$

$$1/U_2 = 1/U_1 + 1/h_d = 1/45$$

$$1/45 = 1/300 + 1/h_d$$

$$1/h_d = 1/45 - 1/300 = 0.0286 - 0.0033 = 0.0253$$

$$h_d = 1/0.0253 = 39.6 \ Btu/(hr)(ft^2)(°F)$$

EVALUATION OF INDIVIDUAL FILM COEFFICIENTS

It was indicated in the preceding section that values of individual film coefficients must in general be based on experimental measurements. Just as with friction factors, it is to be expected that h will depend on the fluid properties, the nature of the flow, and the geometry of the flow system. In fact, the analogy between friction factors and heat transfer coefficients can be developed to give a quantitative relation between the two. With friction factors, we were primarily interested in forced flow through round pipes. Streamline flow could be handled by an exact calculation, and a single empirical correlation for turbulent flow served our purposes. In heat transfer we are concerned with a much wider variety of types of flow and flow system geometries, and the differences from one to another are substantial. Thus, we have streamline and turbulent flow, natural and forced convection, flow inside and outside of pipes, across flat surfaces, etc., and phenomena such as boiling and condensation. In order to take care of such a diversity of situations, it is to be expected that many different empirical correlations will be needed. As with fluid flow, the correlations should be expressed in terms of dimensionless ratios.

Before proceeding to the specific correlations, a consideration of the relative magnitudes of coefficients for different situations will be helpful. It is easy to predict that heat transfer will be favored by forced convection, turbulent flow, and low viscosity as contrasted to natural convection, streamline flow, and high viscosity. Boiling liquids and condensing vapors are found to result in high values of h as compared to ordinary convection.

TABLE 8.2

DIMENSIONLESS RATIOS EMPLOYED IN CONVECTIVE HEAT TRANSFER

Name	Symbol	Group
Reynolds	Re	$DV\rho/\mu$
Prandtl	Pr	$c_p\mu/k$
Nusselt	Nu	hD/k
Stanton	$St = Nu/PrRe$	$h/c_p V\rho$
Grashof	Gr	$L^3\rho^2 g\beta\Delta t/\mu^2$
Graetz	$Gz = RePr(L/D)(\pi/4)$	$\dot{m}c_p/kL$

Table 8.1 lists representative values of h for different situations. The student should study this table sufficiently to retain a clear idea of the relative orders of magnitude of the coefficients. Frequently, it will not be possible to predict an exact value of h. Many times, however, a knowledge of orders of magnitude will allow some resistances to be neglected and permit a satisfactory solution (see Example 4). A knowledge of representative values is also useful for making quick estimations, when the conditions or time available do not justify detailed calculations.

In any processing application, there will always be several heat transfer resistances in series, so that no real benefit is realized from the higher values listed in the table. Dirt or scale deposits can quickly form that will completely nullify the effect of an extremely high film coefficient.

Dimensionless Ratios

The use of dimensionless ratios in describing the behavior of physical systems was discussed in connection with fluid flow. By similar methods, dimensionless ratios significant in describing heat transfer phenomena can be obtained. A list of the more commonly used ratios is given in Table 8.2.

The familiar Reynolds number characterizes flow in a forced convection system. The Reynolds number is not applicable to natural convection, and the Grashof number takes its place. The Grashof number involves the coefficient of volumetric expansion, β, and the temperature difference that is the source of the convection. The volumetric expansion coefficient is defined by the relation

$$\Delta v/v = \beta\Delta t \qquad \text{Eq. 8-14}$$

where Δv is the change in volume resulting from a small temperature change Δt. For a gas obeying the perfect gas law, it can be shown that β is equal to the reciprocal of the absolute temperature, $1/T$.

The Prandtl number is made up entirely of fluid properties and forms an essential part of all general convective heat transfer correlations. The

Nusselt and Stanton numbers are ratios that include h as a factor, and correlations for forced convection can be written in terms of either one. Since the Stanton number has velocity as one of its factors, it cannot be applied to natural convection. The Graetz number is a group that enters into correlations for streamline flow.

The majority of the dimensionless numbers involve some characteristic length. For flow in a round pipe, the characteristic length is the diameter (or radius), and most of the expressions above are in terms of diameter. Other flow systems will have some length that is appropriate. Natural convection frequently involves heat transfer over a flat surface, and here the length of the surface would be used. In streamline flow in a pipe, both the distance from the entrance and the diameter are important, and the ratio L/D is implicitly involved in the Graetz number. Any combination of products or ratios of the dimensionless numbers in Table 8.2 will obviously yield another dimensionless number, and there may thus be more than one way of expressing a particular correlation.

Empirical Correlations

Both by theory and by experiment, it is found that there is a definite relationship among the dimensionless numbers that pertain to a specific convective heat transfer situation. Ordinarily, the Nusselt or Stanton number can be expressed as a power function of two or more other dimensionless numbers in the following form:

$$x = ay^m z^n$$

Although there may be a theoretical basis for the form of the equation, the constants a, m, and n must be determined by experimental measurements.

The problem of establishing a heat transfer correlation is similar to that of establishing the friction factor plot. Because of the greater number of variables involved, heat transfer correlations show greater deviations than is the case with friction factors. Different investigators, who are working with different conditions, may arrive at somewhat different correlations to represent the same situation. An important question is raised by the fact that fluid properties, particularly the viscosity, are dependent on temperature. Should these properties be evaluated at the bulk temperature of the fluid, the temperature of the surface, or some average of the two? Since most of the heat transfer resistance is located in a film that is intermediate in temperature between the surface and the bulk temperatures, the use of an average appears logical, and many correlations are based on properties evaluated at an arithmetic average of the surface and bulk temperatures. Such a correlation is more inconvenient to use than one based on bulk temperature, since a trial-and-error calculation is required to determine the average film temperature. It should be emphasized that there is no "right" answer; an empirical correlation can be set up in any form that is desired. It may be found, however, that some methods will give better agreement with experimental data than others.

When faced with the problem of evaluating h for a particular situation, one must find an appropriate correlation. Correlations for a large number of cases are presented in the engineering literature; one of best reference sources is the well-known text *Heat Transmission,* by McAdams (3rd Edition, McGraw-Hill, 1954). Equations for a few of the more important cases are presented in the following sections. The student should keep in mind that each of these equations does not represent a new theoretical principle that must be understood and memorized. They are all based on the principles just discussed and their use is similar. It is simply a question of selecting the appropriate equation for the particular case.

Turbulent Flow Inside Tubes

The most widely used equation is that of Seider and Tate:

$$Nu = 0.023\ Re^{0.8}Pr^{1/3}(\mu_b/\mu_w)^{0.14} \qquad \text{Eq. 8-15}$$

In this equation, all fluid properties are evaluated at the bulk temperature except for μ_w in the viscosity ratio term, which is evaluated at the wall temperature. This term provides for the effect of temperature on viscosity. If the fluid is being heated, the viscosity in the layer next to the wall is lower than the bulk fluid viscosity. Consequently, there will be greater convection and lower resistance to heat transfer than if the viscosity did not change. Since the ratio μ_b/μ_w is greater than 1.0, a higher Nusselt number (and h) is calculated from Eq. 8-15 than if the viscosity remained constant at the bulk value. Just the reverse applies to cooling, and a lower Nusselt number is calculated.

In the usual case, the fluid film resistance is one of several resistances in series for which the overall temperature difference is known. The wall temperature must be determined by a trial-and-error calculation in which an assumed value of t_w is used for the first determination of h. This first value of h is then used with the series resistance relationships to calculate a new t_w. This process is continued until the assumed and calculated values of t_w agree. Since the viscosity ratio in Eq. 8-15 appears only to the 0.14 power, the calculation is quite insensitive to the numerical values of viscosity. With water, for example, a difference of 100°F between t_w and t_b gives a viscosity ratio of about 2. This factor raised to the 0.14 power is equal to 1.10, resulting in only a 10% change in h. An initial estimation of t_w based on approximate values of the individual resistances will usually be close enough that a repeat calculation for h will not be necessary. In many cases, overall temperature differences will be small, and the viscosity correction can be neglected.

Turbulent Flow Through Other Flow Cross-Sections

As discussed above, some appropriate length must replace the diameter if the flow cross-section is not a completely filled circle. As a general rule, an equivalent diameter equal to four times the cross-sectional area divided by the wetted perimeter will give satisfactory results for calculation of both friction factors and heat transfer coefficients. For a circular pipe, the equivalent diameter is obviously the pipe diameter. Thus,

$$D_e = 4(\pi D^2/4)/(\pi D) = D$$

For a square duct, where L is the length of a side,

$$D_e = 4L^2/4L = L$$

Flow through the annular space between two concentric pipes is frequently encountered in heat transfer applications. In this case,

$$D_e = 4\frac{(\pi/4)(D_2^2 - D_1^2)}{\pi(D_2 + D_1)} = (D_2 - D_1) \qquad \text{Eq. 8-16}$$

Streamline Flow in Tubes

The turbulent flow equations are based on fully-developed flow, that is, the distance from the entrance is great enough that the turbulent velocity and temperature profiles are well established. The length of pipe required to attain the fully-developed condition, called the entrance length, is relatively unimportant in turbulent flow. After flow is fully developed, heat transfer coefficients remain constant except as they may be affected by a change in bulk properties, and they are therefore independent of length. The rapid mixing effects of turbulent eddies do not exist in streamline flow, and entrance lengths are much greater. In fact, it is the entrance region rather than the fully-developed region that is of concern in streamline flow heat transfer. Accordingly, the length of tube is an important variable, and the ratio L/D will appear either explicitly or implicitly in the equations for heat transfer coefficients.

In the calculation of friction factors, we have a simple, exact solution that gives much more reliable answers than can be obtained for turbulent flow. This Poiseuille's law relation, however, applies to fully-developed flow. Convection of heat in streamline flow is more accurately described as conduction in a moving fluid, and exact mathematical solutions can be made. In the entrance region, however, such solutions are exceedingly complex, and they are dependent on external boundary conditions such as the variation in tube wall temperature along its length. In practice, streamline flow will be encountered only with liquids of such high viscosity that it would not be feasible to pump them at turbulent flow velocities. The strong temperature-dependence of viscosity that is usually found in such liquids is the source of additional uncertainties in the calculation of heat transfer coefficients.

A recommended equation for streamline flow is:

$$Nu = 1.86 \ [Re \ Pr \ (D/L)]^{1/3} \ (\mu_b/\mu_w)^{0.14} \qquad \text{Eq. 8-17}$$

In Eq. 8-17, all properties are evaluated at the bulk temperature except for μ_w in the viscosity ratio term. The value of h in the Nusselt number is an average that applies to the length of tube, L. In contrast, Eq. 8-15 gives an h that applies anywhere along the tube, without respect to length. Since h is a function of L in Eq. 8-17, a trial-and-error procedure may be necessary for a complete solution. First, h would be calculated from Eq. 8-17 for an assumed L. This value of h would then be used to calculate a length as is described below in the section on heat exchangers. The procedure is repeated until the assumed and calculated lengths are in agreement.

Equation 8-17 strictly applies only when the tube wall temperature is constant, as would be the case in heating by condensing steam, for example. Furthermore, it does not include effects of natural convection. With large diameters and relatively low viscosities, natural convection can increase h by a several-fold factor. In those situations in which streamline flow prevails in food processing applications, natural convection will usually be unimportant. Equation 8-17 can be considered to predict a conservative, or low, value of h, and can be useful for order-of-magnitude estimations. Because of the many uncertainties involved, it cannot be considered reliable for critical calculations. Such calculations require the use of engineering design procedures that are beyond the scope of this book.

Natural Convection

Because of its limited effectiveness, natural convection would seldom be employed as a direct method of achieving process heat transfer. Whenever processing equipment is operated at a higher or lower temperature than the surroundings, however, there will be natural convection to or from the air. Such convection can cause undesirable heat losses (or gains with refrigerated equipment) and can have a profound effect on the local environment. Our consideration of natural convection will therefore be limited to surfaces that are exposed to a large air space.

In most natural convection heat transfer correlations, the Nusselt number is proportional to the product of the Grashof and Prandtl numbers raised to a fractional power. It is found that turbulent convection is represented by an exponent of $\frac{1}{3}$ and streamline convection by an exponent of $\frac{1}{4}$. The value of the Grashof number serves as a criterion as to whether the convection is streamline or turbulent. For a particular substance, such as air, values of physical properties can be substituted into the dimensionless equations to give simplified, dimensional equations for coefficients. Under the flow conditions most likely to be encountered in practice, the following equations apply to air at atmospheric pressure.

Vertical surfaces; horizontal square plates (heated plate facing up or cooled plate facing down):

$$h = 0.22(\Delta t)^{1/3}$$ Eq. 8-18

Horizontal square plates (heated plate facing down or cooled plate facing up):

$$h = 0.12(\Delta t/L)^{1/4}$$ Eq. 8-19

In Eq. 8-19, L is the length of one side of the square. For plates that are not square, it is suggested that L be taken as the square root of the area.

Horizontal pipes:

$$h = 0.25(\Delta t/D)^{1/4}$$ Eq. 8-20

It is important to remember that Eqs. 8-18, 8-19, and 8-20 are not dimensionless, and the proper units must be used. Temperature must be in °F, and length and diameter in feet.

Condensing Vapors

A saturated vapor condensing on a surface may spread to form a liquid film over the surface, or the condensate may remain as individual drops. A liquid film obviously imposes an additional heat flow resistance, and heat transfer coefficients are smaller for film-type than for dropwise condensation. The condition of the heat transfer surface can be expected to have a pronounced effect. Thus, a dirt deposit may alter the type of condensation as well as creating a resistance. The presence of any non-condensible gas in the vapor causes a marked reduction in heat transfer coefficients.

Because of these variables that cannot be controlled in actual practice, it is not possible to write a reliable equation to predict condensation heat transfer coefficients. Fortunately, the heat transfer resistance of a condensing vapor is usually small compared to other resistances in series with it, and the uncertainty will not be important. For condensing steam, which is the commonest application, 1000 Btu/(hr)(ft^2)(°F) is a conservative value of h. Condensing organic vapors may be expected to have somewhat lower coefficients.

Boiling Liquids

The violent agitation created by vapor escaping from boiling liquids can be expected to result in high heat transfer coefficients. When boiling starts from a heated surface in a liquid, bubbles form at many nucleation sites and grow until they are large enough to break away from the surface and rise through the liquid. If the temperature of the surface is increased, more nucleation sites will become effective, and the number of bubbles will increase. Eventually, the bubbles will form so close to each other that they will coalesce before breaking away. At this point, the surface becomes covered with an insulating film of vapor and the heat transfer coefficient drops markedly. This effect is so substantial that the total heat flow rate will decrease even though the temperature difference increases.

This phenomenon of insulation by a vapor film is illustrated by the familiar behavior of water that is dropped onto a hot metal surface. The water forms into droplets that dance about over the surface and are insulated from it by a film of steam. The critical temperature difference between the surface and the boiling liquid at which the vapor film forms depends on a number of variables, but it will not usually be more than 40° to 50°F. When there are several resistances in series, the overall temperature difference will, of course, be larger than this. Below the critical value, the heat transfer coefficient increases rapidly as the temperature difference increases. For maximum heat flow rates, the temperature should be as close to the critical value as possible without exceeding it. There are no reliable methods of calculating boiling heat transfer coefficients, and equipment design must be based on experience. As in the case of condensation, boiling heat transfer resistances are frequently so low compared to other resistances in series that uncertainties as to exact values are not important.

Estimation of Physical Properties

Use of the above equations for the calculation of heat transfer coefficients requires a knowledge of fluid densities, heat capacities, viscosities, and thermal conductivities. Tables of these properties for a wide variety of materials can be found in many handbooks and engineering textbooks. Most food materials, however, are not definite chemical substances, and data on properties may not be generally available. Most of the liquid food materials of importance in processing applications are aqueous solutions or suspensions. The physical properties are therefore similar to those of water, and it is convenient to express them as ratios to the corresponding properties of water. We are already familiar with specific gravity and specific heat in this regard, and it is logical to extend the method to viscosity and thermal conductivity. Because of the close similarity of the properties to those of water, this method adequately takes care of temperature-dependence.

Specific gravities present very little problem. They are easily measured and are usually given as raw material or product specifications in any processing application. Viscosities are much less available, and they cannot usually be estimated merely from a knowledge of the composition. Some information based on experience or specific measurements will usually be necessary.

If heats of mixing or solution are small, as is usually the case with food materials, the quantity of heat required to raise the temperature of a mixture is equal to the sum of the heat quantities required for the individual components. Thus, lumping all the dissolved or suspended materials together,

$$Q = mc_{av}(t_2 - t_1) = m_w c_w(t_2 - t_1) + m_s c_s(t_2 - t_1)$$

$$\text{sp. ht.} = c_{av}/c_w = m_w/m + (m_s/m)(c_s/c_w)$$

The specific heat of the non-water portion, c_s/c_w, is found to be approximately 0.5 for a very wide range of substances likely to be present in food products. If, as is usually the case, water is the major constituent, little error will be caused by using this constant value of 0.5. Therefore,

$$\text{sp. ht.} = x_w + 0.5\,x_s = (1 - x_s) + 0.5\,x_s = 1.0 - 0.5\,x_s$$

where x_s is the weight fraction of suspended or dissolved material. Experimental measurements have shown that this relationship is also a satisfactory approximation for thermal conductivity. Thus,

$$k_{av}/k_w = 1.0 - 0.5\,x_s$$

The physical properties of most food materials do not vary over a wide range, and the uncertainties arising from the above approximations will usually not have an important effect on the accuracy of calculated heat transfer coefficients. For convenience, the pertinent properties of water are listed in Table 8-3.

Example 6.—Skim milk flowing through a 1-in. stainless steel sanitary tube at a rate of 15 gpm is heated by steam condensing on the outside at a temperature of 220°F. The steam-side heat transfer coefficient is 1500, and the thermal conductivity of stainless steel is 9.4. The milk has a solids content of 9%, a specific gravity of 1.04, and a viscosity 1.5 times that of water. At a point where the bulk temperature of the milk is 100°F, calculate

a) The milk heat transfer coefficient.
b) The milk heat transfer coefficient if a deposit with h_d of 400 is present.

First, the Reynolds number corresponding to the bulk temperature will be calculated to determine whether the flow is turbulent or streamline. If the flow is turbulent, this value of Re is needed in the subsequent calculation.

$$Re = 4\dot{m}/\pi D \mu$$

TABLE 8.3

PROPERTIES OF LIQUID WATER

Tempera- ture °F	Density lb_m/ft^3	Viscosity Centipoise	Thermal Conductivity Btu/(hr)(ft)(°F)	Prandtl Number
32	62.41	1.753	0.3286	13.00
40	62.43	1.526	0.3335	11.13
50	62.41	1.299	0.3392	9.28
60	62.37	1.119	0.3446	7.87
70	62.31	0.975	0.3497	6.75
80	62.22	0.858	0.3545	5.85
90	62.12	0.761	0.3590	5.12
100	62.00	0.680	0.3633	4.52
110	61.86	0.612	0.3673	4.02
120	61.71	0.555	0.3710	3.61
130	61.55	0.506	0.3744	3.26
140	61.38	0.464	0.3776	2.96
150	61.19	0.427	0.3806	2.71
160	60.99	0.395	0.3833	2.49
170	60.79	0.367	0.3857	2.30
180	60.57	0.342	0.3879	2.13
190	60.34	0.320	0.3899	1.99
200	60.11	0.300	0.3916	1.86
210	59.86	0.282	0.3931	1.75
220	59.61	0.266	0.3943	1.65
230	59.35	0.252	0.3953	1.56
240	59.08	0.239	0.3961	1.48
250	58.80	0.228	0.3968	1.41

Source: Based on 1967 ASME Steam Tables.

$$\mu_{water} = 0.680 \text{ centipoise}$$

$$\mu = 1.5(0.680)(2.42) = 2.47 \, lb_m/(ft)(hr)$$

$$\rho_{water} = 62.0 \, lb_m/ft^3$$

$$\rho = 1.04(62.0) = 64.5 \, lb_m/ft^3$$

$$\dot{m} = \left(\frac{15 \, gal}{min}\right)\left(\frac{1}{7.48}\frac{ft^3}{gal}\right)\left(64.5 \, \frac{lb_m}{ft^3}\right)\left(60 \, \frac{min}{hr}\right) = 7760 \, lb_m/hr$$

$$D = 0.902 \text{ in.} = 0.0752 \text{ ft}$$

$$Re = 4(7760)/\pi(0.0752)(2.47)$$

$$= 53{,}000 \text{ (rounded to two significant figures)}$$

For turbulent flow in a round tube, the coefficient is calculated by Eq. 8-15.

$$Nu = 0.023 \, Re^{0.8} Pr^{1/3} (\mu_b/\mu_w)^{0.14}$$

$$Re = 53,000 = 0.53(10^5)$$
$$Re^{0.8} = 0.601(10^4) = 6010$$

From the preceding section,

$$c = k/k_w = 1.0 - 0.5x_s = 1.0 - 0.5(0.09) = 0.955$$
$$k_w = 0.363$$
$$k = 0.955(0.363) = 0.347 \text{ Btu/(hr)(ft)(°F)}$$
$$Pr = c\mu/k = 0.955(2.47)/0.347 = 6.66$$
$$Pr^{1/3} = 1.88$$

In order to evaluate the viscosity ratio term of Eq. 8-15, it is necessary to evaluate a wall temperature. This assumption can be checked by a series resistance calculation after the value of h has been obtained. A reasonable assumption in this case is half way between the steam and the fluid temperatures, or 160°F. As the milk viscosity is a constant factor times the viscosity of water, we can simply use water viscosities in the viscosity ratio term.

$$(\mu_b/\mu_w)^{0.14} = (0.680/0.395)^{0.14} = 1.08$$
$$h = 0.023(k/D) \, Re^{0.8}Pr^{1/3}(\mu_b/\mu_w)^{0.14}$$
$$= 0.023(0.347)(6010)(1.88)(1.08)/0.0752 = 1300 \text{ Btu/(hr)(ft}^2)(°F)$$

To check the temperature assumption, we know that the heat transfer rate is equal to the product of the over-all coefficient and over-all temperature difference and also equal to the product of the inside heat transfer coefficient and the difference between the wall and fluid temperatures. The tube wall is thin enough that the difference in the inside and outside areas can be neglected for this calculation.

$$q/A = U(220 - 100) = h_i(t_w - 100)$$
$$1/U = 1/h_o + x_w/k + 1/h_i$$
$$= 1/1500 + (0.049/12)/9.4 + 1/1300 = 0.00067 + 0.00043 + 0.00077$$
$$= 0.00187$$
$$U = 535$$
$$535(220 - 100) = 1300(t_w - 100)$$
$$t_w = 149°F$$

Using this temperature, the viscosity ratio term now becomes

$$(\mu_b/\mu_w)^{0.14} = (0.684/0.433)^{0.14} = 1.066$$

$$h = 1300(1.066/1.08) = 1280 \text{ Btu/(hr)(ft}^2)(°F)$$

It can be seen that the calculation is quite insensitive to the viscosity correction term. If a reasonable estimate is made for the first trial, a repeat calculation is unnecessary. The accuracy of Eq. 8-15 does not actually justify the refinement made by the check calculation in this case.

In part (b), the dirt deposit constitutes an additional resistance in the calculation of U. Thus, using the first trial value for h_i of 1300,

$$1/U = 0.00187 + 1/400 = 0.00437$$

$$U = 229$$

$$229(220 - 100) = 1300(t_w - 100)$$

$$t_w = 121°F$$

$$(\mu_b/\mu_w)^{0.14} = (0.684/0.559)^{0.14} = 1.03$$

$$h = 1300(1.03/1.08) = 1240 \text{ Btu/(hr)(ft}^2)(°F)$$

Example 7.—Saturated steam at 230°F is flowing through a horizontal 2-in. standard steel pipe (schedule 40). The pipe has a 1-in. layer of magnesia insulation ($k = 0.04$). If the air temperature in the room is 78°F, estimate the temperature of the outer surface of the insulation and the heat loss per foot of pipe.

The diagram below represents the series resistance to heat flow. R_s is

the steam film resistance; R_w, the pipe wall resistance; R_i, the insulation resistance; R_o, the natural convection air film resistance on the outside of the insulation; and t_i, the temperature of the outer surface of the insulation. We can write

$$q = (230 - t_i)/(R_s + R_w + R_i) = (t_i - 78)/R_o$$

The steam film and pipe wall resistances are small and can be neglected with respect to the insulation resistance.

$$1/R_i = k_i A_m/x_i$$

$$1/R_o = h_o A_o$$

where x_i is the insulation thickness, and A_m and A_o are the mean and outside areas of the insulation per foot of length. Therefore,

$$(230 - t_i)k_i A_m/x_i = (t_i - 78)h_o A_o$$

$$230 - t_i = (h_o x_i/k_i)(A_o/A_m)(t_i - 78)$$

The inside diameter of the insulation is the same as the outside diameter of the pipe, or 2.375 in. The outside diameter of the insulation is equal to the inside diameter plus twice the thickness, or 4.375 in. For a fixed length of pipe, the area ratio A_o/A_m is equal to the diameter ratio of D_o/D_m. Since the outside diameter is less than twice the inside diameter, it will be permissible to use an arithmetic rather than a logarithmic mean for D_m.

$$D_m = (2.375 + 4.375)/2 = 3.375$$

Using Eq. 8-20 for natural convection from horizontal pipes,

$$h_o = 0.25 \left(\frac{t_i - 78}{D_o}\right)^{1/4}$$

$$D_o^{1/4} = (4.375/12)^{1/4} = 0.777$$

$$h_o = (0.25/0.777)(t_i - 78)^{1/4} = 0.322(t_i - 78)^{1/4}$$

$$230 - t_i = \left(\frac{0.322(t_i - 78)^{1/4}(1/12)}{0.04}\right)\left(\frac{4.375}{3.375}\right)(t_i - 78)$$

$$230 - t_i = 0.88(t_i - 78)^{1.25}$$

A trial and error solution of the above equation gives $t_i = 124°F$

$$h_o = 0.322(124 - 78)^{1/4} = 0.84$$

For one foot of length, $A_o = \pi D_o$, and

$$q = \pi D_o h_o (t_i - 78) = \pi(4.375/12)(0.84)(46)$$

$$= 44.2 \text{ Btu/hr}$$

HEAT EXCHANGERS

The primary applications of heat transfer coefficients are concerned with the design and performance of heat exchangers. Heat exchangers, which are devices to effect the transfer of heat from a warmer to a colder fluid, can be divided into the two major categories of surface and contact exchangers. In a surface exchanger, the streams are separated by a surface or partition, usually a metal tube or plate. Heat must then flow from one stream, through the partition, and to the other, in the manner indicated in Fig. 8.7, and transfer rates are primarily governed by the individual film coefficients. The separating partition is eliminated in a contact exchanger, and the fluids mix and exchange heat by direct contact. Although this type of heat exchange is very efficient, it can be used only in a few specialized applications, and the remainder of this discussion will be devoted to surface exchangers.

Counter-flow and Parallel-flow Heat Exchangers

These basic categories of heat exchanger operation are most easily visualized by considering the concentric pipe exchanger. In this arrangement, one pipe is placed within a larger pipe, with suitable fittings at the ends to keep the inner pipe centered. One stream flows through the inner pipe and the other through the annular space between the pipes. The common glass chemical laboratory condenser is an exchanger of this type. In counter-flow, the streams enter at opposite ends, and in parallel-flow, they enter at the same end. Although there is a substantial difference in the effectiveness of these two types of operation, the analysis that follows applies equally well to both. The analysis is based on the following postulates:

1. Steady-state flow.

2. The temperature change of each stream varies linearly with the amount of heat transferred. This requirement means that a plot of temperature versus q is a straight line. When only sensible heat is involved, the heat capacities must be constant. The constant temperatures of boiling liquids and condensing vapors constitute a simplified case of the general condition.

3. The overall heat transfer coefficient is constant throughout the length of the exchanger. The fluid properties that affect the individual film coefficients are dependent on temperature and thus change from one end of the exchanger to the other. The resistances of the pipe wall and dirt deposits, however, remain constant, and the variation in the overall coefficient is small in the majority of cases. Satisfactory results will usually be obtained by evaluating fluid properties at the average bulk temperature of the fluid in the exchanger. If the variation in overall coefficient is so large that this approximation is not permissible, it is necessary to divide the exchanger into sections and make a separate calculation for each section.

4. There is no heat exchange with the surroundings. If the temperature of the external surface of the exchanger is substantially higher or lower than the surrounding air temperature, insulation will ordinarily be used to minimize heat loss or gain.

5. There is no heat conduction parallel to the direction of fluid flow. With a very thick pipe wall, it is conceivable that an appreciable amount of heat could be conducted along the pipe, but such a situation would be unusual. With a stream of liquid metal, such as mercury, this assumption of no heat conduction in the direction of flow may not be valid.

Figure 8.8 diagrammatically represents a double pipe exchanger with a counter-flow arrangement. In the following derivation, the subscript 1 refers to the end of the exchanger at which the cold stream enters, and the subscript 2, to the end at which it leaves. Thus, 1 designates the leaving hot stream and 2, the entering hot stream. For parallel flow, the direction of

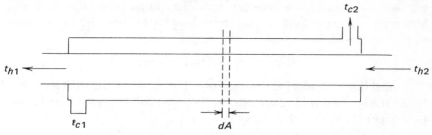

FIG. 8.8. DOUBLE PIPE HEAT EXCHANGER SHOWING COUNTERFLOW

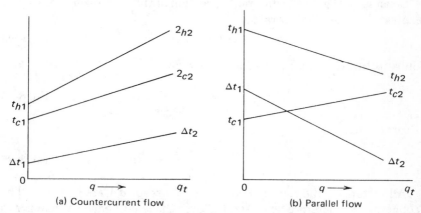

(a) Countercurrent flow   (b) Parallel flow

FIG. 8.9. TEMPERATURE VERSUS HEAT RATE FOR (a) COUNTERFLOW AND (b) PARALLEL
FLOW IN THE HEAT EXCHANGER OF FIG. 8.8

the arrows on the hot stream would be reversed, but 1 would now designate
the entrance and 2 the exit. The dotted lines mark off a differential length
of the exchanger containing the heat transfer area dA. It should be noted
that the heat transfer area is the cylindrical surface of the inner pipe. It is
essential that the heat transfer area be clearly distinguished from the
cross-sectional area for flow, which is designated by the symbol S in these
notes. A differential quantity of heat per unit time, dq, flows across the area
dA from the hot to the cold stream, and the stream temperatures change
by amounts dt_h and dt_c. A heat balance around this section of the exchanger
gives

$$dq = \dot{m}_h c_h dt_h = \dot{m}_c c_c dt_c \qquad \text{Eq. 8-21}$$

Integrating over the length of the exchanger,

$$q_t = m_h c_h (t_{h2} - t_{h1}) = m_c c_c (t_{c2} - t_{c1}) \qquad \text{Eq. 8-22}$$

where q_t is the total amount of heat transferred over the entire length.

Fig. 8.9 shows plots of temperatures of both streams against q for both counter- and parallel-flow arrangements. The constant mass flow rates and heat capacities mean that the plots must be straight lines with slopes given by the expression

$$dt/dq = (t_2 - t_1)/q_t = 1/\dot{m}c$$

The third line on each of the two parts of Fig. 8.9 is Δt, the difference between the hot and cold temperatures. The plots of Δt versus q must also be straight lines, with slopes given by

$$d(\Delta t)/dq = (\Delta t_2 - \Delta t_1)/q_t \qquad \text{Eq. 8-23}$$

Considering again the differential section of the exchanger, dA, we can express the heat transfer rate as

$$dq = U(dA)\Delta t \qquad \text{Eq. 8-24}$$

Substituting dq from Eq. 8-24 into Eq. 8-23,

$$\frac{d(\Delta t)}{U(dA)\Delta t} = \frac{\Delta t_2 - \Delta t_1}{q_t} \qquad \text{Eq. 8-25}$$

Rearranging,

$$\frac{d(\Delta t)}{\Delta t} = \frac{U(\Delta t_2 - \Delta t_1)dA}{q_t} \qquad \text{Eq. 8-26}$$

All factors on the right side of Eq. 8-26 except dA are constant. The equation can therefore be integrated over the length of the exchanger to give

$$\ln(\Delta t_2/\Delta t_1) = UA(\Delta t_2 - \Delta t_1)/q_t$$

Solving for q_t,

$$q_t = \frac{UA(\Delta t_2 - \Delta t_1)}{\ln(\Delta t_2/\Delta t_1)} = UA(\Delta t)_{\text{lm}} \qquad \text{Eq. 8-27}$$

We thus again encounter the familiar expression for a logarithmic mean. As in the previous case of logarithmic mean areas, if the temperature difference ratio is less than 2:1, little error is caused by using an arithmetic mean in place of the logarithmic mean.

A typical heat exchanger calculation will involve the following steps:

1. By a heat balance (Eq. 8-22), establish the flow rates and terminal temperatures of both streams, and calculate the logarithmic mean temperature difference.

2. Calculate an overall heat transfer coefficient from the individual film coefficients and the pipe wall resistance.

3. Substitute the results from the above steps into Eq. 8-27 to obtain the required area.

A common problem is the determination of the amount of heat that can be transferred in an exchanger of known area. The logarithmic term makes it impossible to solve Eq. 8-27 explicitly for exit temperature, and a trial-and-error procedure is indicated. A temperature is assumed and the corresponding area calculated as outlined above. Trials are repeated with different values of assumed temperature until the calculated area agrees with the known area.

The above derivation applies equally well to parallel flow. It is only necessary to substitute the temperatures into the equations so that heat quantities and temperature differences are positive numbers. Whatever the flow arrangement, it is essential that the temperature difference between the hot and cold streams be clearly distinguished from the temperature rise (or drop) of a stream. The difference in temperatures in Eq. 8-22 is an entirely different quantity than the Δt that appears in Eqs. 8-23 to 8-27. In this book, the symbol Δt always refers to a temperature difference between a hot and a cold stream.

Equation 8-27 can be applied to the entire exchanger or to any portion of it. For example, we can calculate by heat balance the temperatures at a point at which half the total heat has been transferred and obtain the corresponding area. In this way, the variation of temperature along the length of the exchanger can be calculated. The results of such calculations would take the form of the curves shown in Fig. 8-10, in which temperature is plotted against length (or area) for the same conditions that are represented in Fig. 8-9. As would be expected, in the region where the temperature difference is large, the change of temperature with area is large. In other words, a large Δt means a large heat transfer rate per unit area. In the opposite limit, if Δt approaches zero, no heat is transferred, and the temperatures do not change with area.

A similar calculation can be used in the situation in which the assumption of a constant U is not permissible. The total heat transfer can be subdivided into portions corresponding to one or more intermediate temperatures of the streams. For each of these sets of temperatures, an overall coefficient and a corresponding area can be calculated. The total area is then the sum of the areas required for the individual portions of the total heat transfer.

For a given heat transfer service, a counter-flow arrangement will always give a higher mean temperature difference and, therefore, a smaller area than parallel flow. The reason for this greater effectiveness of counter-flow can be appreciated by considering what would happen if exchangers of infinite area were used with the entering stream temperatures shown in Figs. 8.9 and 8.10. An infinite area means that, at some point in the exchanger, the two streams must come to the same temperature ($\Delta t = 0$). For parallel flow, this equilibrium temperature must lie between the two en-

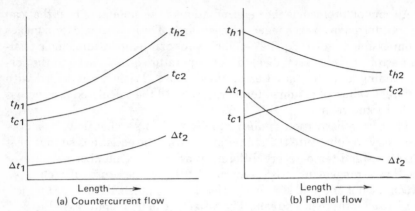

FIG. 8.10.   TEMPERATURE IN THE HOT AND COLD STREAMS AND TEMPERATURE DIF-
FERENCE BETWEEN THE HOT AND COLD STREAMS AS A FUNCTION OF LENGTH FOR THE
HEAT EXCHANGER IN FIG. 8.8

tering temperatures and is the same as would be obtained if the two streams
were mixed together. If the lines in Fig. 8.9b are extended to the right, this
temperature is given by their intersection. On the other hand, zero Δt for
the counter-flow case of Fig. 8.9a will be attained when the hot stream is
cooled to the entering temperature of the cold stream. The hot stream can
actually be cooled to a temperature lower than that at which the cold stream
leaves, even in an exchanger of finite area. Because of this greater effectiveness of counter-flow, a parallel-flow arrangement would never be used
in commercial practice except under some unusual condition in which
factors other than heat transfer rates governed the requirements. If one
or both stream temperatures are constant, as with condensing vapors or
boiling liquids, the direction of flow has no significance, and there is no
difference between counter and parallel flow.

Shell-and-Tube Heat Exchangers

Although concentric pipe exchangers are simple in concept and are easily
constructed in small sizes, they are not practical for the larger areas required
in most industrial applications. Since the length of individual pieces of pipe
that can be used is limited, they must be arranged with a series of hairpin
bends in order to obtain the required area. Such bends require the use of
special fittings and packing glands that are subject to leakage. An exchanger
built up in this manner requires considerable space, and maintenance costs
are excessively high. These problems can be avoided by constructing an
exchanger with a bundle of tubes inside a single shell.

Such a shell-and-tube exchanger is illustrated in Fig. 8.11. The sections
at the ends through which the fluid flowing in the tubes enters and leaves

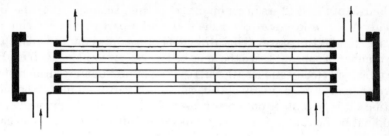

FIG. 8.11.   SINGLE-PASS HEAT EXCHANGER

FIG. 8.12.   2-TUBE-PASS HEAT EXCHANGER

are known as channel sections. The other fluid flows outside the tubes through the shell. It is thus common terminology to refer to the tube-side and shell-side streams. The plates in which the ends of the tubes are sealed are called tube sheets. If the shell-side stream were merely allowed to flow parallel to the tubes throughout the entire cross-section, low velocities and poor heat transfer coefficients would result. Accordingly, the usual practice is to provide a series of baffles so that the fluid must pass back and forth across the tubes. The baffles can be spaced to obtain any desired velocity. Such baffles would obviously not be used if the shell-side fluid were a condensing vapor or a boiling liquid.

The exchanger shown in Fig. 8.11 is termed fixed-tube-sheet as the tube sheets are permanently welded to the shell. This is the simplest type of construction but has the disadvantage that the outsides of the tubes are inaccessible for inspection or cleaning. Furthermore, serious problems can arise from differences in thermal expansion of the shell and tubes. These disadvantages are eliminated by the more costly floating head design, which permits the tube bundle to be completely withdrawn from the shell.

As explained above, the desired shell-side velocities are obtained by means of the baffle spacing. It will usually be found that the tube-side velocity will also be too low if the fluid is allowed to flow through all the tubes in parallel. Accordingly, multi-pass exchangers such as the two-tube-pass exchanger of Fig. 8.12 are in common use. In this exchanger, the tube-side fluid enters and leaves at the same end, and a partition in the channel section divides the passes. This arrangement is equivalent to having half the number of tubes at twice the length. The velocity will be doubled, but the effect of velocity and length will result in approximately an eight-fold increase in pressure drop. By putting additional partitions in both channel sections, it is possible to obtain any desired number of tube passes. A longitudinal baffle can also be placed outside the tubes to provide two shell passes. Construction details of the wide range of available shell-and-tube heat exchanger designs can be found in various engineering references.

Although the shell-side fluid in a single baffle section flows across rather than parallel to the tubes, a large number of baffles in series has the effect of parallel flow. Thus, the exchanger of Fig. 8.11 could be treated as either a parallel- or counter-flow exchanger, depending on the directions of the streams. The two-tube-pass exchanger of Fig. 8.12 can clearly be neither parallel- nor counter-flow, but is a combination of the two. Accordingly, the heat transfer effectiveness will not be as great as for true counter-flow. The exact calculation of the correct mean temperature difference to use in the design of such an exchanger is a rather complicated mathematical problem, but the results are usually expressed as a correction factor, F, applied to the logarithmic mean temperature difference. Values of such correction factors for various arrangements of passes are presented as graphs in many heat transfer references. Figure 8.13 gives the factors for an exchanger with one shell pass and two or more tube passes. The coordinates in this figure are the two terminal temperature differences divided by the difference between the temperatures of the entering hot stream and the entering cold stream. As the figure is symmetrical, it is arbitrary which is considered to be the first temperature difference and which the second. It is undesirable to use a flow arrangement resulting in a factor less than about 0.75. Heat exchanger reference works discuss arrangements for avoiding this situation.

It is not practicable to use the shell side of shell-and-tube exchangers for sanitary service in food processing applications. They are effectively used for heating or cooling with water, steam, or some other heat transfer medium, with the food stream in the tubes, but they are not suitable for exchanging heat between two food streams.

Plate Heat Exchangers

A plate heat exchanger is designed for simplicity of cleaning. It consists essentially of a stack of corrugated stainless steel plates supported on horizontal rails. Heat is exchanged from one stream to another flowing on opposite sides of a plate. In service, the stack is tightly compressed by screws at the ends of the rails, with gaskets between the plates preventing leakage

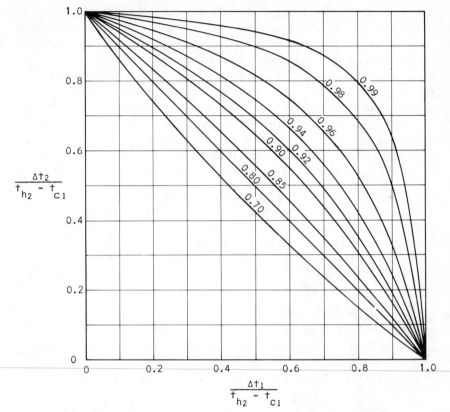

FIG. 8.13.   MEAN TEMPERATURE DIFFERENCE CORRECTION FACTORS FOR 2-TUBE-PASS
EXCHANGER

from the edges. A typical plate size for food use is approximately 1 ft wide
by 3 ft high. Holes (called ports) at the top and bottom of the plates allow
the liquid to pass from one plate to the next. Each plate in general has four
such holes: an inlet and an outlet for each stream. Gaskets around the holes
are used to prevent a stream from entering the passageway between a
particular pair of plates and to allow it to pass on to the next pair. These
gaskets keep the two streams separated and direct them through alternate
pairs of plates. The whole stack is opened for cleaning merely by loosening
the screws at the ends of the rails.

The simplest arrangement is for one stream to flow up through alternate
pairs of plates and the other to flow down through the intervening pairs.
This constitutes a single pass heat exchanger and results in true countercurrent flow. As with shell-and-tube exchangers, it may be desirable to
divide the flow into more than one pass in order to obtain adequate fluid

velocities. By proper arrangement of the ports between the plates, it is possible to provide any desired number of passes for both streams. For example, a stream can flow up through four channels, then down through four, and so on to the end of the stack. It is not necessary that there be the same number of channels for each pass, or that each stream have the same number of passes. With the complex arrangements that can result, true countercurrent flow will obviously not exist; the two streams will necessarily be in parallel flow through some adjacent channels. Because of the many different possible arrangements, it is not feasible to prepare temperature difference correction factor charts such as Fig. 8.13.

The major advantages of plate heat exchangers are as follows:

1. They are compact—a high area is contained in a small volume.
2. They have high efficiency because of the narrow channels for flow.
3. They are easily cleaned.
4. The capacity can be increased or decreased merely by adding or removing plates. It is also possible to change the number of flow passes.
5. Maintenance is simple, although not necessarily inexpensive.

Some disadvantages are:
1. The cost is high compared to tubular exchangers.
2. They are efficient over only a fairly narrow flow range. At flow rates very much below capacity, dead areas develop in the flow channels. In food service, these dead areas can lead to deposit formation and sanitation problems.
3. They cannot be used in high pressure operation. This is not a problem in food service.
4. They are not useful for fluids of high viscosity or consistency.

The primary application of plate heat exchangers is in milk pasteurization, and they are almost exclusively used for this service. Plate exchangers have also been developed that can be used for evaporation.

Mechanically Aided Heat Exchangers

The exchanger types discussed above are obviously unsuitable for high consistency materials such as heavy pastes. No amount of applied pressure will produce satisfactory flow of these materials, and large sections of the exchangers would become filled with a stationary semi-solid mass. With this type of material, it is necessary to provide mechanical assistance to move the fluid past the heat exchange surface. In the most commonly used arrangement, the exchanger consists of a jacketed tube several inches in diameter, fitted with a rotor. Blades attached to the rotor continuously scrape the surface of the tube. The annular space between the tube and the rotor is large enough for the fluid to flow without excessive pressure drop, and the scraping action of the blades provides the necessary mixing and velocity past the surface.

Exchangers of this type may be used for either heating or cooling. One of the most common examples is ice cream freezing. This principle is also applied to evaporation by using open rotors to permit the escape of vapor. In this case, the unit is usually placed in a vertical position so that gravity will assist in moving the fluid along the surface.

Extended Surface Heat Exchangers

As shown in Table 8.1, heat transfer coefficients for gases are usually much lower than for other convection situations. If a gas stream flows on one side of an exchanger and a high-coefficient stream on the other side, the over-all resistance to heat transfer will be made up almost entirely of the gas film resistance. It would therefore be possible to make substantial savings in exchanger cost if the gas film resistance could be reduced. Even at the maximum velocities that can effectively be used, gas film coefficients are still undesirably low. Since the gas film resistance is determined by the product of the coefficient and area, an increase in area is another possibility for reducing the resistance. It is therefore common practice to increase the gas-side area by providing fins or some other protrusions on the surface. In automobile radiators, for example, the air flows through a honeycomb network of thin metal sheet attached to the tubes carrying the water. The total area contacted by the air is many times that on the water side. In an air-cooled engine, fins are cast into the engine block to promote cooling. This extended surface is not as effective as a surface directly separating the two streams, as the heat must flow for a greater distance through the metal before reaching the other side, and the gas side resistance expression must include an effectiveness factor. The determination of such effectiveness factors is the responsibility of the heat exchanger manufacturer and is not of direct concern to the user.

The most common application of extended surface exchangers in the food industry is in refrigeration, where large volumes of air are cooled by an evaporating refrigerant. In dehydration plants, air may be heated by passing it over finned tubes that carry steam.

Example 8.—The skim milk stream of Example 6 is to be cooled from 150°F to 80°F by countercurrent flow of water in a double-pipe exchanger. The inner pipe, through which the milk flows, is a 1-in. stainless steel sanitary tube. The cooling water will enter at 65°F and leave at 75°F. What water flow rate and exchanger length will be required? The milk-side coefficient may be taken as 1300 and the water side as 900 Btu/(hr)(ft^2)(°F), both based on the inside area of the tube.

$$150 \xrightarrow{\text{7760 lb/hr}} 80 \qquad \text{milk side}$$

$$\Delta t = 75 \qquad\qquad \Delta t = 15$$

$$75 \leftarrow 65 \qquad \text{water side}$$

The diagram above represents the given conditions. The mean temperature difference and total heat transferred can be calculated directly.

$$\Delta t_{\text{lm}} = (75 - 15)/\ln(75/15) = 37.3°\text{F}$$

$$q = \dot{m}c(t_1 - t_2) = 7760(0.955)(150 - 80) = 520,000 \text{ Btu/hr}$$

The above expression for q also applies to the water stream.

$$\dot{m}_w(1.0)(75 - 65) = 520,000$$

$$\dot{m}_w = 52,000 \text{ lb/hr}$$

To obtain the exchanger length, we must first calculate the over-all coefficient. Proceeding as in Example 6, except with the water coefficient of 900 replacing the steam coefficient of 1500,

$$1/U_i = 1/900 + (0.049/12)/9.4 + 1/1300 = 0.00231$$

$$U_i = 433 \text{ Btu/(hr)(ft}^2)(°\text{F})$$

By Eq. 8-27,

$$A = q/U\Delta t_{\text{lm}} = 520,000/(433)(37.3) = 32.2 \text{ ft}^2$$

$$= \pi D_i L$$

$$L = 32.2/\pi(0.902/12) = 136 \text{ ft}$$

Example 9.—Air in turbulent flow in a steam-jacketed tube is being heated from 80°F to 170°F by steam condensing at 212°F. If the air flow rate is doubled, estimate the outlet temperature of the air.

The original conditions are represented in the diagram below. A direct approach would be to use these conditions to determine a heat transfer coefficient, and then use this coefficient as a basis for calculating the new temperature. Considerable simplification results if the relationships are set up as ratios.

$$t_s = 212 \rightarrow t_s = 212$$

$$t_1 = 80 \rightarrow t_2 = 170$$

The resistances of the steam film and the tube wall will be negligible compared to the air film resistance. When the velocity is doubled, the air film coefficient will change according to Eq. 8-15. We can therefore write

$$U = h_i = aV^{0.8}$$

$$q = UA\Delta t_{lm} = \dot{m}c(t_2 - t_1)$$

$$q = h_iA\frac{(t_s - t_1) - (t_s - t_2)}{\ln\dfrac{t_s - t_1}{t_s - t_2}} = \dot{m}c(t_2 - t_1)$$

It can be seen that the numerator of the Δt_{lm} expression reduces to $(t_2 - t_1)$ and cancels with the corresponding factor on the right hand side of the equation. By rearranging, we therefore obtain

$$\frac{h_iA}{\dot{m}c} = \ln\frac{t_s - t_1}{t_s - t_2}$$

We can write the same relationship for the new condition, noting that the flow rate is now $2\dot{m}$ and designating the new coefficient and outlet temperature with a prime.

$$\frac{h_i'A}{2\dot{m}c} = \ln\frac{t_s - t_1}{t_s - t_2'}$$

Taking the ratio of these two expressions,

$$\frac{2h_i}{h_i'} = \frac{\ln(t_s - t_1)/(t_s - t_2)}{\ln(t_s - t_1)/(t_s - t_2')}$$

From the relationship of Eq. 8-15,

$$(h_i/h_i') = (V/V')^{0.8} = (1/2)^{0.8}$$

Substituting this expression for h_i/h_i' into the previous equation,

$$\frac{\ln(t_s - t_1)/(t_s - t_2)}{\ln(t_s - t_1)/(t_s - t_2')} = 2^{0.2} = 1.149$$

Substituting the numerical values of temperatures,

$$\ln\frac{132}{212 - t_2'} \quad (1/1.149)\ln(132/42)$$

$$t_2' = 163°F$$

TRANSIENT CONDUCTION

The preceding discussion has been entirely concerned with steady-state heat transfer, that is, the temperature at any point does not change with time. There are many important situations in which steady-state conditions do not prevail, and the problems arising fall into the category of transient heat transfer. For example, the regular day to night changes in temperature create many transient heat transfer problems in agriculture. Any time a processing operation is started, there will be a transient period until steady-state conditions are attained. The need of frequent shut-downs in many food processes for sanitation purposes can make these initial periods an important part of the over-all operation. Cooling or freezing of solid foods is obviously a transient heat transfer process. The most important food application, however, is in thermal processing of foods in individual containers, as in the retorting of canned foods for sterilization. Modern retorting or cooking is, of course, a continuous operation. Cold cans move continuously into one end of the cooker and sterilized cans move out the other. The contents of an individual can, however, undergo transient heating in that they start cold and finish hot.

In the basic problem, an object of initially uniform temperature is placed suddenly in surroundings of a different temperature. It is then required to determine the temperature of the object as a function of time. The mathematical solution to the problem is the same whether the process is one of heating or cooling. Two heat flow resistances are involved: one, ordinarily a convection resistance, between the surrounding medium and the surface of the object; the other, an internal resistance within the object. In the general case, both of these resistances will be effective. There will thus be a temperature difference between the medium and the surface, and the temperature within the object will vary continuously from the surface to the center. In a sterilization process, the can must be left in the cooker long enough for the center to be above a sterilizing temperature for the necessary length of time.

The solution is greatly simplified if the internal resistance is small compared to the external, or surface resistance. For example, if a block of silver is placed in an oven, the natural convection heat transfer resistance from the air to the surface will be high. This high resistance, coupled with the high thermal conductivity of silver, will result in essentially a uniform temperature throughout the block. If a can containing a liquid food is agitated sufficiently to provide good mixing, the temperature throughout the interior will be uniform except for a thin film adjacent to the surface. In this case, the external resistance is a series consisting of the outside convection resistance, the resistance of the container wall, and the inside film resistance. To obtain a solution to this problem, we equate the sensible heat gain from an infinitesimal temperature rise dt to the rate of heat flow multiplied by the corresponding infinitesimal time interval $d\theta$.

$$mcdt = UA(t_o - t)d\theta$$

where m and c are the mass and heat capacity of the object; t_o is the constant temperature of the surrounding medium; t is the uniform temperature of the object; U is the over-all conductance between the medium temperature t_o and the object temperature t, and A is the surface area. Separating the variables in the above equation,

$$\frac{dt}{t_o - t} = \frac{UAd\theta}{mc}$$

Integrating between limits,

$$-\ln\frac{t_o - t}{t_o - t_1} = \frac{UA\theta}{mc} \qquad \text{Eq. 8-28}$$

where t_1 is the initial temperature of the object and t is the temperature after time θ. For a given set of initial conditions, calculation of temperature as a function of time is thus a simple task.

In the general case of a solid or a fluid with no mixing, the assumption of uniform interior temperature does not apply. Temperatures near the surface will obviously change more rapidly than those toward the center. The general solution must therefore give temperature as a function of both time and position. The mathematical derivation is beyond the scope of this text, but the results for a few shapes of objects are given in the heat transfer literature. Such results can be presented in the form of the charts of Fig. 8.14. This figure includes charts for slabs of finite thickness and infinite area, cylinders of infinite length, and spheres. Each chart consists of two sections; the upper section is used for center temperatures and the lower section for average temperatures. Similar charts are available in various references from which the temperature at any interior position can be obtained.

The x coordinate of each chart is given as the dimensionless group $(k/\rho c)$ (θ/r_o^2) or $(k/\rho c)$ (θ/L_o^2), where r_o is the radius of the cylinder or sphere and L_o is one-half the thickness of the slab. The y coordinate is the same temperature ratio group that appears in Eq. 8-28. The physical properties of the substance being heated appears in the ratio $k/\rho c$, which is an important group that always appears in transient heat conduction problems. It is called the thermal diffusivity and has the dimensions of length squared divided by time. The numbers on the families of lines in each chart refer to values of the ratio k/hr_o or k/hL_o, where k is the thermal conductivity of the object and h is the heat transfer coefficient between the constant temperature surroundings and the object. As discussed above, an over-all coefficient U should be used in place of h if there are external resistances in series.

The chart for cylinders applies only to very long cylinders for which the effects of the ends can be neglected. Likewise, the slab chart applies only where edge effects can be neglected. A short cylinder can be considered to be formed by the intersection of a long cylinder with a slab having a thickness equal to the length of the short cylinder. For this case, the y-axis temperature ratio is given by

$$Y_{\text{short cylinder}} = (Y_{\text{infinite cylinder}})/(Y_{\text{infinite slab}})$$

This expression is exact for the center temperature and approximate for the average temperature. Similarly, the value of the temperature ratio for

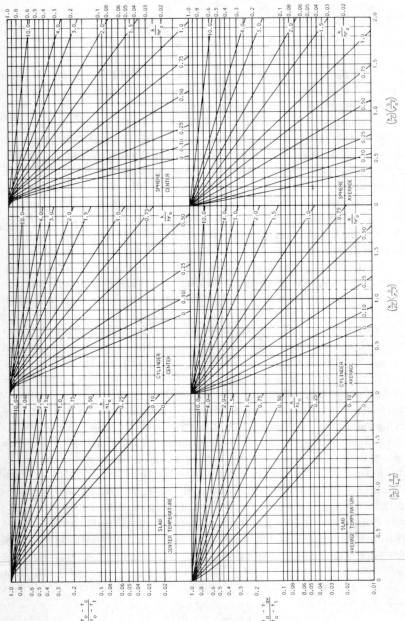

FIG. 8.14.   TRANSIENT HEATING OR COOLING

a rectangular solid is the product of the ratios for three slabs of thicknesses equal to the three dimensions of the solid.

Example 10.—A number 2 can containing 1.25 lb of a liquid with a specific heat of 0.9 and a density of 64 lb/ft^3 will be rotated during processing in such a way that the heat transfer coefficient from the contents to the can wall will be 10 Btu/(hr)(ft^2)(°F). The temperature within the can will be uniform at any instant, except for the laminar layer at the surface. The outside surface coefficient, in the steam atmosphere of the retort, will be 1000. The can, with its contents initially at 160°F, is placed in a retort where the temperature is promptly raised to 240°F. Find the temperature in the can after 5, 10, and 15 minutes. The can has a diameter of 3-5/16 in. and a length of 4-3/16 in.

The thermal resistances of the steam film and the metal wall are completely negligible compared to the resistance of the inside film. In Eq. 8-28, therefore, $U = h = 10$. The total surface area of the can, both the cylindrical portion and the ends, is needed.

$$A = \pi DL + 2(\pi D^2/4) = \pi D(L + D/2)$$

$$= 3.312\pi(4.188 + 1.656)/144 = 0.422 \text{ ft}^2$$

Substituting into Eq. 8-28,

$$-\ln\left(\frac{240 - t}{240 - 160}\right) = \frac{(10)(0.422)\theta}{(1.25)(0.9)} = 3.75\theta$$

where θ is the time in hours. Temperatures calculated from the above equation are as follows:

time, min.	3.75θ	$(240 - t)/80$	t°F
5	0.313	1.368	181.5
10	0.626	1.870	197.2
15	0.938	2.555	208.7

Example 11.—Calculate the center and average temperatures for the conditions of Example 10 on the basis that there is no convection inside the can, with the heat conduction charts. The thermal conductivity is 0.95 times that of water.

We will use the procedure described above for combining values from the slab and cylinder charts.

$$L_o = 4.188/2(12) = 0.175 \text{ ft}$$

$$r_o = 3.312/2(12) = 0.138 \text{ ft}$$

For an average temperature of approximately 200°F, the thermal conductivity of water from Table 8.3 is 0.392.

$$k = 0.95(0.392) = 0.37 \, \text{Btu/(hr)(ft)(°F)}$$

In this problem, there is no longer a film resistance inside the can. The entire resistance between the steam and the contents comes from the steam film and the can wall, for a U of close to 1000. A quick calculation shows that the parameter k/hL_o or k/hr_o is essentially zero.

$$k/\rho c = 0.37/(64)(0.9) = 0.00643 \, \text{ft}^2/\text{hr}$$

$$X_{\text{slab}} = (0.00643/0.175^2)(\theta'/60) = 0.00352 \, \theta'$$

$$X_{\text{cylinder}} = (0.00643/0.138^2)(\theta'/60) = 0.00563 \, \theta'$$

where θ' is time in minutes. Results from the charts are as follows:

	Slab			Cylinder			Product	
θ'	X	Y_c	Y_{av}	X	Y_c	Y_{av}	Y_c	Y_{av}
5	0.0176	1.0	0.91	0.0281	1.0	0.62	1.0	0.564
10	0.0352	1.0	0.85	0.0563	0.97	0.49	0.97	0.416
15	0.0528	1.0	0.79	0.0844	0.9	0.43	0.9	0.340

$$Y = (t_o - t)/(t_o - t_1) = (240 - t)/80$$

Solving the above expression for t, using the product values for Y_c and Y_{av},

θ'	t_c	t_{av}
5	160	195
10	162	207
15	168	213

It is interesting to observe how slowly the center temperature rises compared to the average temperature. It is the center temperature that determines the required cooking time. The advantages resulting from mixing the can contents are obvious.

RADIATION

Radiation is perhaps best visualized as a wave transmission of energy through space. Whatever its source, it is more specifically called electromagnetic radiation because it can be described mathematically in terms of fluctuating electric and magnetic fields. As with any wave motion, radiation has an associated wave length and frequency which determine its character. The product of the length of a wave and the number of waves per second (frequency) gives the radiation velocity which, in a vacuum, has the velocity of light. We can thus write $\lambda\nu = 3.0 \times 10^{10}$ cm/sec, where λ is wave length and ν is frequency.

An alternating electric current flowing through a conductor emits radiation that we call radio or Hertzian waves. The frequency of the alternating current determines the frequency of the radio waves which, in practical applications, is far greater than the common electric power frequency of 60 cycles per second. Radiation also arises from the motion of molecules, atoms, and sub-atomic particles in matter. When energy is supplied to a substance some of these constituents are raised to energetic or "excited" states. The excited particles tend to return spontaneously to the normal state and, in so doing, emit radiation. There are various ways in which the excitation energy can be provided. Fluorescent substances absorb energy from ultraviolet light and emit it as visible light. Bombardment of a substance by electrons produces X-ray radiation. From energy considerations, by far the most important radiation is that arising from thermal agitation of molecules and atoms. The atoms of all matter above a temperature of absolute zero are in a constant motion which results in radiation of energy. As the temperature increases, the motion becomes more rapid and both the frequency and the total energy of the radiation increase. All matter is therefore continuously radiating energy, although the amount radiated at lower temperatures may be too small to be easily detectable. Figure 8.15 shows wave length and frequency ranges for some different categories of electromagnetic radiation.

Radiation and Matter

As pointed out in the previous paragraph, all matter is continuously emitting thermal radiation. For a specific material, this emitted radiation depends only on the temperature and proceeds entirely independently of any incoming radiation or heat flow by other mechanisms. In conduction and convection, we can talk about only a single heat flow stream, from a higher to a lower temperature. In heat exchange by radiation, we must consider the incoming and emitted streams separately; the net exchange is the difference between the two. Of course, any net exchange must always be in the direction from a higher to a lower temperature.

Radiation falling on matter will undergo some combination of absorption, reflection, and transmission. The absorptivity, α, is the fraction of the total radiant energy absorbed; the reflectivity, ρ, is the fraction reflected; and the transmissivity, τ, is the fraction transmitted. By definition, therefore

$$\alpha + \rho + \tau = 1 \qquad \text{Eq. 8-28}$$

It should be realized that the quantities just defined depend very much on the nature of the incoming radiation. For example, ordinary window glass is transparent to visible light, but is quite opaque to ultraviolet and infrared radiation. The walls of a house are opaque to visible light, but readily

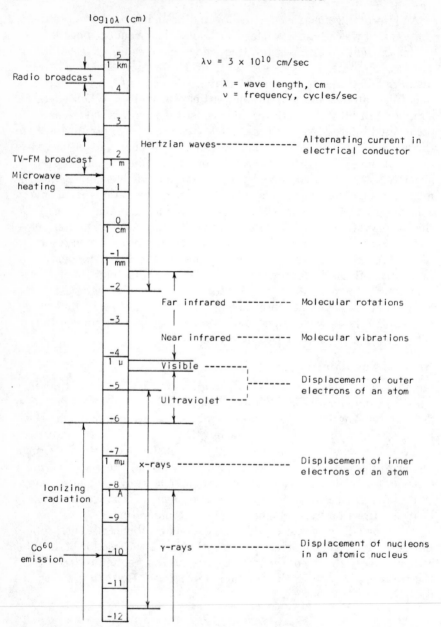

$log_{10}\lambda$ (cm)

$\lambda\nu = 3 \times 10^{10}$ cm/sec

λ = wave length, cm
ν = frequency, cycles/sec

5
1 km

4

Radio broadcast

3

2
1 m   Hertzian waves--------------- Alternating current in
                                       electrical conductor

TV-FM broadcast
Microwave
heating   1

0
1 cm

-1
1 mm

-2

                Far infrared ----------- Molecular rotations
-3

                Near infrared ---------- Molecular vibrations
-4
1 μ
                Visible --------
-5   -------- Displacement of outer
                                                   electrons of an atom
                Ultraviolet ----
-6

-7
1 mμ   x-rays --------------------- Displacement of inner
                                          electrons of an atom
-8
1 Å

Ionizing
radiation   -9

-10
Co⁶⁰   γ-rays ------------------- Displacement of nucleons
emission   in an atomic nucleus

-11

-12

FIG. 8.15. ELECTROMAGNETIC RADIATION SPECTRUM, SHOWING ROUGHLY THE
MECHANISMS BY WHICH VARIOUS TYPES OF RADIATION ARE PRODUCED. 1μ = 1 MICRON
= 10^{-4} CM; 1 Å = 1 ANGSTROM UNIT = 10^{-8} CM

transparent to radio waves. A surface with an absorptivity of 1.0, corresponding to absorption of all incoming radiation, would appear black to the eye, and such an object is called a black body.

Let us consider a number of small objects adjacent to each other in a large isothermal enclosure. At equilibrium, all objects will be at the same temperature and each will be subjected to the same intensity of radiation from the surrounding space in Btu/(hr)(ft^2). At thermal equilibrium, the energy absorbed per unit area by each object must be equal to the energy emitted, and we can write

$$E_1 = \alpha_1 I;\ E_2 = \alpha_2 I;\ E_3 = \alpha_3 I;\ \text{etc.}$$

where E is rate of emission in Btu/(hr)(ft^2), and I is the uniform incoming intensity. Solving each of the above equations for I, we obtain

$$I = E_1/\alpha_1 = E_2/\alpha_2 = E_3/\alpha_3 = \ldots = E_b/\alpha_b \qquad \text{Eq. 8-29}$$

The above relationships show that, in an isothermal system, the ratio of emissive power to absorptivity is the same for all surfaces. Since a black body has maximum absorptivity, it must also have the maximum emissive power. The ratio of the emissive power of a surface to the emissive power of a black body is called the emissivity, ϵ. Also, from Eq. 8-29, this same ratio of emissive powers is equal to the absorptivity. We therefore arrive at the important relationship that, in an isothermal system, the emissivity of any surface is equal to its absorptivity. This statement is a form of Kirchhoff's law.

Emissivity is a property of a surface, and values are tabulated in many heat transfer references. In general, emissivities (and absorptivities) of common surfaces are high, in the vicinity of 0.9. Polished metal surfaces have very low emissivities, and many unpolished metals or metallic paints will have relatively low emissivities. As discussed elsewhere, absorptivity may depend strongly on the wave length of the incident radiation.

Black Body Radiation

True black bodies do not exist in nature. Even a surface such as soot may absorb only about 95% of incoming radiation. For experimental purposes, a "cavity-receiver" can be constructed to approach this ideal as closely as desired. A hollow spherical shell with a small opening is covered on the inside with the best practical black coating. Radiation entering the hole strikes the opposite surface and a small portion is reflected. Except for a very restricted condition, the reflected radiation will not be in a direction to pass out of the hole, but will strike another portion of the surface. In general, many repeated reflections will occur before a ray finally emerges. If 95% of the radiation is absorbed at each reflection, only a few reflections

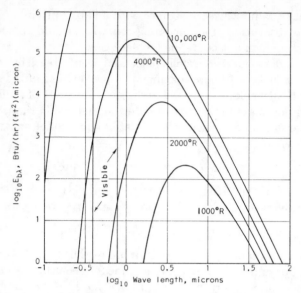

FIG. 8.16.   BLACK BODY MONOCHROMATIC EMISSIVITY POWER

are required to obtain essentially complete absorption. The hole in the shell therefore effectively absorbs all incident radiation and appears as a black surface. The inside surface is, of course, emitting radiation that emerges from the hole, and this must be black body radiation.

It has been shown both experimentally and theoretically that the emissive power of a black body is proportional to the fourth power of the absolute temperature. This relationship, known as the Stefan-Boltzmann law, is written

$$E_b = \sigma T^4 \qquad\qquad \text{Eq. 8-30}$$

for E in Btu/(hr)(ft^2) and T in °R, the proportionality constant σ has the value 0.1713×10^{-8} Btu/(hr)(ft^2)(°R^4).

The statement was made previously that the frequency of thermal radiation increases (or the wave length decreases) as the temperature rises. A warm object, such as an electric iron, emits infrared radiation. We can feel it from a distance, but not see it in a dark room. At higher temperatures, we see a dull red glow, showing that the wave length is getting into the red end of the visible region. With further increase in temperature, as with an incandescent electric light, the radiation is getting well into the visible region and approximates white light. Sunlight corresponds to a temperature of about 10,000°F.

Black body radiation at any temperature is, of course, not at a single wave length, but theoretically includes the entire range of wave lengths from zero

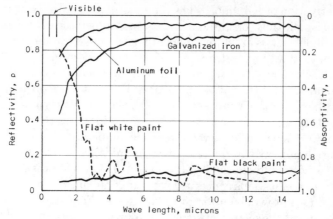

FIG. 8.17. MONOCHROMATIC ABSORPTIVITY OF VARIOUS SURFACES

to infinity, generating a continuous spectrum. The amount of energy toward the ends of the spectrum is very small, and most of it is concentrated in a central region that gives the radiation its predominant characteristic (such as color). This spectral distribution of black body radiation is given by Planck's law and is represented in Fig. 8.16. In Fig. 8.16, emissive power *per unit wave length* is plotted on a logarithmic scale against wave length for several temperatures of the emitting surface. The energy emitted over any wave length band is equal to the width of the band times the average height of the curve in that region, or just the area under the curve. The total energy as given by Eq. 8-30 is the area under the curve between the wave length limits of zero and infinity.

The curves in Fig. 8.16 do not intersect, showing that the energy emitted at all wave lengths increases as temperature increases. It can also be seen that the maximum points of the curves shift toward shorter wave lengths as temperature increases, in agreement with the above discussion.

Non-black Surfaces

Absorptivity and emissivity as defined previously are total or average values that apply to the entire spectrum. Actually, these quantities are strongly dependent on wave length for many materials. Thus, as mentioned, glass absorbs strongly in the infrared and ultraviolet, but not in the visible region. Most white surfaces, such as white paint, snow, etc., are obvious reflectors of visible light but are good absorbers of infrared. Figure 8-17 shows absorptivity as a function of wave length for several surfaces. The total absorptivity of a surface represents an integrated value of this monochromatic absorptivity.

The derivation of Kirchhoff's law for equality of total absorptivity and emissivity is valid only for surfaces at the same temperature. It can be shown that Kirchhoff's law is exact for monochromatic emissivity and absorptivity regardless of the temperatures of the source and receiver. In general, however, the total absorptivity and emissivity will not be equal if the source and receiver are at different temperatures. For example, consider the absorptivity curve for the white lacquer in Fig. 8-17. If this surface is exposed to sunlight, its absorptivity is seen to be something less than 0.2. On the other hand, the surface is at a relatively low temperature and will emit radiation predominantly in the range of 8–10 microns. At this wave length, the absorptivity (and emissivity) is almost 0.9. This effect is particularly important in applications concerned with solar radiation, where the source and receiver are at widely different temperatures. For example, glass walls readily transmit the energy of solar radiation. The glass is opaque to the low temperature radiation on the interior, and the heat is retained inside. Conduction and convection heat exchange, of course, proceeds independently of radiation effects.

Industrial and process radiant heat transfer applications usually are at lower temperatures, and the absorptivities of most of the commonly encountered surfaces are not strongly dependent on wave length. In these applications, it is usually a satisfactory approximation to use a constant absorptivity, independent of wave length. Indeed, sufficient detailed information is seldom available for a more exact determination. If the monochromatic absorptivity and emissivity are independent of wave length, the total absorptivity is equal to the total emissivity under all conditions, regardless of the nature of the incoming radiation. A surface having this property of constant monochromatic absorptivity is called a gray body.

Net Radiant Interchange

In processing applications, we will usually be concerned with the net exchange of radiant heat between two surfaces. In treating this problem, we must first recognize that a radiating surface sends out rays in all directions. If two surfaces of finite area are some distance apart, only a fraction of the total radiation leaving one surface will strike the other. This fraction does not depend on temperatures or emissivities, but only on the geometrical relation of the two surfaces. If the surfaces are gray rather than black, there will be reflected rays as well as direct radiation.

Consider a quantity or "bundle" of radiation leaving surface 1 at a particular instant of time. Of this quantity, a certain fraction will strike surface 2, and the remainder will pass into the surrounding space. A portion of the radiation striking surface 2 will be absorbed and the remainder will be reflected. A portion of the reflected radiation will strike surface 1, where it again will be either absorbed or reflected. This process of repeated absorption and reflection will continue until the entire quantity of radiation initially leaving surface 1 has been absorbed by surface 2, reabsorbed by surface 1, or lost into the surrounding space. The original quantity of radiation emitted is proportional to $\sigma T_1{}^4 A_1$. The continued reflections and absorptions depend on the geometrical arrangement and the emissivities (absorptivities) of both surfaces. Each bundle of radiation initially emitted by surface 1 will behave the same way, and for the total radiation emitted by surface 1 that is eventually absorbed by surface 2 we can write

$$q_{1-2} = \sigma T_1^4 A_1 F_{12}$$

where F_{12} is a factor that depends on the emissivities of both surfaces and on their geometrical relationship. Similarly, for surface 2

$$q_{2-1} = \sigma T_2^4 A_2 F_{21}$$

The net heat transfer is the difference between these two quantities, or

$$q_{net} = \sigma T_2^4 A_2 F_{21} - \sigma T_1^4 A_1 F_{12} \qquad \text{Eq. 8-31}$$

Equation 8-31 applies only to black or gray surfaces. If emissivity varies with wave length, a much more complicated calculation is required. When $T_2 = T_1$, there can be no net exchange, but Eq. 8-31 must still apply. Setting the equation equal to zero, we obtain

$$A_2 F_{21} = A_1 F_{12} \qquad \text{Eq. 8-32}$$

Since the factor F does not depend on temperature for either black or gray surfaces, Eq. 8-32 is valid for all temperatures, not just for the limiting case of equal temperatures, and we have the general relation

$$q_{net} = \sigma(T_2^4 - T_1^4) A_1 F_{12} \qquad \text{Eq. 8-33}$$

One of the most common cases of radiant interchange is that of an object completely surrounded by a large surface. A piece of equipment in a room radiating to the walls would correspond to this case. It is obvious that all the radiation leaving the object strikes the other surface. Because the surface is large compared to the object, a negligible part of the radiation striking the outer surface will be reflected back to the object. Most of the reflected rays will travel back and forth across the large surface until they are absorbed. Therefore, all of the radiation leaving the object will be absorbed by the surrounding surface, and we can write

$$q_{1-2} = \sigma T_1^4 A_1 \epsilon_1$$

and therefore, $F_{12} = \epsilon_1$. As always, $A_1 F_{12} = A_2 F_{21}$, so

$$q_{net} = \sigma(T_1^4 - T_2^4) A_1 \epsilon_1 \qquad \text{Eq. 8-34}$$

Solutions for a large number of geometrical arrangements are presented in the heat transfer literature. One of the more useful solutions applies to two concentric spheres or two concentric cylinders of infinite length. For this case,

$$1/F_{12} = 1/\epsilon_1 + (A_1/A_2)(1/\epsilon_2 - 1) \qquad \text{Eq. 8-35}$$

In Eq. 8-35, subscript 1 applies to the inner surface. If A_2 becomes very large compared to A_1, the second term on the right drops out, and Eq. 8-35 reduces to the case considered previously for which $F_{12} = \epsilon_1$. For the case of infinite parallel planes, $A_1 = A_2$ and

$$1/F_{12} = 1/\epsilon_1 + 1/\epsilon_2 - 1 \qquad \text{Eq. 8-36}$$

Equivalent Conductance for Radiation

It is frequently convenient to express radiant heat transfer rate as the product of a conductance and a temperature difference, just as is done with conduction and convection. Thus,

$$q = h_r A_1(t_1 - t_2) = \sigma(T_1^4 - T_2^4)A_1 F_{12} \qquad \text{Eq. 8-37}$$

An expression for h_r can be obtained by noting that the fourth power temperature difference can be factored as follows:

$$(T_1^4 - T_2^4) = (T_1^2 + T_2^2)(T_1 + T_2)(T_1 - T_2)$$

Substituting into Eq. 8-37, we obtain

$$h_r/F_{12} = \sigma(T_1^2 + T_2^2)(T_1 + T_2) \qquad \text{Eq. 8-38}$$

Figure 8.18 is a graph of h_r/F_{12} as calculated fromEq. 8-38. With the aid of this figure, radiant heat transfer rates can be obtained without the necessity of calculating the fourth powers of the absolute temperatures. The chart is particularly useful when radiant heat transfer is in parallel or series with convection or conduction. It is then possible to combine radiation resistances with other resistances in the usual series or parallel resistance relationships. Observation of Fig. 8.18 shows that, at temperatures up to a few hundred °F, h_r is not very sensitive to temperature. Thus, a sufficiently accurate value of h_r can frequently be obtained even though both temperatures are not precisely known. This fact permits considerable simplification when one of the temperatures is the unknown quantity being calculated.

Example 10.—The top of a vegetable dehydrator is constructed of sheets of $\frac{1}{4}$-in.-thick asbestos-cement covered with a 1-in. layer of insulation. On a certain day, the air temperature of the building in which the dehydrator is located is 70°F, and the ceiling temperature is 40°F. If the air temperature inside the dehydrator is 155°F, what is the heat loss per sq. ft. through the top? The following information is available:

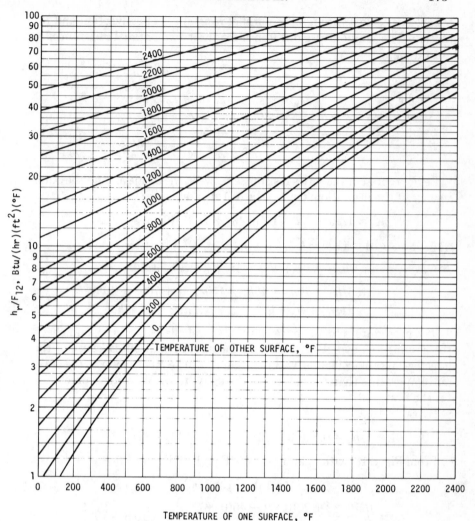

FIG. 8.18.   EQUIVALENT CONDUCTANCE FOR RADIATION

Heat transfer coefficient from hot air to inside surface—10 Btu/(hr) (ft^2)(°F)

Thermal conductivity of asbestos-cement—0.43 Btu/(hr)(ft)(°F)

Thermal conductivity of insulation—0.05 Btu/(hr)(ft)(°F)

Emissivity of outer surface of insulation—0.96

The following diagram represents the thermal resistance combination for this situation. Note that the inside air film, the asbestos-cement, and the insulation form a series resistance path. From the outside of the insulation, heat is lost through the parallel resistances of convection and radiation. The temperature difference for these two parallel resistances is not the same.

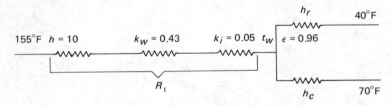

Let R_1 represent the series resistance between the inside air and the outer surface of the insulation. On a basis of 1 ft^2 area,

$$R_1 = 1/10 + 0.25/(12)(0.43) + 1/(12)(0.05) = 1.82$$

$$q/A = (155 - t_w)/R_1 = h_c(t_w - 70) + h_r(t_w - 40)$$

$$t_w(h_c + h_r + 1/R_1) = 155R_1 + 70h_c + 40h_r$$

$$t_w = \frac{155/R_1 + 70h_c + 40h_r}{1/R_1 + h_c + h_r} = \frac{155/1.82 + 70h_c + 40h_r}{1/1.82 + h_c + h_r}$$

The procedure is to assume a value of t_w, calculate h_c and h_r, and check the assumed t_w by substituting into the above equation. Because of the effective layer of insulation, we know that t_w will be much closer to the outer air temperature than to that inside the dehydrator. We will assume 80°F for the first trial.

By Eq. 8-18,

$$h_c = 0.22(80 - 70)^{1/3} = 0.22(2.15) = 0.47$$

From Fig. 8.18, with t_1 and t_2 of 80°F and 40°F, and $F_{12} = \epsilon$

$$h_r = 1.0\epsilon = 1.0(0.96)$$

$$t_w = \frac{155/1.82 + 70(0.47) + 40(0.96)}{1/1.82 + 0.47 + 0.96} = 156.5/1.98 = 79°F$$

This answer is close enough to the assumed value of 80°F that a repeat calculation is unnecessary. The calculation clearly shows the simplification resulting from use of the equivalent conductance for radiation. The solution could have been obtained by the direct use of Eq. 8-34, but it would not have been possible to obtain a simple expression for t_w, and a much lengthier calculation would have been required.

The heat flux is obtained by substituting values for t_w and R_1 in the expression given above:

$$q/A = (155 - t_w)/R_1 = (155 - 79)/1.82 = 42 \text{ Btu/(hr)(ft}^2)$$

Example 11.—A warehouse for storing food products is to have a new roof. It is desired to maintain an inside temperature no greater than 85°F during the summer months, and a question has been raised as to the most effective roof treatment for minimizing radiant heat gain from the outside. The following alternatives are being considered:

	Short Wave Absorptivity (For Solar Radiation)	Long Wave Emissivity
Unpainted galvanized iron	0.65	0.23
Aluminum sheet	0.26	0.04
Aluminum paint	0.35	0.45
White paint	0.18	0.85
Asbestos-cement	0.59	0.96

List the above materials in the order of their effectiveness in reducing radiant heat gain. The solar radiation intensity may be taken as 330 Btu/(hr)(ft^2).

We will consider only radiant heat interchange between the roof and the sky. To determine relative effectiveness, all surfaces will be compared on the basis of the same roof temperature. Under identical exposures, the poorer surfaces would get hotter, but we are not asked to determine the actual temperatures. The net interchange to be minimized is the difference between the incoming solar radiation that is absorbed and the long wave radiation emitted, per sq. ft. of surface.

$$q_{net} = 330\alpha_{short} - \sigma T^4 \epsilon_{long}$$

For a roof temperature of 120°F,

$$q_{net} = 330\alpha_{short} - 0.1713(580/100)^4 \epsilon_{long}$$

$$= 330\alpha_{short} - 194\epsilon_{long}$$

The results of this calculation for the different surfaces are as follows:

	$330\alpha_{short}$	$194\epsilon_{long}$	q_{net}	rank
Galvanized iron	215	45	170	5
Aluminum sheet	86	8	78	4
Aluminum paint	116	87	29	3
White paint	59	165	−106	1
Asbestos cement	195	186	9	2

The situation on the inside surface, where only long wave radiation is involved, is different. Here, the surfaces would rank in the order of their long wave emissivities. It can thus be seen that the most effective roof would be aluminum sheet painted white on the outside.

PROBLEMS

1. Estimate the thermal conductivity of avocado (moisture content 64.7%) at 28°C. Compare your answer to the experimental value, 0.429 watts/(meter)(K).

2. A cold room for hardening ice cream has an 8 in. thick insulated wall made from a material which has an average thermal conductivity of 0.024 Btu/(ft)(hr)(°F). The inner wall temperature is 10°F and the outer wall temperature is 70°F. What is the rate of heat transfer through one square foot of wall?

3. Water at 32°F is freezing in a container with insulated walls. The bottom of the container (2 ft wide, 4 ft long) is kept at −4°F.

   (a) What is the rate of ice formation (lb_m/hr) when the ice layer is 4 inches thick? Neglect sensible heat of the ice.

         Latent heat of fusion of ice = 144 Btu/lb

         Thermal conductivity of ice = 1.5 Btu/(ft)(hr)(°F)

         Thermal conductivity of water = 0.35 Btu/(ft)(hr)(°F)

   (b) What is the heat flux in this problem?

   (c) What is the driving force in the equation for heat flux?

   (d) What is the resistance to heat transfer?

4. An apparatus for measuring thermal conductivity consists of a stainless steel slab heated as shown. The two plates are maintained at different temperatures so there is a steady heat flux. Temperatures, T_1, T_2 and T_3 are measured. The side walls are insulated as shown. Find k for the meat.

Data: For stainless steel

$$k = 12.5 \frac{Btu}{(hr)(ft)(F°)}$$

$T_1 = 120°F$
$T_2 = 118°F$
$T_3 = 97°F$

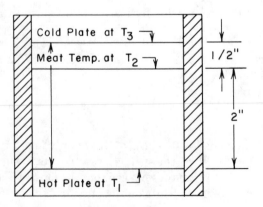

5. An experimental drum drier operates in a vacuum (no air present) at 6 psia. A fruit slurry is spread on the drum (which is heated from the inside) in a layer 0.25 in. thick. When the slurry is first applied, near the top of the drum, water is evaporating from the surface of the slurry at a rate of 1×10^{-4} lb_m/sec per square foot of surface.

(a) What is the heat flux in this region of the drier?
(b) What is the temperature of the drying surface? (Assume thermal equilibrium between surface and vapor).
(c) If the thermal conductivity of the slurry is 0.31 Btu/(ft)(hr)(°F), what is the temperature of the slurry next to the metal drum?

6. Strawberries consist of about 11% solids and 89% water. In the literature you find two experimental values of thermal conductivity for strawberries at 80°F:

Source A	0.267	Btu/(hr)(ft)(°F)
Source B	0.780	Btu/(hr)(ft)(°F)

Which value do you think is more reliable? Why?

7. The 4 in. thick insulating wall on a freezing tunnel is held to a support structure by metal fasteners. If the inside wall temperature is −100°F and the outside wall temperature is 60°F calculate the rate of heat gain through a 100 sq ft area, held by 100 fasteners. The fasteners can be considered rods with a circular cross sectional area of 1.0×10^{-4} ft, and k of 100 Btu/(hr)(ft)(°F). The k for the insulation is 0.020.

8. A 4-in. layer of insulating brick has temperatures on the two faces of 1600°F and 200°F. The thermal conductivities at these temperatures are 0.080 and 0.050 Btu/(hr)(°F), respectively. It may be assumed that thermal conductivity varies linearly with temperature.

(a) What is the heat flow rate per sq ft of wall area?
(b) Sketch a curve of temperature versus distance through the wall.
(c) What is the temperature at the mid-point of the wall?

9. A furnace wall is made up of a 2-in. layer of fire brick, a 4-in. layer of insulating brick, and a 3-in. layer of ordinary brick. Measurements indicate that there is a heat loss of 300 Btu/(hr)(ft²). If the outside temperature is 100°F, estimate the inside surface temperature. Thermal conductivities of the bricks are as follows:

	temp., °F	k
Fire brick	392	0.58
	1832	0.95
Insulating brick	392	0.050
	1400	0.113
Ordinary brick		0.40 (constant)

10. Thermal conductivities of liquids can be measured by a comparison method as shown in the sketch. The ends and sides of the cell are constructed of some conventional plastic material, and any desired liquid is placed in the open space. The cell is then placed between two plates that are maintained at two different constant temperatures, and temperatures are observed by thermocouples as indicated after equilibrium is reached. In one such test, the following temperatures were observed:

	Water in Cell	Tomato Concentrate in Cell
t_1	76°F	78°F
t_2	90°F	89°F
t_3	112°F	108°F

From these data, calculate the ratio of the thermal conductivity of tomato concentrate to that of water.

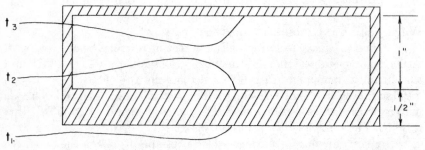

11. Problems involving heating or cooling of fruit such as oranges can be simplified by considering the peel to consist of a spherical shell which provides all of the resistance to heat transfer. Derive an expression for the correct mean area to be used for steady state conduction through a spherical shell of inside radius r_1 and outside radius r_2.

12. Steam at 10 psi gage is being condensed inside a 20 ft length of stainless steel tubing 1 in. o.d. and ¾ in. i.d. The outside of the tube is exposed to air at 70°F. If steam is condensed at a rate of 8 lb/hr, estimate the value of the heat transfer coefficient between the outside tube surface and the air. The coefficient of the steam on the inside may be taken as 2000 Btu/(hr)(ft²)(°F). The thermal conductivity of stainless steel is 9.4 Btu/(hr)(ft)(°F).

13. The walls of a vegetable dehydrator are made of ¼ in.-thick asbestos-cement sheets having a thermal conductivity of 0.43 Btu/(hr)(ft)(°F). In operation, the air temperature inside the dehydrator is 160°F, and the room temperature outside the dehydrator is 85°F. It is estimated that the heat transfer coefficient between the air and the inside surface is 15 Btu/(hr)(ft²)(°F), and between the outside surface and the room air is 3.0 in the

same units. It is desired to reduce the heat loss from the dehydrator to $\frac{1}{4}$ of its present value by adding a layer of mineral insulation ($k = 0.05$) to the outside. What thickness of insulation will be required?

14. What is the rate of convection heat loss from the side walls of a cylindrical cooking vessel (3 ft outside diameter and 4 ft high)? The outside of the vessel insulation, facing ambient air, is found to be 120°F, and the air temperature is 60°F. Assume a heat transfer coefficient of 0.74 Btu/(ft^2)(hr)(°F).

15. A steel tube of 1 mm wall thickness is being used for an ammonia condenser in a refrigeration plant. If the water side coefficient is estimated at 1500 kcal/(m^2)(hr)(°C) and the conductivity of steel is 40 kcal/(m)(hr)(°C), calculate the overall heat transfer coefficient. Assume the surface coefficient for condensing ammonia is 5000 kcal/(m^2)(hr)(°C).

16. Calculate the rate of heat transfer to a vegetable purée in a simple heat exchanger. Steam is condensing at 5.3 psig on one side of a stainless steel surface [$k = 12$ Btu/(hr)(ft)(°F), 0.24 in. thick]. The surface heat transfer coefficients are 2000 Btu/(hr)(ft^2)(°F) for the condensing steam and 28.5 Btu/(hr)(ft^2)(°F) on the purée side. The bulk temperature of the purée is maintained at 200°F by stirring. The heat transfer surface is 6 sq ft.

17. A milk formula is to be canned aseptically at a rate of 5000 lb$_m$/hr. The formula will be heated in an exchanger at 300°F for sterilization and then cooled by water in another (counter-current) exchanger to 100°F. The exchanger available for cooling has an area of 25 ft^2, and it is estimated that it will operate with an overall heat transfer coefficient of 400 Btu/(hr)(ft^2)(°F). If the water enters at 70°F, what water flow rate will be required? The milk formula has a specific heat of 0.90.

18. Steam at 65.3 psig is to be used to provide heat to boil water at atmospheric pressure. The flat heat transfer area is 10 ft^2. If 665 lb$_m$/hr of water must be evaporated, what is the maximum thickness of copper that can be used? Assume the heat transfer coefficients are 2000 Btu/(hr)(ft^2)(°F) on the steam side and 1000 Btu/(hr)(ft^2)(°F) on the water side. k for copper equals 200 Btu/(hr)(ft)(°F).

19. In an evaporator the heat from the condensing steam crosses a metal surface to the boiling feed. A single effect vacuum evaporator concentrates milk from 12% solids to 36% solids. Find the quantity of steam required per hour and the heat transfer surface area of the evaporator.

Milk feed rate = 1000 lb$_m$/hr.

Pressure in evaporator = 10 psia.

Steam pressure = 30 psig.

Feed temperature = 70°F.

Overall heat transfer coefficient = 300 Btu/(hr)(ft^2)(°F).

Neglect boiling-point rise.

20. A single effect evaporator is required to concentrate a solution from 10% solids to 30% solids at the rate of 500 lb of feed per hour. If the pressure in the evaporator is 10 lb/in.^{2} abs., and if steam is available at 30 lb/in.^{2} gage, calculate the quantity of steam required per hour and the area of heat transfer surface if the overall heat transfer coefficient is 300 Btu/(ft^2) (hr)(°F). Assume that the temperature of the feed is 65°F, and that the boiling point of the solution under the pressure of 10 lb/in.^{2} abs. is 195°F. Assume, also, that the specific heat of the solution is 1 Btu/lb°F and the latent heat of vaporization of the solution is the same as that for water under the same conditions.

21. Pear purée is being concentrated in a continuous vacuum evaporator with a heating surface of 50 sq ft. Steam condensing at 5 psi gage is used as the heating medium, and the vacuum is such that the boiling temperature is 110°F. Initially, the evaporation rate is 2500 lb/hr, but after several hours the rate drops to 1500 lb/hr because of the formation of a deposit by the purée. Estimate the value of the heat transfer coefficient for the deposit.

22. Chilled water for the condenser of a low temperature evaporator is provided by a refrigeration unit. In the chiller, the water flows through copper tubes with ¾ in. outside diameter and $\frac{1}{32}$ in. wall thickness at a rate of 20 gpm through each tube. Refrigerant boils on the outside of the tubes at a temperature of 33°F and with a heat transfer coefficient of 1200. At a point where the bulk temperature of the water is 60°F, calculate the water film heat transfer coefficient. The thermal conductivity of copper is 220.

23. Use the Sieder and Tate equation to estimate the film heat transfer coefficient for water being cooled as it flows in a 1.0 in. i.d. pipe at 20 gal/min. The water temperature is 100°F, the wall temperature is 50°F. Example 6 will serve as a useful guide.

24. Water, in turbulent flow in a pipe, is being heated. The inside film heat transfer coefficient is 500 Btu/(hr)(ft^2)(°F). Estimate how the heat transfer coefficient would change if the inside pipe diameter were doubled, keeping the mass flow rate the same and maintaining turbulent flow.

25. Air at 1000°F is flowing at a Reynolds number of 10,000 through a horizontal 1 in. type L copper [k = 220 Btu/(hr)(ft)(°F)] tube (see Table 8.5 for dimensions). Two inch thick insulation (k = 0.04) surrounds the tube. Room temperature is 50°F. Assume steady state and neglect the variation of k with temp. for the tube and insulation. Using appropriate correlations, estimate

(a) outside film heat transfer coefficient
(b) inside film heat transfer coefficient
(c) heat loss per foot of tube lgngth
(d) outside surface temp of insulation

(This problem requires a table of properties for air.)

26. A laboratory furnace with an insulating wall 6 in. thick and an inside surface temperature of 1500°F is losing heat by natural convection to air

at 78°F. Estimate the rate of heat loss per square foot of vertical wall. The insulation has a thermal conductivity of 0.05 at 200°F and 0.08 at 1800°F.

27. Tomato pulp is to be heated from 60°F to 175°F at a rate of 400 lb/hr in a heat exchanger consisting of a length of jacketed stainless steel sanitary tubing. Heat is provided by steam condensing at 215°F in the jacket. It is desired that the maximum inside wall temperature not exceed 200°F at any point in the exchanger. What tubing diameter will be required to satisfy these conditions? The following data apply:

Condensing steam coefficient—1500 Btu/(hr)(ft^2)(°F)
Specific heat of tomato pulp—0.95
Density—64 lb$_m$/ft^3
Thermal conductivity—0.95 times thermal conductivity of water
Viscosity—5 times viscosity of water

28. Calculate the length of 1-in. tubing required to heat the tomato pulp in Problem 27.

29. Water flowing at 10,000 lb$_m$/hr inside a 0.10 ft i.d. pipe at steady state is heated from 80°F to 220°F by steam condensing at 250°F on the outside of the pipe. Assume the pipe is 0.06 in. thick copper [k = 200 Btu/(hr) (ft)(°F)] and the steam side heat transfer coefficient is 2000 Btu/(hr) (ft^2)(°F). Assuming no vaporization occurs on the water side, find or estimate

(a) The heat transfer rate q (from an energy balance).
(b) The water side heat transfer coefficient. For purposes of calculating μ_w you may assume the average wall temperature is 240°F. For other properties use the average temperature between the inlet and outlet.
(c) The length of pipe necessary. Use log mean temperature difference between steam and water as in Eq. 8-27 of the heat exchanger section.

30. A liquid-to-liquid counterflow heat exchanger is used to heat a cold fluid from 120°F to 310°F. Assuming that the hot fluid enters at 500°F and leaves at 400°F, calculate the log mean temperature difference for the heat exchanger.

31. Repeat Problem 30 assuming the heat exchanger is a two-tube pass, one-shell-pass heat exchanger. To solve this problem you must determine a correction factor F between 0.7 and 0.99 from the curves in Fig. 8.13 and multiply F times Δt_{lm}.

32. A corn syrup stream flowing at a rate of 75,000 lb per hour is to be heated by steam. Available for this purpose is a 2-tube pass heat exchanger containing 25 stainless steel tubes per pass. The tubes are ¾ in. o.d., 0.049 in. wall thickness, and 20 ft long. If the corn syrup enters the tubes at 100°F and the temperature of the condensing steam outside the tubes is 220°F, to what temperature can the syrup be heated? The syrup has a specific

gravity of 1.3, a specific heat of 0.85, a thermal conductivity 0.85 times that of water, and a viscosity 10 times that of water. The condensing steam film coefficient may be taken as 1500, and the thermal conductivity of stainless steel is 9.4.

This problem requires a trial and error solution. First assume a value for the final temperature t_2. Then calculate h_i and U. Finally calculate t_2 from Δt_{lm} and q (from heat balance). Compare to your first guess and repeat if necessary.

33. In an experimental study of heat transfer coefficients, a sugar solution is pumped through a steam-jacketed stainless steel 1-in. sanitary tube. Steam condenses on the outside at atmospheric pressure. In two separate tests, the following data were obtained:

	I	II
flow rate, lb/hr	5000	2500
inlet temp., °F	70	70
outlet temp., °F	120	131

The specific heat of the solution is 0.95. On the basis of the data, estimate the inside film coefficient of heat transfer for each of the two tests. It may be assumed that the steam film coefficient remains unchanged and that the inside film coefficient depends on velocity according to Eq. 8-15.

34. One thousand lb per hour of sugar solution is to be cooled from 170°F to 100°F by water in a counter-flow exchanger. Cooling water is available at 75°F and will leave the exchanger at 85°F. The viscosity of the syrup is such that the average overall heat transfer coefficient is 250 Btu/(hr)(ft²)(°F) between syrup temperatures of 170°F and 130°F, but only 100 Btu/(hr)(ft²)(°F) between 130°F and 100°F. It is thus not permissible to use a constant U-value for the entire exchanger. If the specific heat of the syrup is 0.90, what is the required area of the exchanger?

35. A glass jar is cooled at the end of a canning operation by immersing it in water at 70°F. Assume the thermal conductivity of the jar (and the cap) is 0.40 Btu/(hr)(ft²)(°F), the wall thickness is 0.12 in., and the heat transfer coefficients on the inside and outside are 10 and 50 Btu/(hr)(ft²)(°F), respectively. Estimate the rate of heat transfer at a time when the well-stirred liquid contents of the jar are at 240°F. The surface area of the jar is 144 sq in.

36. (a) Using symbols, write an energy balance for the jar cooling in Problem 35 in terms of an overall heat transfer coefficient and the heat capacity. (b) What type of process is this? (c) What heat capacity should you use?

37. (a) In a study of transient heat conduction, a plastic sphere of 1-in. diameter is dropped into a water bath held at a constant temperature of 180°F. A thermocouple at the center of the sphere showed an initial tem-

perature of 70°F and a temperature of 127°F after a time of 6 minutes. The plastic material has a thermal conductivity of 0.11, a specific heat of 0.4, and a specific gravity of 1.2. From these data, estimate the value of the heat transfer coefficient from the water to the sphere. (b) A similar experiment is now conducted in which a 1-in. diameter hollow sphere made of thin copper is filled with a fruit purée. With the same water bath and initial temperatures as before, the center temperature now rises to 122°F in 6 minutes. The purée has a specific heat of 0.95 and a specific gravity of 1.06. Estimate the thermal conductivity of the purée. Convection inside the sphere can be neglected.

38. A steam jacketed kettle of hemispherical shape, 3 ft i.d., is being used to heat a tomato concentrate. The wall of the kettle is stainless steel with a thickness of $\frac{1}{8}$ in. Saturated steam at 5 psi gage is used for heating, and the steam side heat transfer coefficient may be taken as 1000. The kettle is equipped with a stirrer that keeps the contents well agitated and results in an inside heat transfer coefficient of 80. The density of the concentrate is 70 lb/ft³, and the specific heat is 0.85. If the kettle is initially filled with this material at a temperature of 70°F, what length of time will be required for the concentrate to reach a temperature of 200°F?

39. Tomato juice to be used for a hot fill canning operation is held at 212°F in a tank 2.0 ft in diameter and 4.0 ft high. The tank is full when a line failure closes down the cannery. To try to save the juice ice water at 32°F is circulated in a jacket on all sides of the tank. Estimate the average temperature and the temperature at the tank center after 20 hours. Assume:

Cooling by conduction in the juice (no mixing).

Cylindrical tank uniformly cooled on ends and sides.

Negligible resistance to heat transfer in tank wall and on brine side.

$$\text{Thermal diffusivity of juice} = \alpha = \frac{k}{\rho c} = 7.0 \times 10^{-3} \frac{\text{ft}^2}{\text{hr}}$$

40. Butter is packed in 1 ft × 1 ft × 1 ft cube-shaped boxes and cooled uniformly from each face. The overall heat transfer coefficient through the container walls and air film is 2.4 Btu/(hr)(ft²)(°F). If the butter is originally at 70°F, cold room is at 0°F find the time necessary to cool the center of each butter cube to 24°F.

Approximate properties of butter:

$k = 0.12$ Btu/(hr)(ft)(°F)

$\rho = 60$ lb$_m$/ft³

$c_p = 0.5$ Btu/lb$_m$ °F

41. The cold boxes in Problem 41 are returned to the processing room which is maintained at 70°F. Assuming the box surfaces are at 0°F, write the empirical correlations and estimate the air-side film heat transfer coefficient

(a) to one of the vertical sides of a box

(b) to the top of a box

42. A thin soup having the same properties as water (ρ = 60 lb_m/ft^3, k = 0.39, μ = 0.30 centipoise, c_p = 1.0) is to be heated with stirring in a steam-jacketed hemispherical kettle (3 ft diameter). The steam is under pressure (240°F) and the top of the kettle is perfectly insulated. If the initial temperature of the soup is 140°F and the overall heat transfer coefficient is 120 Btu/(hr)(ft^2)(°F), estimate the center temperature of the soup after one hour.

43. (a) Neglecting the thermal resistance of the metal steam jacket in Problem 42, estimate the heat loss by radiation from the hemispherical part of the outside of the kettle. It is a cold day and the walls, floor and ceiling are about 40°F. Assume the emissivity of the stainless steel kettle is 0.2 and the absorptivity of the walls, etc., is 0.8. The surface area of the kettle is 14.1 ft^2 and of the walls, etc., is about 24,000 ft^2. (b) Would the radiation heat loss be greater, less or the same if the kettle were painted black? Why? (c) Would the calculated radiation heat loss be greater, less, or the same if the walls were considered black bodies? Why?

44. Calculate the net heat transfer by radiation to a loaf of bread in an oven at a uniform temperature of 350°F. The emissivity of the surface of the loaf is 0.85; the total surface area of the loaf is 100 in.^{2} and the surface temperature of the loaf is 212°F.

45. Calculate the rate of heat transfer to a single sealed can of product in a vacuum oven at a time when the surface temperature is 40°F. The diameter of the can is 6 in., the height is 6 in. and the emissivity is 0.1. The oven walls are at 1540°F.

46. (a) A water container is adjacent to a steam boiler. In order to help keep the water cool, should the outside surface of the container be painted white or covered with aluminum foil? (b) Which covering should be used if the container is located in the sun (instead of near the boiler)? Use Fig. 8.16 and 8.17 of the radiation section.

47. Estimate the heat flux from a Steriflamme burner to a can (a) by radiation; (b) by convection; at a time when the can surface temperature is 240°F. You may treat the can surface as if it were flat so that the flame and can are parallel surfaces of equal area. You may also assume the flame is a black body at 2540°F, the heat transfer coefficient from the flame to the can is about 2 Btu/(hr)(ft^2)(°F) and the emissivity of the can surface is 0.05.

48. Calculate the net rate of heat transfer by radiation to a potato surrounded by catalytic heaters at 2000°F. Assume that the surface temperature of the potato is 212°F, the surface area is 60 sq in. and the emissivity of the potato surface is 0.70.

49. The outer surface of a drier loses heat to the surroundings by radiation and convection. Under conditions where the heat transfer coefficient

for convection is $h_c = 1.0$ Btu/(hr)(ft^2)(°F) and the emissivity of the drier surface is 0.5, which method of heat transfer is removing most heat? The surface temperature is 340°F and the surroundings are at 40°F. Show your calculations.

50. A blancher box 6 ft wide and 36 ft long has a top cover plate of aluminum-painted galvanized iron. The box is in a room with an air temperature of 85°F and is heated by steam to a temperature of 210°F. The average wall and ceiling temperature of the room is 65°F. Estimate the steam consumption in pounds per hour resulting from heat loss from the top of the box by convection and radiation. The emissivity of the surface is 0.66.

51. At a certain point in a continuous belt dehydrator, the temperature of the material on the belt is 130°F and the air temperature is 165°F. The air flow rate is such that the convective heat transfer coefficient is 20 Btu/(hr)(ft^2)(°F), both to the material on the belt and to the walls of the dehydrator. If the dehydrator is well insulated so that heat losses can be neglected, estimate the rate of heat transfer to the material by convection from the air and by radiation from the top surface. For the purposes of this calculation, the top surface and the belt may be considered to be infinite parallel planes. All emissivities are 0.9.

Hint: You can calculate the temperature of the top surface by recognizing that since no heat transfers through the insulated top, at steady state the rate of heat transfer to the top surface by convection must equal the rate of heat transfer away from the top by radiation. It is convenient here to make use of the form:

$$Q \text{ radiation} = h_r(t_1 - t_2)$$

where h_r may be obtained from Fig. 8.18 in the text.

52. A bare thermocouple located on the axis of a pipe is being used to measure the temperature of a stream of hot exhaust gas. The thermocouple indicates a temperature of 800°F, and the pipe wall temperature is found to be 200°F. Estimate the true temperature of the air flowing past the thermocouple. The convective heat transfer coefficient between the air and the thermocouple may be taken as 30 Btu/(hr)(ft^2)(°F), and all emissivities are 0.90.

SYMBOLS

A	area perpendicular to direction of heat transfer or Angstrom unit $= 10^{-8}$ cm
a	constant
A_m	mean area for heat transfer
c	heat capacity
cm	centimeter
c_p	heat capacity at constant pressure

D diameter

Dimensionless numbers

    Gr Grashof number = $L^3 \rho^2 g \beta \Delta t / \mu^2$

    Gz Graetz number = $RePr(L/D)(\pi/4) = \dot{m} c_p / kL$

    Nu Nusselt number = hD/k

    Pr Prandtl number = $c_p \mu / k$

    Re Reynolds number = $DV\rho/\mu$

    St Stanton number = $Nu/PrRe = h/c_p V \rho$

E radiation energy flux, usually Btu/(hr)(ft^2)

E_b radiation energy flux for a black body

$E_{b\lambda}$ radiation energy flux for a black body at one wave length

F_{12} factor for combined emissivities and space relationship of bodies 1 and 2

g gravitational acceleration

h conductance film coefficient of heat transfer, Btu/(hr)(ft^2)(°F)

h_r equivalent conductance for radiation

I intensity of radiation flux, usually Btu/(hr)(ft^2)

k thermal conductivity, Btu/(hr)(ft)(°F)

$k/\rho c_p$ thermal diffusivity

L characteristic length dimension, e.g., length of a cylinder, side of a square, etc.

L_o one half the thickness of the slab

ln   natural logarithm of a number

m a constant or mass

$\dot{m}$ mass flow rate

n constant

Q quantity of heat, Btu

q rate of heat transfer, Btu/hr

q_{1-2} total radiation emitted by surface 1 that is absorbed by surface 2

q_{2-1} total radiation emitted by surface 2 that is absorbed by surface 1

q_{net} net heat transfer by radiation between two surfaces

R resistance, °F hr/Btu

R_t total resistance

r radial direction in a cylinder

r_o radius of a cylinder or sphere

T absolute temperature

t temperature

t' intermediate temperature

t_s surface temperature

t_1 initial temperature or at point 1

t_2 temperature at point 2

U	overall heat transfer coefficient, Btu/hr ft^2 °F
V	velocity
v	volume
X	x-coordinate in Fig. 8-14 $(h/\rho c)(\theta/r_o^2)$
x	weight fraction, general function, or dimensionless group
Y	y-coordinate in Fig. 8-14 $(t_o - t)/(t_o - t_1)$
y	general function or dimensionless group
z	general function or dimensionless group

Subscripts

av	average
b	bulk or black body
c	cold side
d	deposit
e	equivalent
h	hot side
i	inside or insulation
lm	logarithmic mean
m	mean
o	outside
s	solids or steam
w	wall or water
α	absorptivity
β	coefficient of thermal expansion
Δt	temperature difference between a hot stream and a cold stream, also temperature difference causing natural convective heat transfer
$(\Delta t)_{lm}$	logarithmic mean temperature difference $(\Delta t_2 - \Delta t_1)/\ln(\Delta t_2/\Delta t_1)$
Δv	change in volume
Δx	path length, usually for heat transfer
ϵ	emissivity, dimensionless
θ	time
λ	wave length of radiation
μ	viscosity or micron = 10^{-4} cm
μ_b	fluid viscosity at bulk temperature
μ_w	fluid viscosity at wall temperature
ρ	reflectivity or density
σ	Stefan-Boltzman constant, 0.1713×10^{-8} Btu/(hr)(ft^2)(°R^4)
τ	transmissivity, dimensionless

CHAPTER 9

Mixtures of Gases and Vapors[1]

INTRODUCTION

There is no firm distinction between the terms gas and vapor. Gas is the more general term, and a substance in the gaseous state that is at or near a condition of condensation may be called a vapor. Thus, we think of steam as a vapor because water is a liquid at ordinary conditions. We might talk about the vapor rising from a container of liquid nitrogen, but nitrogen escaping from a high-pressure cylinder would certainly be called a gas.

Most food processing applications involving mixtures of gases occur at or near atmospheric pressure, and perfect gas behavior is a valid approximation. The following discussion will therefore be based on perfect gas behavior for all substances in the gaseous state. Reference should be made to Chapter 4 for a discussion of the perfect gas law.

COMPOSITION RELATIONSHIPS

The composition of gas mixtures can, as in the case of any kind of mixture or solution, be expressed in terms of weight fraction or weight per cent. Because of the simple relationship among pressure, volume, and temperature that results when mole units are used, there are frequently special advantages in using mole fraction rather than weight fraction for gas compositions. In the thermodynamics chapter, it was pointed out that a mixture of fixed composition, such as air, can be treated as a single gas with an average molecular weight calculated from the molal concentrations of the constituents.

One of the consequences of the perfect gas law as applied to mixtures is that each constituent in a volume of gas can be considered independently as though it occupied the entire volume. Thus, for a mixture of gases A, B, and C, we can write

$$P_a = N_a RT/V$$

$$P_b = N_b RT/V$$

$$P_c = N_c RT/V \qquad \text{Eq. 9-1}$$

and for the mixture considered as a whole,

$$P = N_t RT/V = (N_a + N_b + N_c)RT/V \qquad \text{Eq. 9-2}$$

---

[1] Symbols used in this chapter are listed and defined at the end of the chapter.

where the total moles, N_t, is the sum of the moles of the individual constituents.

The pressures P_a, P_b, and P_c, which are the pressures the individual gases would have if each one occupied the entire volume independently of the others, are called partial pressures. Comparing the sum of the three Eqs. 9-1 with Eq. 9-2 shows that

$$P = P_a + P_b + P_c \qquad \text{Eq. 9-3}$$

or the sum of the partial pressures in a gas mixture is equal to the total pressure. The relationship expressed by Eq. 9-3 is known as Dalton's law. It is exact for a mixture of perfect gases and can be used as an approximation for a mixture of real gases. If any one of Eqs. 9-1 is divided by Eq. 9-3, the common factor RT/V cancels, and we have the result

$$P_a/P = N_a/N_t = x_a \qquad \text{Eq. 9-4}$$

The partial pressure of a gas in a mixture is thus equal to its mole fraction times the total pressure.

In the above discussion, we considered the pressures of the individual constituents if each is measured at the volume and temperature of the mixture. We can also consider the volumes of the individual gases if each is measured at the total pressure and temperature of the mixture. Thus,

$$V_a = N_a RT/P$$
$$V_b = N_b RT/P$$
$$V_c = N_c RT/P \qquad \text{Eq. 9-5}$$

and for the total,

$$V = N_t RT/P \qquad \text{Eq. 9-6}$$

In this case, each individual volume is equal to the total volume times the mole fraction.

The term, volume per cent, is frequently used in expressing gas compositions. This quantity is simply the partial volume as defined above divided by the total volume (and multiplied by 100). Equations 9-5 and 9-6 show that gas volume per cent is the same as mole per cent. This equality of volume and mole per cent does not apply to liquid mixtures or solutions.

If a gas mixture is in equilibrium with a pure liquid phase of any one of its constituents, the vapor pressure-temperature relation for that material must be satisfied. This condition means that the partial pressure of the substance in the gas phase must be equal to the pressure of the saturated vapor at the temperature of the system.

Example 1

A container partially filled with water at 100°F is open to the atmosphere. At equilibrium, what is the partial pressure and mole fraction of water vapor in the air above the liquid?

At equilibrium, the air is saturated with water vapor, and the partial pressure of the vapor is equal to the vapor pressure of 0.949 psia. The total atmospheric pressure is 14.7 psia, so that

$$x_w = P_w/P = 0.949/14.7 = 0.0646$$

Example 2

A closed cylinder fitted with a piston contains dry air at 150°F and atmospheric pressure. A small quantity of liquid is introduced into the cylinder and the system allowed to come to equilibrium. At this condition, a few drops of liquid still remain. If the temperature remains at 150°F, what is the total pressure and mole fraction of water vapor? If the piston is moved so that the volume is one-half of its original value, with the temperature remaining constant, calculate the total pressure and mole fraction of water vapor.

In all cases, the vapor space is in equilibrium with liquid water at 150°F, so the partial pressure of water vapor is equal to the saturated vapor pressure of 3.72 psia. The pressure of the air in the cylinder initially is 14.7 psia, and the addition of water does not change this value. Therefore,

$$P = P_w + P_a = 3.72 + 14.7 = 18.4 \text{ psia}$$

$$x_w = P_w/P = 3.72/18.4 = 0.202$$

After compression, the total moles of air in the cylinder is unchanged. For one-half of the original volume, the perfect gas law states that the pressure of air must be doubled. The pressure of water vapor does not change, since it must remain equal to the saturated vapor pressure. Therefore,

$$P_a = 2(14.7) = 29.4 \text{ psia}$$

$$P = P_w + P_a = 3.72 + 29.4 = 33.1 \text{ psia}$$

$$x_w = P_w/P = 3.72/33.1 = 0.112$$

Since the water vapor pressure cannot rise above the saturation value of 3.72 psia, it is necessary that some water condense out of the vapor phase during the compression process.

The above discussion and the remainder of this chapter are limited to the case of a pure liquid phase. If the gas were ammonia instead of air, for example, some of it would dissolve in the liquid water, and the equilibrium relationships would change. This type of situation is encountered in distillation processes, which are not discussed in this book.

PSYCHROMETRY

The subject of psychrometry is concerned with the behavior of mixtures of condensible vapors with non-condensible gases, and more specifically with the air-water system. The principles have important applications in humidification and dehumidification, evaporative cooling, air conditioning, dehydration, and many natural phenomena involving evaporation and condensation of water.

Psychrometric Definitions

Dew point.—If an air-water vapor mixture is cooled at constant pressure, the partial pressure of each component will remain constant until the temperature is lowered to the saturation temperature corresponding to the partial pressure of water vapor. At this point, the water vapor will be in a saturated state, and any further cooling will result in condensation. The temperature at this condition is called the dew point.

Humidity.—Y (sometimes called absolute humidity, specific humidity, or humidity ratio) is defined as the number of pounds of water vapor carried by one pound of dry air. This figure multiplied by 7000 gives grains of moisture per pound of dry air (there are 7000 grains in one pound-mass), thus

$$Y = \frac{m_w}{m_a} = \frac{M_w P_w V/RT}{M_a P_a V/RT} = \frac{M_w P_w}{M_a P_a} = \frac{18.02}{28.98} \frac{P_w}{P - P_w} = 0.622 \frac{P_w}{P - P_w}$$

Eq. 9-7

Example 3.—Compute the humidity of saturated air at 100°F and a total pressure of 1 atm. From the steam tables,

$$P_w = P_s = 0.949 \text{ psia}$$

$$Y_s = \frac{(0.622)(0.949)}{14.7 - 0.949} = 0.0429 \text{ lb } H_2O/\text{lb dry air}$$

A curve representing humidity of saturated air as a function of temperature is shown in Fig. 9.1.

Relative humidity.—This term, rh, is defined as the ratio of the actual partial pressure of water vapor in the air to the pressure of saturated water vapor at the same temperature. At the dew point, the relative humidity is 1.0. Relative humidities are frequently multiplied by 100 to express them as percentages.

$$\text{rh} = P_w/P_s$$

Eq. 9-8

Example 4.—Compute the humidity of air with a relative humidity of 60% at 100°F.

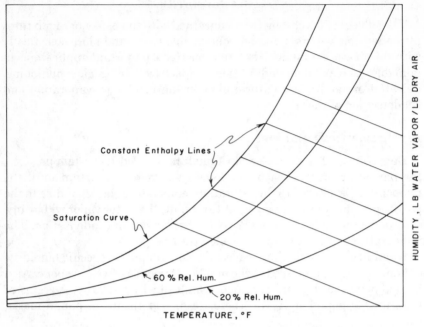

FIG. 9.1. SCHEMATIC OF THE AIR-WATER VAPOR PSYCHROMETRIC CHART

$$P_s = 0.949 \text{ psia}$$

$$\bullet \quad P_w = 0.6 \times 0.949 = 0.569 \text{ psia}$$

$$Y = \frac{0.622 \times 0.569}{14.7 - 0.569} = 0.0250$$

Figure 9.1 shows humidity plotted against temperature for several different values of relative humidity. Note that the 100% relative humidity line is identical to the humidity curve for saturated air mentioned above.

Humid heat.—C_s is the number of Btu necessary to raise the temperature of 1 lb of dry air and the water vapor it contains 1°F at constant pressure. Over the range of conditions usually involved in psychrometric calculations, the specific heats of air and water vapor are substantially constant at 0.24 and 0.45 Btu/lb°F, respectively. Therefore,

$$C_s = 0.24 + 0.45\, Y \qquad\qquad \text{Eq. 9-9}$$

Total enthalpy.—H is the enthalpy of 1 lb of dry air and the water vapor it contains, expressed as Btu per pound of dry air,

$$H = H_a + Y H_g \qquad\qquad \text{Eq. 9-10}$$

The enthalpy must be based on some fixed reference states for air and water. Because psychrometric calculations do not involve chemical reactions, the reference temperature need not be the same for air and water. If saturated liquid at 32°F is chosen as the reference state for water, enthalpies of water can be taken directly from the steam tables. It will be shown later, however, that increased accuracy for certain types of calculations will be obtained if some other reference temperature is chosen. It is convenient to use 0°F as the reference temperature for air. If this selection is made,

$$H_a = 0.24\,t$$

where t is in degrees Fahrenheit.

Example 5.—Compute the enthalpy of the air in the previous example

$$H_a = 0.24 \times 100 = 24.0\ \text{Btu/lb}$$

From steam tables,

$$H_g\ (\text{sat. steam at } 100°\text{F}) = 1105\ \text{Btu/lb}$$

$$H = 24.0 + 0.0250 \times 1105 = 51.6\ \text{Btu/lb dry air}$$

This calculation neglects the effect of pressure on enthalpy of steam. At these low pressures, the resulting error is negligible. In this manner, the enthalpy can be computed for any condition of moist air. Lines of constant enthalpy are shown on Fig. 9.1.

Adiabatic Saturation

Consider a long horizontal pipe, partially filled with water, and thermally insulated from the surroundings. Let air flow at a constant rate through the pipe above the surface of the water. It is postulated that the water temperature is uniform and that the pipe is long enough that the air leaving is in equilibrium with the water.

If the entering air is at a different temperature from the water, heat will be transferred from the warmer to the colder stream, and the temperatures of both will tend to change. If the entering air is dry, water will evaporate into the air, and the water will be cooled. Water will condense out of the air if it is sufficiently humid, and heat will be released. After the air has flowed for a sufficient length of time, steady state will be achieved, and there will be no further change in the water temperature. The air temperature and humidity, of course, change as the air flows through the pipe. The air will leave the pipe at the temperature of the water and will be saturated with water vapor at that temperature.

The equilibrium temperature which is attained is obviously dependent on the temperature and humidity of the entering air, but not on the air flow rate or the initial temperature of the water. In order to make the system completely steady state, let water at the equilibrium temperature be admitted at a rate sufficient to compensate for that lost by evaporation.

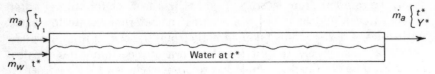

FIG. 9.2. THE ADIABATIC PROCESS

We will now develop equations which describe the adiabatic saturation temperature.

The steady state conditions are represented in Fig. 9.2. Since this is a steady flow process with no work, heat, or changes in kinetic or potential energy, it must take place at constant enthalpy. Equating the total enthalpy of the discharge air to the enthalpies of the air and water entering,

$$\dot{m}_a H^* = \dot{m}_a H_1 + \dot{m}_w h_f^* \text{ and } H^* = H_1 + \frac{\dot{m}_w}{\dot{m}_a} h_f^*$$

By conservation of mass,

$$\dot{m}_w = \dot{m}_a (Y^* - Y_1) \text{ and } H^* = H_1 + (Y^* - Y_1) h_f^* \qquad \text{Eq. 9-11}$$

The second term on the right side of Eq. 9-11 is relatively small. As the reference temperature for enthalpies of water is arbitrary, h_f^* can be made zero by proper choice of reference temperature. For most engineering calculations, the adiabatic saturation process may therefore be considered to take place at constant total enthalpy. A knowledge of the total enthalpy of the air is thus sufficient to establish the adiabatic saturation temperature.

For many purposes, it is convenient to have an expression of Eq. 9-11 in terms of sensible and latent heat quantities. In the humidification process, the change in enthalpy is equal to the sum of the sensible and latent heat changes, or approximately

$$H^* - H_1 = 0 = C_s(t^* - t_1) + \lambda(Y^* - Y_1) \qquad \text{Eq. 2-12}$$

The above expression is approximate because both C_s and λ vary as the humidity and temperature change during the process. Furthermore, the second term on the right side of Eq. 9-11 has been neglected. A rigorous derivation shows that Eq. 9-12 is exact if C_s is taken as the value of the entering air and λ corresponds to temperature t^*. Accordingly, rearrangement of Eq. 9-12 gives

$$\frac{t^* - t_1}{Y^* - Y_1} = -\frac{\lambda^*}{C_{s1}} \qquad \text{Eq. 9-13}$$

The adiabatic saturation temperature can be calculated from either Eq. 9-11 or Eq. 9-13 by a trial-and-error method if Y_1 and t_1 are known. A value of t^* is assumed, from which Y^* and H^*, corresponding to saturated air at

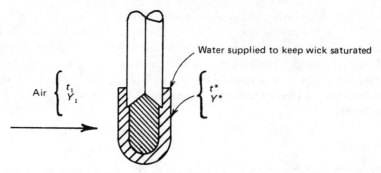

FIG. 9.3. THE WET BULB PROCESS

t^*, can be calculated and checked by substitution into Eq. 9-11 or Eq. 9-13. The calculation is repeated until the assumed t^* gives results that agree with one of the equations.

Lines calculated from Eq. 9-13 for fixed values of t^* can be plotted on the coordinates of Fig. 9.1. Eq. 9-11 shows that such lines will correspond closely to the lines of constant enthalpy that are already plotted on the figure. For practical calculations, the difference between true adiabatic saturation lines and constant enthalpy lines can be neglected. Such a plot eliminates the necessity for the trial-and-error calculation described above, as the value of t^* is found simply by following one of these lines from t_1 and Y_1 up to the saturation curve.

Wet Bulb Temperature

Consider a thermometer as shown in Fig. 9.3 which has a wick wet with water covering the bulb. If unsaturated air is blown past the bulb, or if the thermometer is moved through air, water will evaporate from the wick and cause cooling. This effect is readily observed by wetting one's finger and blowing on it. At the same time, because of the temperature drop of the bulb, heat will be transferred from the air to the bulb. Note that his process is quite different from the adiabatic saturation process. The time of contact of air with water is so short that the temperature and humidity of the air are essentially unchanged.

Eventually a state of dynamic equilibrium will be reached, after which time the temperature of the wet bulb will remain constant. At this condition, the heat transferred from the air to the wet bulb must be equal to the total latent heat of vaporization of the water that is evaporating. The temperature of the water and the bulb is not changing, and there is no other heat source.

The rate of heat transfer is given by the product of a heat transfer coefficient (thermal conductance) and the temperature driving force

$$q/A = h(t_1 - t^*)$$

The water evaporating from the wick must diffuse out through an air film by much the same mechanism as the heat flows in. The rate of evaporation (mass transfer) can be expressed as the product of a mass transfer coefficient and a humidity driving force. The humidity at the surface is that of saturated air at the temperature of the wet bulb. If the main body of air were also saturated, obviously no water vapor could pass into the air. We may therefore write

$$\dot{m}_w/A = k_y(Y^* - Y_1)$$

Equating the total latent heat of vaporization to the heat transferred,

$$\lambda^* \dot{m}_w = q$$

$$\lambda^* k_y(Y^* - Y_1) = -h(t^* - t_1)$$

$$\frac{t^* - t_1}{Y^* - Y_1} = -\frac{\lambda^* k_y}{h} \qquad\qquad \text{Eq. 9-14}$$

The coefficients h and k_y are both functions of the nature of flow of air past the bulb and of certain physical properties of the air-water system.

It is found experimentally for the air-water system that for average conditions the ratio h/k_y is approximately equal to C_s. Comparison of Eqs. 9-13 and 9-14 shows that, if this equality holds, the wet bulb temperature has the same value as the adiabatic saturation temperature. For the air-water system, the two temperatures are usually considered to be the same, and no distinction is made. It should be emphasized that approximate equality of h/k_y to C_s for air-water is entirely fortuitous. If we are dealing with mixtures of alcohol vapor and air, for example, the equality does not hold, and the wet bulb temperature is not equal to the adiabatic saturation temperature.

Wet bulb temperatures are frequently measured with a sling psychrometer. This instrument has two thermometers mounted close to each other on a board. One of the thermometers has a wick around the bulb which is kept wet with water. The board is free to rotate about a handle fixed on the end away from the bulbs. The psychrometer is whirled rapidly through the air until the wet bulb temperature remains unchanged. The wet and dry bulb temperatures are thus obtained simultaneously under the same conditions. Equation 9-14 shows that knowledge of the wet and dry bulb temperatures is sufficient to establish the air humidity.

Psychrometric Charts

A chart constructed similarly to Fig. 9.1 is of considerable assistance in

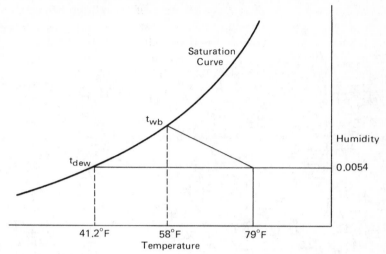

FIG. 9.4 WET AND DRY BULB TEMPERATURES, HUMIDITY, AND DEW POINT
FOR EXAMPLES

psychrometric calculations. Such a chart is Fig. 9.4. In particular, a chart eliminates the need for trial-and-error calculations involving adiabatic humidification or wet bulb temperatures. It should be remembered, however, that such a chart is merely an aid to calculation and presents no new information. Greater accuracy may be required than is obtainable with a chart, and the exact equations must then be used.

Psychrometric charts are widely available, both in the engineering literature and from manufacturers of air conditioning equipment. In addition to the basic lines shown in Fig. 9.1, these charts include a variety of other information. There will usually be lines of constant volume of moist air in cu ft per lb of dry air. Humidities are frequently expressed as grains rather than pounds of water vapor.

Psychrometric relationships depend on the atmospheric pressure, and a chart must be based on a specific value, usually the standard atmosphere pressure of 14.7 psi. Some charts include a table of corrections to be applied when the atmospheric pressure differs from the standard value. For extensive calculations at a reduced pressure, as at a high elevation, it is convenient to construct a chart for the particular atmospheric pressure desired.

Example 6.—A sling psychrometer shows a wet bulb temperature of 58°F and a dry bulb temperature of 79°F. Determine the humidity, the relative humidity, and the dew point by calculation and by using the chart in Fig. 9.5. At 58°F,

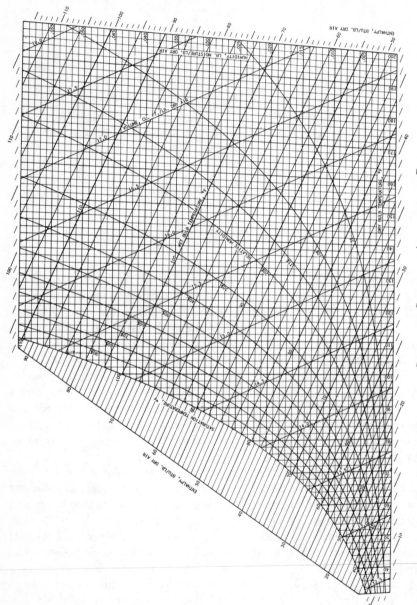

FIG. 9.5. PSYCHROMETRIC CHART FOR STANDARD ATMOSPHERIC PRESSURE

$$P_{sat} = 0.238 \text{ psi (from steam tables)}$$

$Y^* = 0.622P_s/(14.7 - P_s) = 0.622(0.238)/(14.7 - 0.238) = 0.01024 \text{ lb}$
$H_2O/\text{lb dry air}$

$$\lambda^* = 1061 \text{ Btu/lb}$$

Using Eq. 9-13,

$$(t_1 - t^*)C_{s1} = (Y^* - Y_1)\lambda^*$$

$$(79 - 58)(0.24 + 0.45Y_1) = (0.01024 - Y_1)1061$$

$$Y_1 = 0.00544 \text{ lb } H_2O/\text{lb dry air}$$

$$= 0.00544(7000) = 38.1 \text{ grains } H_2O/\text{lb dry air}$$

Using Eq. 9-7,

$$0.00544 = 0.622P_w/(14.7 - P_w), \text{ therefore } P_w = 0.128 \text{ psi}$$

$$P_s = 0.49 \text{ psi at } 79°F$$

$$\text{rh} = P_w/P_s = 0.128/0.49 = 0.261$$

The dew point is the temperature at which the saturated vapor pressure is equal to the water partial pressure of 0.128 psi. From the steam tables,

$$t_d = 41.2°F$$

To use the chart in Fig. 9.5 follow a wet bulb line from the saturation curve at 58°F to the point of intersection with a dry bulb temperature of 79°F, as illustrated in Fig. 9.4. At this point, the chart shows

$$Y = 0.0054 \text{ lb } H_2O/\text{lb dry air and rh} = 26\%$$

The dew point corresponds to cooling at constant humidity and is found by following a horizontal line at a humidity of 0.0054 lb H_2O/lb dry air to the intersection with the saturation curve and reading the corresponding temperature.

$$t_d = 41.2°F$$

Example 7.—The air in example 6 is heated from 79° to 100°F. How much heat is required per pound of dry air?

For heating at constant humidity, only sensible heat is involved, and we can write

$$Q = C_s(t_2 - t_1)$$

$$C_s = 0.24 + 0.45(0.0054) = 0.242 \text{ Btu/lb°F}$$

$$Q = 0.242(100 - 79) = 5.1 \text{ Btu/lb}$$

We can also obtain the heat requirement by reading the change in enthalpy from the chart in Fig. 9.5. Following constant enthalpy lines from the points representing the air at the two temperatures,

$$H_2 = 30.0 \text{ and } H_1 = 25.0$$

$$Q = H_2 - H_1 = 30.0 - 25.0 = 5.0 \text{ Btu/lb}$$

HUMIDITY MEASUREMENT

Inspection of the psychrometric chart shows that knowledge of any two of the four properties, dry bulb temperature, wet bulb temperature, dew point, and relative humidity is sufficient to completely specify the condition of the air. Dry bulb temperature can always easily be measured, and a determination of any one of the remaining three will provide the necessary information.

As discussed above, a wet bulb temperature measurement is quite simple, and this is the most commonly used humidity determining method. In addition to the sling psychrometer, a variety of commercial instruments are available in which an air stream is blown or aspirated past stationary wet and dry bulb thermometers. The disadvantage of the wet bulb method is that it depends on a certain relationship of heat and mass transfer coefficients that can actually vary according to the conditions of measurement. Humidity determinations by the wet bulb method are therefore subject to appreciable error.

There are several types of instruments that respond directly to relative humidity. One of these is the common hair hygrometer, in which the length of a hair depends on the amount of moisture absorbed from the surrounding air. The change in length is transmitted to a pointer through a mechanical linkage. Also in this category are sensing elements containing hygroscopic salts whose electrical resistance depends on moisture content. All instruments in the relative humidity group are secondary instruments in that they must be calibrated against some known standard.

A dew point measurement serves as a simple and reliable primary humidity standard. It is based on an exact thermodynamic principle and does not depend on a somewhat uncertain physical relationship as does the wet bulb temperature. Dew points can easily be measured to within 1°F by observing the temperature at which fog forms on a polished surface.

There are also a variety of analytical instruments that employ some chemical or physical method to give a direct measure of the amount of moisture in an air sample. Such instruments may be capable of high accuracy, but they are, for the most part, considerably more complex and expensive than the simple methods described above.

COOLING BY EVAPORATION

One of the most common applications of psychrometric principles is in cooling by evaporation. In an evaporation cooler, a stream of warm air is contacted with cool water to provide a supply of cool air. In a cooling tower, warm water is cooled by contacting it with a stream of air. Since both of these applications obtain their cooling effect by evaporation, a low air humidity or a large difference between the wet and dry bulb temperatures will lead to more effective performance.

Evaporative Coolers

Evaporative cooling is a widely used and inexpensive method of providing cool air in air conditioning applications. The essential components of an evaporative cooler are a fan for moving the air; a chamber containing some kind of packing where the air contacts the water; and a pump for recirculating the water. In operation, water is pumped from a reservoir at the bottom of the chamber and is either sprayed into the top of the chamber or allowed to run down over the packing. In small coolers, the packing may be simply a pad of excelsior. If open sprays are used, the air stream then flows through the packing, which serves to remove droplets and provide additional contact between air and water. Excess water flows from the bottom of the packing back into the reservoir.

The process taking place in the cooler is a simple adiabatic humidification. The water in the reservoir soon comes to the adiabatic saturation, or wet bulb temperature, and only enough water must be added to make up that lost by evaporation. The time of contact would not ordinary be sufficient for the air to reach equilibrium with the water, and the condition of the air will therefore follow an adiabatic humidification path that stops short of saturation. For example, the actual change in temperature of the air that passes through the cooler might be 80% of the difference between the dry bulb and wet bulb temperatures of the entering air.

Evaporative coolers are obviously most effective in desert areas, where temperatures may be high but humidities are low. They are of little use in humid climates. These coolers will always result in an increase in humidity of the conditioned space. When the ambient humidity is low, this increase will not be objectionable. The temperature in the conditioned space must always be higher than that of the cooled air, and the heat load is removed as sensible heat as the temperature of the cooled air stream increases from the temperature leaving the cooler to the room temperature. Even though air from the cooler is saturated, heating it to room temperature brings it below saturation. If ambient humidities are so high that evaporative cooling is ineffective, cool air must be provided by heat exchange in some kind of refrigeration system. In refrigerated air conditioning, the air will ordinarily be cooled below its initial dew point, and moisture will be condensed. Refrigerated air conditioning thus lowers the humidity of the conditioned space rather than raising it as is the case for evaporative cooling.

Cooling Towers

Most processing plants require substantial quantities of cooling water. Plants located adjacent to natural water supplies such as oceans, lakes, or rivers have commonly used such water for cooling and returned it to the source. In inland waters, at least, this practice is coming under increasing criticism because of the "thermal pollution" or temperature increase of natural water bodies resulting from a large number of processing operations. In areas where there is no immediately accessible natural water supply, it has never been economical to use appreciable quantities for cooling on a once-through basis. It is therefore important to have an economical method to cool water that has been heated in processing operations so that it can be reused.

The typical cooling tower is a vertical rectangular structure filled with packing in the form of wood slats or grids. The most common type is the induced draft tower, which has fans at the top to draw air up through the packing. The warm water to be cooled trickles down over the packing countercurrent to the air flow and collects in a sump at the bottom. The process differs from that of an evaporative cooler in that the water temperature is not constant but decreases continuously from the top to the bottom of the tower. The air is not being adiabatically humidified and its wet bulb temperature does not remain constant.

The calculation of the required height of cooling tower to accomplish a specified lowering of the water temperature is somewhat analogous to the calculation of the area of a counterflow heat exchanger. However, the combination of sensible and latent heat effects and the simultaneous transfer of both mass and heat between the two streams result in a much more complex process, and quantitative treatment is beyond the scope of this text. Even without detailed calculations, it is easy to understand that, given sufficient air rate and tower height, the lower limit of water cooling is the wet bulb temperature of the entering air. In contrast to an evaporative air cooler, a cooling tower can be effective even though the entering air is saturated, as long as the temperature is low enough. As the air rises through the tower, it is warmed by sensible heat transfer and thus increases its moisture holding capacity. Such operation can lead to fog formation and poor performance, however.

Example 8.—An evaporative cooler is to maintain a room temperature of 85°F. Outside air will enter the cooler at 100°F and 20% rh and will achieve 85% of the approach to the wet bulb temperature in the cooler. If the total heat input to the room is 5000 Btu/hr, calculate the volume of outside air that must be passed through the cooler and the relative humidity of the air in the room.

Air entering cooler

$$t_1 = 100°F, rh = 20\%$$

from Fig. 9.5, wet bulb = 69°F, humid volume = 14.3 ft^3/lb

The condition of the air leaving the cooler lies on the wet bulb (or adiabatic humidification) line of the entering air at a temperature that is 85% of the distance from the entering to the wet bulb temperature.

$$t_1 - t_2 = 0.85 \ (t_1 - t^*) = 0.85 \ (100 - 69) = 26.4°F$$

$$t_2 = 100 - 26.4 = 73.6°F$$

from Fig. 9.5, $Y_2 = 0.0142$ lb H_2O/lb dry air

The heat load in the room is absorbed in heating the cool air from 73.6°F to the room temperature of 85°F.

$$q = \dot{m}C_s(85 - 73.6)$$
$$C_s = 0.24 + 0.45Y = 0.24 + 0.45(0.0142) = 0.246 \ \text{Btu/lb°F}$$

$$5000 = \dot{m} \ (0.246)(11.4), \text{therefore} \ \dot{m} = 1780 \ \text{lb/hr}$$

volumetric flow rate = (1780 lb/hr)(14.3 ft^3/lb)(1/60 min/hr)

$$= 424 \ \text{ft}^3/\text{min}$$

The relative humidity of the room air is found from Fig. 9.5 by following a line of constant humidity from the cooler exit condition of 69°F wet bulb and 73.6°F dry bulb to the room temperature of 85°F. This assumes that no moisture is added to the room from any other source.

from Fig. 9.5, rh = 55%

Explanation of Psychrometric Chart

On Fig. 9.5 it will be observed that the temperature grid lines are not parallel but diverge from the bottom to the top. This construction is used so that the wet bulb temperature and constant enthalpy lines will be exactly straight. Wet bulb temperatures are considered to be identical to adiabatic saturation temperatures and are calculated from Eq. 9-11. In order to avoid confusion, constant enthalpy lines are not drawn across the chart but are given by the scales on the two sides. To read an enthalpy, a straightedge is laid across the chart with the ends at the same enthalpy on both sides. A fine line drawn or scratched on a piece of transparent paper or plastic will give more accurate results than a solid straightedge. The constant volume lines on the chart are calculated by a simple application of the perfect gas law.

PROBLEMS

1. Find the state factors listed below for air at 85°F dry bulb and 65°F wet bulb:
   (a) relative humidity
   (b) absolute humidity
   (c) dew point
   (d) humid volume
   (e) enthalpy

2. Atmospheric air has a temperature of 90°F and a dew point of 53°F.
   (a) What is the relative humidity when the air is cooled to 60°F without addition or removal of water vapor?
   (b) How many pounds of water could be removed if 10.0 cubic feet of 90°F air is cooled to 40°F?

3. One pound of dry air contains 0.05 lb of water vapor/lb dry air. The temperature of the mixture is 110°F, the pressure is 14.7 psia. Compute:
   (a) the partial pressure of water vapor
   (b) the absolute humidity if saturated at 110°F
   (c) the relative humidity if the temperature increases to 114°F at constant pressure and humidity.

Verify your calculations by using the psychrometric chart in Fig. 9.5.

4. If moist air is compressed, the partial pressure of water vapor will increase and the dew point is correspondingly higher. If this new dew point is higher than the initial temperature of the air, moisture can be separated by cooling the compressed air back to its original temperature. Expansion back to low pressure will then provide a supply of dried air. It is desired to produce a supply of air with a dew point of 32°F at atmospheric pressure by compressing air at 70°F and 50% relative humidity and cooling the compressed air back to 70°F. To what pressure must the air be compressed? If the dried air comes to a temperature of 70°F after expanding, what will the relative humidity and wet bulb temperature be?

5. A food processor is operating a dehydration plant at a high elevation where the atmospheric pressure is 10 psi abs. On a particular day, the outside air had a wet bulb temperature of 56°F and a dry bulb temperature of 70°F. What was the humidity of the air in lb moisture per lb dry air? The approximation that wet bulb temperature is equal to adiabatic saturation temperature is valid regardless of the atmospheric pressure.

6. Green onions are to be dried from 75% to 15% moisture (wet basis) in an intermediate stage of a continuous belt dehydrator. Hot air entering the dehydrator at 160°F is made up of a mixture of atmospheric air (80°F and 30% rh) and a recycle stream. The total air flow rate in the dehydrator (fresh air plus recycle) is to be 220 pounds of dry air per pound of dry solid. It is desired that the temperature of the air leaving the dehydrator be 15°F higher than its wet bulb temperature. It may be assumed that the wet bulb temperature of the air remains constant throughout the dehydrator. Determine the proportions of fresh air and recycle necessary to give the desired condition of the air leaving.

7. For an experimental study, it is desired to have a supply of air at 90°F and 70% rh. This air is to be provided by blowing atmospheric air through a saturator that is maintained at the proper temperature (not an adiabatic saturator), then heating the saturated air at constant humidity to 90°F. If the atmospheric air is at 80°F and 30% rh, determine:

(a) The temperature at which the saturator should be operated.
(b) The pounds of water evaporated in the saturator per pound of dry air.
(c) Btu per pound of dry air required in the heater.

8. Diced bell peppers with an initial solids content of 10% are to be dried to a final moisture content of 15% (wet basis) in a counterflow continuous belt dehydrator. Atmospheric air at 90°F and 30% relative humidity will be heated to 165°F for the drying operation. It is desired that the relative humidity of the air leaving the dehydrator not exceed 70%. It may be assumed that the adiabatic saturation temperature of the air remains constant throughout the dehydrator.

(a) Calculate the pounds of dry air required per pound of dry solid.
(b) If one ton per hour of wet material is fed to the dehydrator, how many Btu per hour must be supplied to the air heater?

9. One-half ton per hour of diced carrots are to be dehydrated in a parallel flow dehydrator from 85% to 20% moisture content (wet basis). Atmospheric air at 80°F and 60% humidity is heated to 200°F at a rate of 400 lb of dry air per lb of dry matter.

(a) What is the temperature of the air leaving if the wet bulb temperature remains constant?
(b) A practical rule observed in commercial dehydrator operation is that the dry bulb temperature of the air will drop 5°F for each 0.001 increase humidity. Using this rule, what is the temperature of the air leaving the dehydrator?
(c) How many Btu/hr are required to heat the air?
(d) Repeat the problem with the same total air rate (dry basis) made up of 50% fresh air and 50% recirculated air.

SYMBOLS

A	area, ft^2
C_s	humid heat, Btu/(lb)(°F)
H	enthalpy of air water-vapor mixture, Btu/lb
H_a	enthalpy of dry air, Btu/lb
h	surface coefficient of heat transfer, Btu/(hr)(ft^2)(°F)
h_f	enthalpy of saturated water, Btu/lb
h_g	enthalpy of saturated steam, Btu/lb
h_f^*	enthalpy of water at adiabatic saturation temperature, Btu/lb
k	mass transfer coefficient, lb/(hr)(ft^2)
M_a	molecular weight of air = 28.98 lb-moles
M_w	molecular weight of water = 18.02 lb-moles
m_a	mass of air, lb
m_w	mass of water, lb
$\dot{m}_a$	flow rate of air, lb/hr
$\dot{m}_w$	flow rate of water, lb/hr
N	number of pound moles, weight in pounds divided by molecular weight
P	absolute pressure, psia (lb/in.² absolute)
P_a	partial pressure of a, psia
q	heat flux, Btu/hr
R	universal gas constant, 10.73 (ft^3)(lb)/(in^2)(lb-mole)(R°)
rh	relative humidity in percent
T	absolute temperature, °R = °F + 460
t	temperature, °F
t^*	temperature at adiabatic saturation, °F
V	gas volume, ft^3
V_a	partial volume of gas a, ft^3
X_a	mole fraction of gas a
Y	humidity, lb H_2O/lb dry air (also called absolute or specific humidity)
Y^*	humidity at adiabatic saturation, lb H_2O/lb dry air
λ	latent heat of evaporation, Btu/lb
λ^*	latent heat of evaporation at adiabatic temperature, Btu/lb

CHAPTER 10

Refrigeration[1]

INTRODUCTION

Storage of food at low temperatures, either in the frozen or unfrozen state, is one of the oldest methods used to prevent spoilage. In cold climates, the low temperature is available directly from the surroundings. Where such natural cooling is not available, some source of artificial cooling must be provided. Refrigeration can thus be defined as the production and maintenance in a space of a temperature lower than that of the surroundings. Maintenance of the low temperature means that the refrigeration system must be capable of absorbing the quantity of heat that leaks in from the surroundings or arises from a material to be cooled. In conventional practice, this heat is absorbed, either directly or indirectly, as a latent heat of fusion or vaporization of some substance that melts or vaporizes (or sublimes) at low temperature.

In the earlier part of this century, ice was the principal means of refrigeration, and the iceman on his route was a daily sight. Ice is still a convenient means of portable refrigeration, and large quantities of agricultural produce are kept cold with ice while being shipped to market. Solid carbon dioxide (dry ice), which sublimes rather than melts, is used on a limited scale when lower temperatures are required. More recently, liquid nitrogen has come into use as a portable refrigerant.

Applications of the above types are essentially batch operations, and the low temperature is maintained only as long as the supply of refrigerant lasts. Continually renewing the supply is inconvenient and, in large scale applications, costly. What is desired is a machine that will operate continuously with a suitable energy supply to remove heat from refrigerated space.

VAPOR COMPRESSION REFRIGERATION

By far the most common method of refrigeration is the vapor compression system. The applications of this system range from small household and portable refrigerators to large industrial installations. It is the low cost mass production of small refrigeration units that has made possible in this country the widespread use of home refrigerators, freezers, and air conditioners. Vapor compression systems absorb heat as latent heat of vaporization of a liquid that boils at low temperature. Instead of being discarded,

---

[1] The symbols used in this chapter are listed and defined at the end of the chapter.

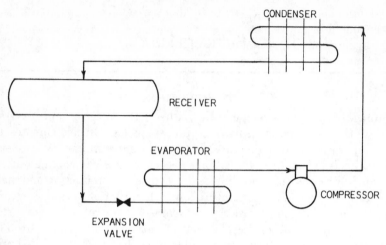

FIG. 10.1. BASIC VAPOR COMPRESSION CYCLE

however, the vapor that forms is recycled by compression and condensation back to a liquid.

Figure 10.1 shows the elements of such a refrigeration cycle. Liquid refrigerant vaporizes at low temperature and pressure in the evaporator in absorbing heat from the space or material to be cooled. Vapor flows from the evaporator to the compressor, where it is compressed to a pressure high enough that it can be condensed with the available cooling water or ambient air. In other words, the temperature of the saturated vapor at the compressor discharge pressure must be at least several degrees higher than the cooling water or ambient air temperature. After condensation, saturated liquid passes to the receiver, which serves both as a storage vessel and as a means of smoothing out any fluctuations in the operation of the cycle. The pressure in the receiver is the same as at the compressor discharge and, since there is vapor space above the liquid, the liquid must be saturated at that pressure. Liquid from the receiver flashes across the expansion valve to the evaporator pressure. The term, flash, refers to the sudden expansion of a vaporizable liquid to a lower pressure. The liquid is now saturated at the pressure and temperature of the evaporator. The heat removed in reducing the liquid temperature between the receiver and the evaporator is absorbed as latent heat of vaporization in the flash operation. Liquid is now back in the evaporator to complete the cycle.

Refrigerants

In principle, any chemically stable substance that can exist as a liquid and vapor in the temperature range of interest can be used as a refrigerant. Other obviously desirable characteristics are that it be low cost, non-toxic, non-flammable, and non-corrosive. The saturation pressure in the condenser should be low so as to simplify mechanical design, but the pressure in the evaporator should not be less than atmospheric. If the evaporator is operated below atmospheric pressure, air can leak into the system and raise the pressure in the condenser. The desired evaporator temperature will thus be an important consideration in selection of a refrigerant.

Although a number of substances have been used in the past as refrigerants, there are only two basic ones in common use today. One is ammonia, and the other is a group of halogen-substituted hydrocarbons, or halocarbons. Ammonia has several advantages, but it is poisonous in high concentrations and has an objectionable odor even in very low concentrations. Since it is virtually impossible to avoid some leakage, the use of ammonia is limited to commercial installations in which the fumes can be tolerated. The halocarbons, which were introduced under the trade name of Freon, are by far the most widely used refrigerants. By varying the substituted halogen atoms, materials covering a wide range of vapor-pressure vs. temperature can be obtained. The two most common are Refrigerant 12 (R-12), dichloro-difluoromethane; and Refrigerant 22 (R-22), monochloro-difluoromethane.

The halocarbons have all the advantages listed above except for low cost. They have the disadvantage of a relatively low latent heat of vaporization. This requires a higher circulation rate in order to handle a given refrigeration duty but does not inherently reduce efficiency. Halocarbons have the important advantage of being compatible with a hermetically sealed system, in which the refrigerant comes into contact with the windings of the motor driving the compressor. All modern domestic refrigerators now use these sealed units.

Thermodynamics of Vapor Compression Cycle

Calculations of heat and work effects in the vapor-compression cycle require a knowledge of the thermodynamic properties of the refrigerant. As discussed in the chapter on Thermodynamic Properties, such compilations are available for all common refrigerants, either in tabular or chart form. A particularly useful graphical representation is the pressure-enthalpy diagram. As shown in Fig. 10.2, pressure (usually on a logarithmic scale) is plotted on the vertical axis and enthalpy on the horizontal axis. The lines for saturated liquid and saturated vapor and the critical point are as indicated. In the two phase region, inside the saturation loop, a constant pressure line is also a constant temperature line. In the subcooled liquid and superheated vapor regions, constant temperature lines are close to vertical. This is merely an expression of the fact that enthalpy depends primarily on temperature and changes very little with changes in pressure.

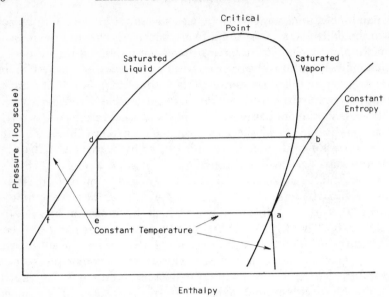

FIG. 10.2. VAPOR COMPRESSION CYCLE ON PRESSURE ENTHALPY DIAGRAM

An important part of the diagram in refrigeration calculations is the constant entropy line in the superheated region. As was pointed out in the Thermodynamic Properties chapter, entropy is a concept of the second law and its discussion is beyond the scope of this text. However, the second law shows that the ideal process of a frictionless, adiabatic compression corresponds to constant entropy. In this application, we are using entropy merely to follow the path of a process and are not concerned with numerical values of entropy. For a perfect gas, a frictionless adiabatic compression (or expansion) is represented by the expression Pv^γ = constant, where γ is the heat capacity ratio c_p/c_v. This expression is derived without reference to entropy or the second law. For our purposes, the constant entropy lines on the charts could just as well be labeled "ideal compression lines." If a table of properties rather than a chart is being used, it will be necessary to refer to the numerical value of entropy to the extent necessary to ascertain that it remains constant.

We will now follow the path of the simple refrigeration cycle described above on the pressure-enthalpy diagram. Saturated vapor at point a leaves the evaporator and is compressed along the constant entropy (or ideal compression) line to point b. The vapor passes into the superheated region on compression, and the temperature at b is well above the saturation temperature at point c at the same pressure. Even though the gas is hot, the amount of heat lost from a compressor is usually small compared to the work, and the assumption of an adiabatic process is reasonable. The temperature at b can be read from the chart. If the vapor were a perfect gas, we could calculate the final temperature using the adiabatic compression formula in the previous paragraph together with the perfect gas law.

In refrigeration calculations, we will make extensive use of the first law of thermodynamics for steady flow systems. Kinetic and potential energy effects are insignificant in the present application, and we can rewrite Eq. 3-11 as

$$Q - W_s = \Delta H \qquad \text{Eq. 10-1}$$

For an adiabatic compression, $Q = 0$, and the work of compression is equal to the change in enthalpy. Since work is done on the system, W_s is a negative quantity. Using a basis of one pound of refrigerant,

$$-W_s = h_b - h_a \qquad \text{Eq. 10-2}$$

The work calculated by Eq. 10-2 is an ideal or frictionless quantity, and we must divide by a compressor efficiency to get the actual work. The efficiency will depend on the type of compressor and must be known from experience. A mechanical efficiency in the range of 75–90% is reasonable for a reciprocating compressor.

The hot gas leaving the compressor at point b is cooled and condensed at constant pressure in the condenser. It should be noted that the step from b to c in the superheat region is not constant temperature. The temperature is, of course, constant in the two phase region from c to d. Referring to Eq. 10-1, we note that there is no shaft work and that the heat transferred is equal to the change in enthalpy.

$$-Q_c = h_b - h_d \qquad \text{Eq. 10-3}$$

Since heat is lost from the system, Q is a negative quantity. The enthalpy difference from b to c represents sensible heat of the superheated vapor, and the difference from c to d is the latent heat of vaporization.

Saturated liquid leaving the receiver at point d is expanded or throttled across the expansion valve to point e. There is no work done in this simple throttling process, and any heat transferred to the valve is negligible. Eq. 10-1 therefore shows that the process from d to e is constant enthalpy, or $h_d = h_e$. Point e lies inside the two phase region, and the fluid leaving the expansion valve is therefore a mixture of liquid and vapor. Enough vapor must form so that the latent heat of vaporization absorbs the heat necessary to cool the fluid from the receiver to the evaporator temperature. The fraction of vapor can be calculated from Eq. 4-2 by using enthalpy in place of volume.

$$x = (h_e - h_f)/(h_a - h_f) \qquad\qquad \text{Eq. 10-4}$$

The evaporation process is represented by the step from e to a. As in the condenser, the heat is equal to the change in enthalpy.

$$Q_e = h_a - h_e \qquad\qquad \text{Eq. 10-5}$$

This enthalpy difference represents the refrigeration effect on the cycle.

Because the vapor entering the compressor and the liquid flowing to the expansion valve are saturated, the simple cycle described above is said to operate under saturated conditions. Many deviations from this simple cycle are encountered in practice. The vapor at a may be superheated before entering the compressor; the compression path ab might not lie along a constant entropy line; the liquid leaving the receiver may be subcooled before entering the expansion valve. Various modifications of the basic cycle can be employed. Discussion of such variations and modifications is beyond the scope of this text. An understanding of the basic cycle described here will provide a basis for those with particular interests in refrigeration to utilize the detailed information presented in specialized references.

Rating of Refrigeration Systems

As a carryover from the past, the capacity of a refrigeration system may be expressed in terms of an equivalent quantity of ice. On this basis, one ton of refrigeration is defined as the capacity equivalent to the consumption of one ton of ice in a 24 hr period. Since ice has a latent heat of fusion of 144 Btu/lb, a ton of refrigeration is equal to 288,000 Btu per day, 12,000 Btu/hr, or 200 Btu/min. A capacity in tons is not a sufficient specification for a refrigeration unit, since the performance will also depend on both the condenser and evaporator temperatures. A more useful specification is the compressor horsepower, which is a measure of the physical size of the equipment.

It is intuitively obvious that a lower evaporator temperature and a higher condenser temperature will place greater demands on the system. Inspection of Fig. 10-2 shows that increasing the distance between the lines bd and ae representing the condenser and evaporator conditions will increase the work required $(h_b - h_a)$ compared to the quantity of refrigeration $(h_a - h_e)$. A measure of this effect is given by the coefficient of performance (CP), which is defined as the ratio of the refrigeration to the work required. In terms of Fig. 10.2,

$$\text{CP} = (h_a - h_e)/(h_b - h_a)$$

Another frequently used expression is horsepower per ton of refrigeration. This quantity is the reciprocal of the CP multiplied by factors to convert

Btu to horsepower and ton units. Since 42.42 Btu/min = 1 horsepower and 200 Btu/min = 1 ton,

$$\text{Hp/ton} = (200/42.42)(1/CP) = 4.71/CP$$

The CP depends on the condenser temperature, the evaporator temperature, and the properties of the refrigerant. As the two temperatures move closer together, the work of compression decreases, and the CP increases. If the temperatures were the same, no work would be required, and the CP would be infinite. This is merely saying that a refrigeration unit is not needed. A steep slope of the constant entropy line reduces the enthalpy difference $h_b - h_a$ and thereby increases the CP. It is in this regard that the properties of the refrigerant are important. For a condenser temperature of 86°F and an evaporator temperature of 5°F, most common refrigerants have values of CP between about 4.6 and 5.0. Accordingly, 1 horsepower will provide about 1 ton of refrigeration because Hp/ton = 4.71/CP.

System Components

This section includes a brief discussion of components of vapor compression systems in order to provide a better basis for understanding the operating principles. No attempt is made to give details of the wide variety of types and arrangements of equipment that are in use.

Compressor.—Any standard type of compressor can be used, and refrigeration compressors are basically no different from those used for other purposes. By far the most common type is the reciprocating compressor. Rotary and centrifugal compressors may be used in applications where their characteristics have particular advantages.

Condenser and evaporator.—These components are simply heat exchangers that operate with substantially a constant temperature on the refrigerant side. Condensers may be either air or water cooled. Air cooled condensers are provided with fins on the outside of the tubes and, except for some household refrigerators, are equipped with fans for air movement. Evaporators may take a variety of forms. For cooling air, they are similar to air-cooled condensers, with the refrigerant flowing inside finned tubes. For cooling liquids, some kind of tubular exchanger is used with the refrigerant either inside or outside the tubes. With refrigerant inside the tubes, whether liquid or gas is being cooled, liquid refrigerant may enter one end of the tubes directly from the expansion valve and refrigerant vapor pass directly from the other end to the compressor. Alternatively, in a flooded system, the tubes are connected to a reservoir in which a level of liquid refrigerant is maintained at the evaporator pressure. The liquid line from the expansion valve and the vapor line to the compressor are connected to the reservoir rather than directly to the tubes. In another arrangement, a tube bundle can be immersed in a pool of refrigerant held in

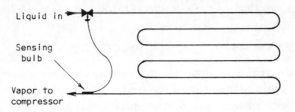

(a)   Evaporator coil with thermostatic expansion valve.

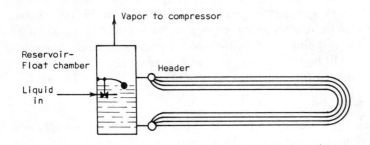

(b)   Flooded evaporator with refrigerant in tubes.

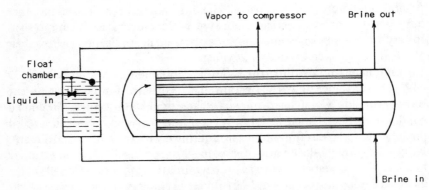

(c)   Shell-and-tube brine chiller with refrigerant in shell

FIG. 10.3. TYPICAL EVAPORATOR ARRANGEMENTS

an outer shell. Refrigerant boiling outside the tubes will then cool a liquid that flows through the tubes. Fig. 10.3 shows some evaporator arrangements.

Controls.—There are basically two variables to be controlled in a refrigeration system: the quantity of heat removed and the temperature. The former is controlled by the refrigerant flow rate and the latter by the compressor operation. The expansion valve controls the flow of refrigerant to the evaporator. In a flooded system, the expansion valve will be some kind of float valve that acts to maintain a constant liquid level in the reservoir. In non-flooded systems, in which the evaporator does not include a liquid reservoir, thermostatic expansion valves are customarily used. The opening of such a valve is controlled by the action of a temperature sensing bulb attached to the vapor line leaving the evaporator. This bulb is usually filled with the liquid refrigerant used in the system and is connected by a small-diameter tube to the closed side of a diaphragm that operates the valve stem. If the temperature in the vapor line rises, indicating that more refrigerant is needed, the vapor pressure of the liquid in the bulb increases and acts against the diaphragm to increase the valve opening. A drop in the vapor line temperature has the opposite effect. These valves are usually set to maintain a few degrees of superheat in the vapor going to the compressor so as to insure that no liquid will be carried over.

In small systems such as household refrigerators, a fixed length of capillary tube is commonly used in place of an expansion valve. This is a simple and low cost arrangement, but it lacks flexibility to operate efficiently over a wide range of loads and it requires careful matching of the system components.

The temperature level of refrigeration is basically controlled by the volumetric capacity of the compressor to handle vapor from the evaporator. The compressor must be sized to meet the maximum requirement. If the load is reduced, a controller acts to limit the compressor capacity correspondingly. In effect, the compressor maintains the desired low temperature by pumping away vapor as it is formed. The expansion valve matches the load by admitting liquid at the necessary rate.

The most common method of temperature control is to start and stop the compressor according to the system requirements. Usually a temperature sensing element in the refrigerated space activates the switch of the motor driving the compressor. An alternative method is to activate the motor switch by the evaporator pressure. In either case, there is a set range for temperature or pressure, above which the compressor is stopped and below which it is started. In larger systems, it is generally undesirable to start and stop the entire compressor capacity in this manner. In a system of more than one compressor, the control function can be handled by one compressor, while the others operate continuously. With multi-cylinder compressors, provision can be made for the control device to take individual cylinders out of operation by holding their suction valves open. Other means of control are to by-pass gas from the compressor discharge back to the suction or to vary the compressor speed. With centrifugal compressors, a throttling valve on the suction line is sometimes used for evaporator pressure control.

ABSORPTION REFRIGERATION

A major part of the expense of a vapor compression system, for equipment, operation, and maintenance, is associated with the compressors. Equation 3-10 shows that the work of compression in a steady flow process is proportional to the volume of fluid handled. Because of the high volume of vapor as compared with liquid, pumping a liquid is much simpler and less expensive operation than compressing a vapor. In the absorption refrigeration system, the refrigerant is moved from the evaporator pressure to the condenser pressure by a liquid pump in place of a vapor compressor.

Absorption refrigeration accomplishes the above result by absorbing the refrigerant vapor from the evaporator in some suitable liquid carrier, pumping this liquid stream to the condenser pressure, and using heat to evaporate or distill the refrigerant from the carrier at the elevated pressure. The vapor released from the carrier then passes to the condenser, and the rest of the system is similar to vapor compression. A variety of combinations of refrigerant and absorbing liquid are possible. The most common is the system of ammonia as the refrigerant and water as the carrier. The only other system in common practice uses water as the refrigerant and a concentrated solution of lithium bromide in water as the carrier. Water has two disadvantages as a refrigerant: (1) it cannot be used at temperatures below 32°F and (2) the very low evaporator pressure increases the problem of air leaks into the system and requires very large diameter vapor piping. The lithium bromide system is used in air conditioning applications where the odor of escaping ammonia vapor could create a problem.

Although pumping costs are small compared to vapor compression costs, absorption refrigeration requires substantial pieces of process equipment both to absorb the vapor at low pressure and to regenerate it from the carrier at high pressure. The absorption step releases the heat of condensation of the vapor plus any heat of solution, and this heat must be removed by air or cooling water in a suitable heat exchange arrangement. In the regeneration step, heat must be supplied to vaporize the refrigerant from the carrier. With the ammonia-water system, a distillation column is needed in addition in order to remove water vapor from the ammonia. Because of these demands for heating and cooling and the associated equipment costs, absorption refrigeration is economical on an industrial scale only where there is a supply of essentially free waste heat.

The Servel Electrolux household refrigerator is an ammonia-water absorption system that uses a unique arrangement to eliminate the liquid pump. An atmosphere of hydrogen gas is maintained in the vapor space in the evaporator, at a sufficient pressure that the total pressures in the evaporator and condenser are essentially the same. Ammonia vapor readily dissolves in the absorber, but the hydrogen is insoluble in water and remains behind. A liquid seal prevents hydrogen from getting into the condenser, where the ammonia must be at the total pressure in order to condense. Liquid circulation between the absorber and regenerator is accomplished by gravity, with the assistance of a vapor lift from the ammonia vapor released in the regenerator. The absorber and condenser have fins on the outer surfaces, and heat is removed by natural circulation of air. The only outside energy required is a source of heat at the regenerator. Since this system has no moving parts, there is nothing to wear out, and it is the only household system available in areas where there is no electricity for operation of mechanical refrigerators. The development of low cost and dependable mechanical refrigeration systems has made the Servel system economically non-competitive in areas where there is electric power. The Servel would be even less competitive in larger sizes, and any industrial operation would always have electric power available.

THERMOELECTRIC COOLING

Thermoelectric cooling takes advantage of the principle by which thermocouples are used to measure temperature. A thermocouple consists essentially of two wire strands of dissimilar metals that are soldered or welded together at the ends. If the two junctions are held at different temperatures, an electromotive force will arise that will cause a current to flow continuously through the wire loop. If one of the wires is cut and the cut ends connected to the terminals of a potentiometer, no current will flow and the potential difference between the junctions can be measured. This potential difference varies directly with the temperature difference between the junctions and thus gives a basis for temperature measurement.

If we connect the cut ends of the same wire loop to a source of direct current, the resulting current flow causes heat to be absorbed at one junction and released at the other. The wire couple can thus be used as a refrigerating device by placing the heat absorbing end in the space to be cooled and by using air or water cooling to remove the heat released at the other end. Developments in semiconductors in recent years have provided materials that give a much greater thermal effect than ordinary thermocouple wires, and thermoelectric cooling devices are now practical. They have the advantage of no moving parts and, since they do not depend on any gravity flow of fluids, will operate in any position. They are thus ideally suited for use aboard aircraft or space vehicles. They are expensive, however, and have a lower efficiency than conventional refrigeration systems, so their use is limited to specialized applications. They are commercially available as coolers for constant temperature laboratory baths, and small portable refrigerators have been manufactured.

VACUUM COOLING

In vapor compression refrigeration, the warm liquid from the receiver flashes through the expansion valve and drops in temperature to a value in equilibrium with the evaporator pressure. Any vaporizable liquid can be cooled in this manner, by allowing it to flash or spray into a space where the pressure is held at a low enough value to be in equilibrium with the desired temperature. For continuous operation, the low pressure must be maintained by removing the vapor formed in the flash operation. Flash cooling has its widest application to water or water-containing materials. Hot water under pressure at a temperature above the normal boiling point can be cooled to 212°F by allowing it to flash to atmospheric pressure. In this case, the vapor formed will merely escape to the atmosphere.

In order to cool water below 212°F by this process, it is necessary to maintain a vacuum. The vapor formed must be removed from the vacuum space by compressing it to atmospheric pressure. Water can easily be cooled to the freezing point in this manner. The cost of the cooling process is essentially that of compressing the vapor. Because of the low absolute pressures involved, the volume of vapor to be compressed will be high. If an ample supply of steam is available, steam ejectors will usually be the preferred method for compressing the vapor. Where steam is not available, the compression can be accomplished with centrifugal compressors. With steam ejectors, particularly, it is not practicable to recover the vapor. Any volatiles from food materials that escape with the water vapor will thus be lost.

Many times, the available cooling water will not be at a low enough temperature for some processing requirement, and the vacuum cooling process may be the most effective means of obtaining the desired low temperature. In essence, all that is needed is a vacuum tank and an ejector or compressor for handling the vapor. There must, of course, be a pump to remove the water from the tank and provide sufficient pressure to circulate it through the processing plant.

Vacuum or flash cooling can be applied to aqueous food liquids as well as to water. Sanitation considerations are of particular importance in such applications because of the possibility of microorganisms entering through any leaks in the reduced pressure region. Vacuum cooling has also been successfully applied to solid foods, particularly in cooling of lettuce from the field. Up to two freight car loads of lettuce in cartons are placed in a chamber which is then evacuated either by steam ejectors or centrifugal compressors. A period of about 20 to 30 minutes is required to evaporate enough water to reduce the temperature essentially to 32°F. This process is suitable only for leafy or porous produce that will permit the water vapor to escape readily. Vacuum cooling has been used on a smaller scale with spinach, celery, cauliflower, and sweet corn.

DIRECT CONTACT WITH LIQUID REFRIGERANT

In the usual refrigeration cycle, the refrigerant operates in a closed system, and cooling is effected across some kind of heat exchange surface. Much greater rates of heat transfer can be obtained by direct contact of refrigerant with the material to be cooled. Direct contact by cold water or ice is, of course, a standard method of cooling solid materials. This same principle can be extended to use of vaporizable liquid refrigerants.

The process is simplest if the refrigerant does not have to be recovered. With the use of solid CO_2, for example, the CO_2 vapor formed merely escapes to the atmosphere. In a continuous cooling or freezing process for solid food products, however, we would prefer a refrigerant that is liquid at atmospheric pressure for ease in handling and for making effective contact with the product. The refrigerant obviously must be a substance that is approved for food use and that would have no undesirable effects on product quality. Ammonia and sulfur dioxide are thus immediately eliminated.

One appropriate refrigerant in common use today is liquid nitrogen. In recent years, the basic oxygen process has come into wide use in steel making. The large quantities of nitrogen available as a by-product from oxygen production have led to the development of commercial processes and equipment for freezing of foods with liquid nitrogen. In essence, liquid nitrogen is simply sprayed over the food on a moving belt, and the nitrogen gas passes to the atmosphere. The very low temperature of liquid nitrogen at atmospheric pressure ($-321°F$) creates some problems. In order to use the nitrogen efficiently, sensible heat must be recovered from the gas before it is allowed to escape to the atmosphere. This is accomplished by allowing the gas to pass along a tunnel countercurrent to the entering food conveyor. Because of the poor heat transfer coefficients with low velocity gas streams, the tunnel must be of appreciable length and adds to the cost of the installation. Furthermore, the very low temperature is a disadvantage rather than an advantage in the main section where the liquid spray contacts the food. As pointed out in the discussion of boiling in the heat transfer chapter, too large a temperature difference actually reduces the rate of heat transfer. The liquid droplets become surrounded by a film of vapor that insulates them from the warmer surface. Liquid nitrogen spray on the food acts in much the same way as water droplets on a hot stove. It would be wasteful, of course, to bring the food completely down to the liquid nitrogen temperature. When the food leaves the freezer, there is a substantial temperature gradient from the surface into the center. It is allowed to remain in the freezer only for the time required to bring the average temperature down to the desired value.

Liquid nitrogen can be used effectively in transport of frozen food. Here, the problem is simply that of maintaining a low temperature rather than

TABLE 10.1

THERMODYNAMIC PROPERTIES OF SATURATED REFRIGERANT-12

Temp (°F)	Press (psia)	Volume (cu ft/lb) Liquid v_f	Vapor v_g	Enthalpy (Btu/lb) Liquid h_f	Vapor h_g	Entropy (Btu/lb·°R) Liquid s_f	Vapor s_g
-40	9.31	0.01056	3.875	0.00	72.91	0.0000	0.1737
-38	9.80	0.01059	3.692	0.42	73.13	0.0010	0.1734
-36	10.32	0.01067	3.520	0.84	73.35	0.0020	0.1731
-34	10.86	0.01063	3.357	1.27	73.58	0.0030	0.1729
-32	11.42	0.01065	3.204	1.69	73.80	0.0040	0.1726
-30	12.00	0.01067	3.059	2.11	74.02	0.0050	0.1723
-28	12.60	0.01070	2.921	2.54	74.23	0.0059	0.1720
-26	13.23	0.01072	2.792	2.96	74.45	0.0069	0.1718
-24	13.89	0.01074	2.669	3.38	74.67	0.0079	0.1715
-22	14.56	0.01076	2.553	3.81	74.89	0.0089	0.1713
-20	15.27	0.01079	2.443	4.24	75.11	0.0098	0.1710
-18	16.00	0.01081	2.339	4.66	75.33	0.0108	0.1708
-16	16.75	0.01083	2.240	5.09	75.55	0.0118	0.1706
-14	17.54	0.01086	2.146	5.52	75.76	0.0127	0.1703
-12	18.35	0.01088	2.057	5.94	75.98	0.0137	0.1701
-10	19.19	0.01091	1.973	6.37	76.20	0.0146	0.1699
-8	20.06	0.01093	1.892	6.80	76.41	0.0156	0.1697
-6	20.96	0.01096	1.816	7.23	76.63	0.0165	0.1695
-4	21.89	0.01098	1.744	7.66	76.84	0.0174	0.1693
-2	22.85	0.01101	1.675	8.09	77.06	0.0184	0.1691
0	23.85	0.01103	1.609	8.52	77.27	0.0193	0.1689

Temp (°F)	Press (psia)	Volume (cu ft/lb) Liquid v_f	Vapor v_g	Enthalpy (Btu/lb) Liquid h_f	Vapor h_g	Entropy (Btu/lb·°R) Liquid s_f	Vapor s_g
60	72.73	0.01191	0.5584	21.77	83.41	0.0462	0.1648
62	74.81	0.01195	0.5411	22.22	83.60	0.0470	0.1647
64	77.24	0.01198	0.5245	22.68	83.79	0.0479	0.1646
66	79.73	0.01202	0.5085	23.13	83.98	0.0488	0.1645
68	82.28	0.01205	0.4931	23.59	84.17	0.0496	0.1644
70	84.89	0.01209	0.4782	24.05	84.36	0.0505	0.1643
72	87.56	0.01213	0.4638	24.51	84.55	0.0513	0.1643
74	90.29	0.01216	0.4500	24.97	84.73	0.0522	0.1642
76	93.09	0.01220	0.4367	25.44	84.92	0.0530	0.1641
78	95.95	0.01224	0.4238	25.90	85.10	0.0539	0.1640
80	98.87	0.01228	0.4114	26.37	85.28	0.0548	0.1639
82	101.86	0.01232	0.3994	26.83	85.46	0.0556	0.1638
84	104.92	0.01236	0.3878	27.30	85.64	0.0565	0.1638
86	108.04	0.01240	0.3766	27.77	85.82	0.0573	0.1637
88	111.23	0.01244	0.3658	28.24	86.00	0.0581	0.1636
90	114.49	0.01248	0.3553	28.71	86.17	0.0590	0.1635
92	117.82	0.01252	0.3452	29.19	86.35	0.0598	0.1635
94	121.22	0.01256	0.3354	29.66	86.52	0.0607	0.1634
96	124.70	0.01261	0.3259	30.14	86.69	0.0615	0.1633
98	128.24	0.01265	0.3168	30.62	86.86	0.0624	0.1632
100	131.86	0.01269	0.3079	31.10	87.03	0.0632	0.1631

2	24.88	0.01106	1.546	8.95	77.49	0.0203	0.1687
4	25.94	0.01108	1.487	9.38	77.70	0.0212	0.1685
6	27.04	0.01111	1.430	9.82	77.91	0.0221	0.1683
8	28.17	0.01113	1.376	10.25	78.12	0.0230	0.1682
10	29.34	0.01116	1.324	10.68	78.34	0.0240	0.1680
12	30.54	0.01119	1.275	11.12	78.55	0.0249	0.1678
14	31.78	0.01121	1.228	11.55	78.76	0.0258	0.1677
16	33.06	0.01124	1.183	11.99	78.97	0.0267	0.1675
18	34.38	0.01127	1.140	12.43	79.18	0.0276	0.1673
20	35.74	0.01130	1.099	12.86	79.39	0.0285	0.1672
22	37.14	0.01132	1.060	13.30	79.59	0.0294	0.1670
24	38.57	0.01135	1.022	13.74	79.80	0.0303	0.1669
26	40.06	0.01138	0.986	14.18	80.01	0.0312	0.1668
28	41.58	0.01141	0.952	14.62	80.21	0.0321	0.1666
30	43.15	0.01144	0.919	15.06	80.42	0.0330	0.1665
32	44.76	0.01147	0.887	15.50	80.62	0.0339	0.1664
34	46.42	0.01150	0.857	15.94	80.83	0.0348	0.1662
36	48.12	0.01153	0.828	16.38	81.03	0.0357	0.1661
38	49.87	0.01156	0.800	16.83	81.23	0.0366	0.1660
40	51.67	0.01159	0.774	17.27	81.44	0.0375	0.1659
42	53.51	0.01162	0.748	17.72	81.64	0.0383	0.1657
44	55.41	0.01165	0.723	18.16	81.84	0.0392	0.1656
46	57.35	0.01168	0.700	18.61	82.04	0.0401	0.1655
48	59.35	0.01171	0.677	19.06	82.24	0.0410	0.1654
50	61.39	0.01175	0.655	19.51	82.44	0.0418	0.1653
52	63.49	0.01178	0.634	19.96	82.63	0.0427	0.1652
54	65.65	0.01181	0.614	20.41	82.83	0.0436	0.1651
56	67.85	0.01185	0.595	20.86	83.02	0.0444	0.1650
58	70.12	0.01188	0.576	21.31	83.22	0.0453	0.1649

102	135.56	0.01274	0.2994	31.58	87.20	0.0641	0.1631
104	139.33	0.01278	0.2911	32.07	87.36	0.0649	0.1630
106	143.18	0.01283	0.2830	32.55	87.52	0.0658	0.1629
108	147.11	0.01288	0.2752	33.04	87.68	0.0666	0.1629
110	151.11	0.01292	0.2677	33.53	87.84	0.0675	0.1628
112	155.19	0.01297	0.2604	34.02	88.00	0.0683	0.1627
114	159.36	0.01302	0.2533	34.52	88.16	0.0691	0.1626
116	163.61	0.01307	0.2464	35.01	88.31	0.0700	0.1626
118	167.94	0.01312	0.2397	35.51	88.46	0.0708	0.1625
120	172.35	0.01317	0.2333	36.01	88.61	0.0717	0.1624
122	176.85	0.01323	0.2270	36.52	88.76	0.0725	0.1623
124	181.43	0.01328	0.2209	37.02	88.90	0.0734	0.1623
126	186.10	0.01334	0.2150	37.53	89.04	0.0742	0.1622
128	190.86	0.01339	0.2092	38.04	89.18	0.0751	0.1621
130	195.71	0.01345	0.2036	38.55	89.32	0.0759	0.1620
132	200.64	0.01350	0.1982	39.07	89.46	0.0768	0.1619
134	205.67	0.01356	0.1929	39.59	89.59	0.0776	0.1619
136	210.79	0.01362	0.1878	40.11	89.72	0.0785	0.1618
138	216.01	0.01368	0.1828	40.63	89.84	0.0793	0.1617
140	221.32	0.01375	0.1780	41.16	89.97	0.0802	0.1616
142	226.72	0.01381	0.1733	41.69	90.09	0.0811	0.1615
144	232.22	0.01387	0.1687	42.23	90.20	0.0819	0.1614
146	237.82	0.01394	0.1642	42.77	90.32	0.0828	0.1613
148	243.51	0.01401	0.1599	43.31	90.43	0.0837	0.1612
150	249.31	0.01408	0.1556	43.85	90.53	0.0845	0.1611
152	255.20	0.01415	0.1515	44.40	90.64	0.0854	0.1610
154	261.20	0.01422	0.1475	44.95	90.74	0.0863	0.1609
156	267.30	0.01430	0.1436	45.51	90.83	0.0872	0.1608
158	273.51	0.01437	0.1398	46.07	90.92	0.0880	0.1607

Source: E. I. DuPont Nemours & Co.

freezing the food. Liquid nitrogen in an insulated truck or freight car vaporizes as needed into an air stream that is distributed throughout the car by fans. The expense and space requirements of a mechanical refrigeration system are thus eliminated.

More recently, direct contact systems have been developed for use of halo-carbon refrigerants. The refrigerant contacts the food directly and evaporates at atmospheric pressure. Because of the high cost of the refrigerant, vapors are not permitted to escape but are condensed on the evaporator of a conventional vapor-compression system. Refrigerant 12, which has been approved in the United States for food use in this system, has an atmospheric boiling point of $-21.6°F$ and thus avoids the disadvantages of the extremely low temperature of liquid nitrogen. The physical size of the equipment is much less because of higher heat transfer coefficients and because the long section for recovering sensible heat from the vapor is not required. There is a small loss of refrigerant, but the overall cost of the process is reported to be substantially less than that of the liquid nitrogen process.

Example 1

A controlled temperature storage room is maintained at $20°F$ by an R-12 refrigeration unit with evaporator and condenser temperatures of $10°F$ and $90°F$, respectively. The refrigeration load is 25 tons, and the unit operates under saturated conditions.

(a) Calculate the refrigerant circulation rate, the CP, and the compressor horsepower. Assume a compressor efficiency of 85%.

(b) If cooling water enters the condenser at $75°F$ and leaves at $85°F$, what is the water circulation rate?

Calculations of the refrigeration cycle will be made with reference to Fig. 10.2. From Table 10.1 and Fig. 10.4 for R-12,

Evaporator pressure = 29.34 psia ($10°F$)

Condenser pressure = 114.5 psia ($90°F$)

$h_a = 78.34$ Btu/lb, $h_b = 88.70$ Btu/lb, $h_c = 86.17$ Btu/lb, $h_d = h_e = 28.71$ Btu/lb

For 25 tons of refrigeration,

$q = \dot{m}_r Q_e = 25(200) = 5000$ Btu/min $= \dot{m}_r(h_a - h_e) = 49.6 \dot{m}_r$

$\dot{m}_r = 5000/49.5 = 101$ lb/min refrigerant flow rate

Power requirement

$CP = Q_e/W_s = (h_a - h_e)/(h_b - h_a) = 49.6/10.4 = 4.8$

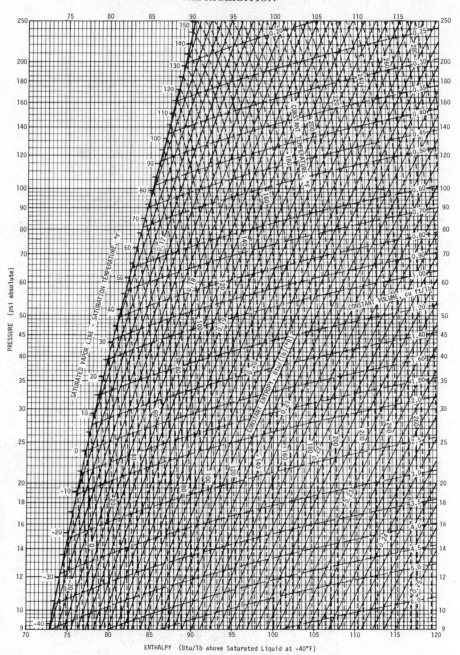

FIG. 10.4. PRESSURE-ENTHALPY DIAGRAM FOR REFRIGERANT-12

TABLE 10.2

THERMODYNAMIC PROPERTIES OF SATURATED AMMONIA

Temp (°F)	Press (psia)	Volume (cu ft/lb) Liquid v_f	Volume (cu ft/lb) Vapor v_g	Enthalpy (Btu/lb) Liquid h_f	Enthalpy (Btu/lb) Vapor h_g	Entropy (Btu/lb°R) Liquid s_f	Entropy (Btu/lb°R) Vapor s_g
−40	10.41	0.02322	24.86	0.0	597.6	0.0000	1.4242
−38	11.04	0.02327	23.53	2.1	598.3	0.0051	1.4193
−36	11.71	0.02331	22.27	4.3	599.1	0.0101	1.4144
−34	12.41	0.02336	21.10	6.4	599.9	0.0151	1.4096
−32	13.14	0.02340	20.00	8.5	600.6	0.0201	1.4048
−30	13.90	0.02345	18.97	10.7	601.4	0.0250	1.4001
−28	14.71	0.02349	18.00	12.8	602.1	0.0300	1.3955
−26	15.55	0.02354	17.09	14.9	602.8	0.0350	1.3909
−24	16.42	0.02359	16.24	17.1	603.6	0.0399	1.3863
−22	17.34	0.02364	15.43	19.2	604.3	0.0448	1.3818
−20	18.30	0.02369	14.68	21.4	605.0	0.0497	1.3774
−18	19.30	0.02373	13.97	23.5	605.7	0.0545	1.3729
−16	20.34	0.02378	13.29	25.6	606.4	0.0594	1.3686
−14	21.43	0.02383	12.66	27.8	607.1	0.0642	1.3643
−12	22.56	0.02388	12.06	30.0	607.8	0.0690	1.3600
−10	23.74	0.02393	11.50	32.1	608.5	0.0738	1.3558
−8	24.97	0.02398	10.97	34.3	609.2	0.0786	1.3516
−6	26.26	0.02403	10.47	36.4	609.8	0.0833	1.3474

Temp (°F)	Press (psia)	Volume (cu ft/lb) Liquid v_f	Volume (cu ft/lb) Vapor v_g	Enthalpy (Btu/lb) Liquid h_f	Enthalpy (Btu/lb) Vapor h_g	Entropy (Btu/lb°R) Liquid s_f	Entropy (Btu/lb°R) Vapor s_g
40	73.32	0.02533	3.971	86.8	623.0	0.1885	1.2618
42	76.31	0.02539	3.823	89.0	623.4	0.1930	1.2585
44	79.38	0.02545	3.682	91.2	623.9	0.1974	1.2552
46	82.55	0.02551	3.547	93.5	624.4	0.2018	1.2519
48	85.82	0.02557	3.418	95.7	624.8	0.2062	1.2486
50	89.19	0.02564	3.294	97.9	625.2	0.2105	1.2453
52	92.66	0.02571	3.176	100.2	625.7	0.2149	1.2421
54	96.23	0.02577	3.063	102.4	626.1	0.2192	1.2389
56	99.91	0.02584	2.954	104.7	626.5	0.2236	1.2357
58	103.7	0.02590	2.851	106.9	626.9	0.2279	1.2325
60	107.6	0.02597	2.751	109.2	627.3	0.2322	1.2294
62	111.6	0.02604	2.656	111.5	627.7	0.2365	1.2262
64	115.7	0.02611	2.565	113.7	628.0	0.2408	1.2231
66	120.0	0.02618	2.477	116.0	628.4	0.2451	1.2201
68	124.3	0.02625	2.393	118.3	628.8	0.2494	1.2170
70	128.8	0.02632	2.312	120.5	629.1	0.2537	1.2140
72	133.4	0.02639	2.235	122.8	629.4	0.2579	1.2110
74	138.1	0.02646	2.161	125.1	629.8	0.2622	1.2080

−4	27.59	0.02408	9.991	38.6	610.5	0.0880	1.3433
−2	28.98	0.02413	9.541	40.7	611.1	0.0928	1.3393
0	30.42	0.02419	9.116	42.9	611.8	0.0975	1.3352
2	31.92	0.02424	8.714	45.1	612.4	0.1022	1.3312
4	33.47	0.02430	8.333	47.2	613.0	0.1069	1.3273
6	35.09	0.02435	7.971	49.4	613.6	0.1115	1.3234
8	36.77	0.02441	7.629	51.6	614.3	0.1162	1.3195
10	38.51	0.02446	7.304	53.8	614.9	0.1208	1.3157
12	40.31	0.02452	6.996	56.0	615.5	0.1254	1.3118
14	42.18	0.02457	6.703	58.2	616.1	0.1300	1.3081
16	44.12	0.02463	6.425	60.3	616.6	0.1346	1.3043
18	46.13	0.02468	6.161	62.5	617.2	0.1392	1.3006
20	48.21	0.02474	5.910	64.7	617.8	0.1437	1.2969
22	50.36	0.02479	5.671	66.9	618.3	0.1483	1.2933
24	52.59	0.02485	5.443	69.1	618.9	0.1528	1.2897
26	54.90	0.02491	5.227	71.3	619.4	0.1573	1.2861
28	57.28	0.02497	5.021	73.5	619.9	0.1618	1.2825
30	59.74	0.02503	4.825	75.7	620.5	0.1663	1.2790
32	62.29	0.02509	4.637	77.9	621.0	0.1708	1.2755
34	64.91	0.02515	4.459	80.1	621.5	0.1753	1.2721
36	67.63	0.02521	4.289	82.3	622.0	0.1797	1.2686
38	70.43	0.02527	4.126	84.6	622.5	0.1841	1.2652

76	143.0	0.02653	2.089	127.4	630.1	0.2664	1.2050
78	147.9	0.02660	2.021	129.7	630.4	0.2706	1.2020
80	153.0	0.02668	1.955	132.0	630.7	0.2749	1.1991
82	158.3	0.02675	1.892	134.3	631.0	0.2791	1.1962
84	163.7	0.02683	1.831	136.6	631.3	0.2833	1.1933
86	169.2	0.02691	1.772	138.9	631.5	0.2875	1.1904
88	174.8	0.02699	1.716	141.2	631.8	0.2917	1.1875
90	180.6	0.02707	1.661	143.5	632.0	0.2958	1.1846
92	186.6	0.02715	1.609	145.8	632.2	0.3000	1.1818
94	192.7	0.02723	1.559	148.2	632.5	0.3041	1.1789
96	198.9	0.02731	1.510	150.5	632.7	0.3083	1.1761
98	205.3	0.02739	1.464	152.9	632.9	0.3125	1.1733
100	211.9	0.02747	1.419	155.2	633.0	0.3166	1.1705
102	218.6	0.02455	1.375	157.6	633.2	0.3207	1.1677
104	225.4	0.02463	1.334	159.9	633.4	0.3248	1.1649
106	232.5	0.02472	1.293	162.3	633.5	0.3289	1.1621
108	239.7	0.02481	1.254	164.6	633.6	0.3330	1.1593
110	247.0	0.02490	1.217	167.0	633.7	0.3372	1.1566
112	254.5	0.02499	1.180	169.4	633.8	0.3413	1.1538
114	262.2	0.02508	1.145	171.8	633.9	0.3453	1.1510
116	270.1	0.02517	1.112	174.2	634.0	0.3495	1.1483
118	278.2	0.02526	1.079	176.6	634.0	0.3535	1.1455
120	286.4	0.02536	1.047	179.0	634.0	0.3576	1.1427
122	294.8	0.02545	1.017	181.4	634.0	0.3618	1.1400
124	303.4	0.02555	0.987	183.9	634.0	0.3659	1.1372

Source: U.S. Bureau of Standards Circular *142*.

Hp/ton = 4.71/CP = 4.71/4.8 = 0.982

Theoretical power = 0.982(25) = 24.5 hp

Actual power = theor. power/eff. = 24.5/0.85 = 28.8 hp

Condenser duty

$q = \dot{m}_r Q_c = \dot{m}_r(h_b - h_d) = 100.8(60.0) = 6048$ Btu/min

$= \dot{m}_w(1.0)(85 - 75)$

$\dot{m}_w = 6048/10 = 605$ lb/min water flow rate

Example 2

An ammonia refrigeration system is to be used to cool brine to 0°F. Cooling water is available at 60°F. The evaporator and condenser will operate on a 10°F temperature differential (evaporator temperature 10° below cold brine temperature and condensed refrigerant 10° above entering cooling water). The compressor is driven by a 5 hp motor. If the motor is not to be operated above rated load, what is the maximum cooling capacity in tons and the corresponding refrigerant circulation rate? Assume a compressor efficiency of 85% and saturated conditions for the refrigerant leaving the condenser and evaporator.

Referring to Fig. 10.2 and using Table 10.2 and Fig. 10.5 for ammonia

$h_a = 608.5$ Btu/lb (−10°F saturation temp., 23.7 psia)

$h_b = 718.6$ Btu/lb (70°F saturation temp., 128.8 psia)

$h_d = h_e = 120.5$ Btu/lb

Compressor performance

Power delivered = 5(0.85) = 4.25 hp

= 4.25(42.4) = 180.2 Btu/min

Power used $= \dot{m}_r W_s = \dot{m}_r(h_b - h_a) = 105.1 \, \dot{m}_r$

$\dot{m}_r = 180.2/105.1 = 1.715$ lb/min

Cooling capacity

$Q_e = h_a - h_e = 488$ Btu/lb

$q = \dot{m}_r Q_e = 1.715(488) = 836.9$ Btu/min

= 836.9/200 = 4.18 tons

PROBLEMS

1. An R-12 refrigeration system operating under saturated conditions, with a condenser temperature of 80°F and an evaporator temperature of

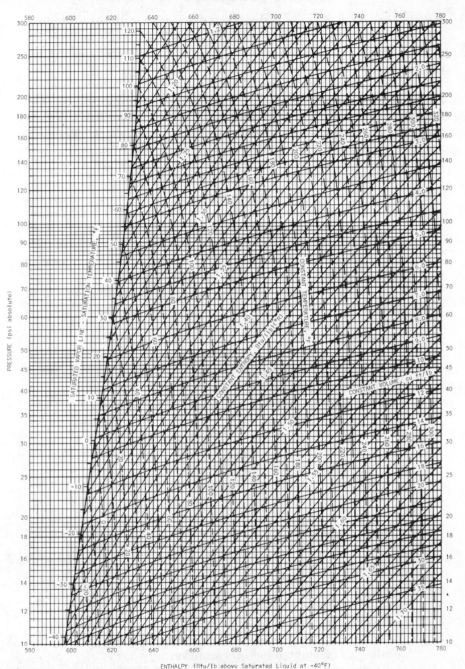

ENTHALPY (Btu/lb above Saturated Liquid at -40°F)

FIG. 10.5. PRESSURE-ENTHALPY DIAGRAM FOR AMMONIA.
BASED ON U.S. BUREAU OF STANDARDS CIRCULAR 142

−10°F, has a 5 ton capacity limited by the compressor. In the winter, the cooling water temperature is lower and the condenser can be operated at 65°F. Estimate the capacity and coefficient of performance under these conditions.

2. An ammonia refrigeration system is operated with two evaporators, having evaporating temperatures of −20°F and 25°F, respectively. The condenser temperature is 80°F and saturated conditions exist. A back pressure control valve is used to maintain the pressure on the high temperature evaporator. If the heat loads on the low and high temperature evaporators are 15,000 and 30,000 Btu/hr, respectively, calculate:

(a) the compressor horsepower, assuming 85% efficiency

(b) the heat removed in the condenser

(c) repeat the calculation for total horsepower, using two independent systems for the two evaporators.

3. How many tons of refrigeration are required to cool 2000 lb of 3.5% milk from 98°F to 38°F in 15 minutes? Compare this cooling process with that required to cool 2000 lb of freshly harvested apples.

4. How many tons of refrigeration are required to freeze 2000 lb per hour of ice cream mix when the mix enters at 38°F and the ice cream leaves at 21°F? The mix composition is 18% fat, 16% sugar and 44% total solids. Neglect energy from the dasher or heat gain from the room.

5. A one-ton ammonia refrigeration system has an evaporating temperature of −5°F and condensing temperature of 85°F. Calculate the following for saturated conditions:

(a) volume of vapor to be compressed per minute (theoretical compressor displacement rate)

(b) the horsepower required for a thermal efficiency of 85%

(c) the capacity in tons if the evaporating temperature if raised to 20°F without any change in compressor capacity

6. Work problem 5 with R-12 as the refrigerant. Compare the two systems.

SYMBOLS

C	constant, dimensionless
c_p	specific heat at constant pressure, Btu/lb°F
c_v	specific heat at constant volume, Btu/lb°F
h_a	enthalpy of saturated vapor entering compressor, Btu/lb
h_b	enthalpy of super-heated vapor leaving compressor, Btu/lb
h_c	enthalpy of saturated high-pressure vapor, Btu/lb
h_d	enthalpy of saturated high-pressure liquid, Btu/lb
h_e	enthalpy of wet evaporating liquid entering evaporator, Btu/lb

h_f enthalpy of saturated low-pressure liquid, Btu/lb

$\dot{m}_r$ refrigerant flow rate, lb/min

$\dot{m}_w$ water flow rate, lb/min

P   pressure, psia

Q   heat transferred across the boundary of a system, Btu/lb

Q_c heat transferred from condenser, Btu/lb

Q_e heat transferred to evaporator, Btu/lb

q   heat flux, Btu/min

v specific volume, ft^3/lb

W_s work done on refrigerant in compressor, Btu/lb

χ fraction of vapor after expansion, dimensionless

γ heat capacity ratio, c_p/c_v

ΔH change in enthalpy in a system

CHAPTER 11

Mass Transfer[1]

INTRODUCTION

If there are differences in concentrations of constituents throughout a solution, there will be a tendency for movement of material to produce a uniform concentration. Such movement may occur in gas, liquid, or solid solutions. Movement resulting from random molecular motion is called diffusion. In liquids and gases, movement may also result from convection. For example, if an open container of ammonia is placed in one corner of a room, the odor will soon be detected throughout the entire room. In this case, there is a combination of molecular diffusion and convection. If a lump of sugar is placed in a glass of water, the sugar will eventually dissolve and spread into all parts of the volume. Convection would be less important and could be avoided almost completely with proper care. In solid solutions, there can obviously be no convection and all movement is by molecular diffusion. Although rates are relatively low, diffusion in solids is a common phenomenon. Hydrogen gas will diffuse through certain metals. Special steels are produced by allowing carbon or other substances to diffuse in from the surface. Organic solvents may diffuse through the walls of plastic containers.

The movement of matter as described above is termed mass transfer. Mass transfer always arises from differences in concentrations in solutions and is to be distinguished from bulk conveying by pumping, etc., or from purely mechanical processes such as mixing, screening or filtration. There are many examples in food processing of operations utilizing mass transfer. Some of these are: humidification and dehumidification, dehydration, distillation, absorption, extraction, ion exchange, and reverse osmosis. The application of mass transfer theory to process design and analysis of these operations is a complex engineering subject. A fundamental treatment is beyond the scope of this text, however, some appreciation of the basic principles can be of very substantial assistance in understanding a wide variety of processing problems.

Diffusion

Molecular diffusion is analogous to heat transfer by conduction. In both cases, the process is caused by random molecular motion. The driving force

---

[1] The symbols used in this chapter are listed and defined at the end of the chapter.

for conduction of heat is temperature difference, or temperature gradient, as expressed by Fourier's Law in Eq. 8-1. The driving force for mass diffusion is concentration difference; the basic relationship is called Fick's Law and can be written as follows:

$$\dot{m}_a/A = -D(dC_a/dx)$$ Eq. 11-1

In this equation, $\dot{m}_a$ is the diffusion rate of component a in mass per unit time, A is the area perpendicular to the direction of diffusion, C_a is concentration in mass per unit volume, and x is distance in the direction of diffusion. The constant D is called the diffusion coefficient, or diffusivity. By substituting conventional units for the quantities in Eq. 11-1, we can determine the units and dimensions of diffusivity. Thus,

$$\frac{lb_m}{hr\,(ft^2)} = D\left(\frac{lb_m}{ft^3}\right)\left(\frac{1}{ft}\right)$$

Rearranging and cancelling in the above expression, we find that D has units of ft^2/hr, or more generally, dimensions of length squared divided by time. Note that the unit of mass used in Eq. 11-1 is immaterial, as long as both the diffusion rate and concentration are in terms of the same unit. Furthermore, mass can be expressed in pound-moles or gram-moles as well as pounds or grams.

Diffusivity is a physical property just as is thermal conductivity, and its value will be dependent on the temperature, pressure, and composition of the system. Thermal conductivity, however, is a property of a substance or material, whereas diffusivity is a property of a system. Both the diffusing substance and the medium through which it is diffusing must be specified in order to fix the value. Many more studies have been made on diffusion in gases than in liquids and solids, and tables of diffusivities for binary gas mixtures are available in various references. There is a single diffusivity for a given pair of gases, regardless of which is considered to be diffusing and which is the stationary component. Diffusion in gases can be treated by principles of kinetic theory, but liquid and solid systems are less well understood and must be treated on a more empirical basis.

Equation 11-1 can be integrated for steady-state, unidirectional diffusion through an area of constant cross-section to give

$$\dot{m}_a/A = D(C_1 - C_2)/(x_2 - x_1)$$ Eq. 11-2

Equation 11-2 is valid in fluid systems only when there is no significant bulk flow. This restriction obviously applies to convection currents, but there is also a common situation in which bulk flow can arise purely from molecular diffusion. To explain this phenomenon, let us first consider a mixture of two gases in free space. If there is a concentration gradient for gas A in one direction, there must be an equivalent concentration gradient for gas B in the opposite direction. If the total pressure is uniform throughout the system, the moles of gas A diffusing in one direction must be equal to the moles of gas B diffusing in the opposite direction. If the diffusion rates were not equal, the total number of moles per unit volume would become different in different parts of the system. This would not be possible, since the perfect gas law requires that the molal concentration be the same at constant pressure and temperature.

Now consider an example in which water is evaporating from a liquid surface and diffusing into the air space above it. As before, there will be a concentration gradient for air in the opposite direction, and air must diffuse toward the surface. There can be no net diffusion of air, however, since air cannot pass into the liquid. Therefore, there must be a bulk flow of gas away from the surface sufficient to equalize the diffusion of air toward the surface. In effect, this bulk flow carries water vapor with it and results in a higher transport of water vapor than would occur with the same concentration gradient in the absence of the water surface barrier. Equation 11-1 must be modified to allow for this bulk flow, and Eq. 11-2 does not apply. The magnitude of this effect depends on the ratio of the partial pressure of the diffusing substance (water vapor in this case) to the total pressure. In wet bulb thermometry at ordinary temperatures, for example, the water vapor pressure is so low compared to atmospheric pressure that the effect can be neglected.

A major problem in measuring gaseous diffusion rates is eliminating the effects of convection. The most reliable method, where it is applicable, utilizes a capillary tube partially filled with a vaporizable liquid. The tube is held in a vertical position in an inert gas atmosphere at a controlled constant temperature. A gentle stream of the inert gas passes over the mouth of the tube to carry away vapor that diffuses through the gas above the liquid level. The rate of diffusion is the rate of evaporation as obtained by observing the drop in liquid level over a period of time. The concentration of the vapor at the liquid surface is obtained from the known vapor pressure-temperature relationship, and the concentration at the mouth of the tube is zero.

This is actually an unsteady state diffusion problem, since the length of diffusion path is continuously increasing as the liquid level drops. However, the drop in level occurs so slowly that the steady state equation applies to the conditions existing at any point in time. Furthermore, it can easily be shown that the proper length of diffusion path to be used in Eq. 11-2 is the arithmetic average of the initial and final lengths. It is important that the tube diameter be uniform but, as shown in the following example, the diameter need not be known.

Example 1.—A capillary tube containing water is held in a dry air atmosphere at 77°F. The water level is initially 2 cm from the top and drops to 3 cm after 117 hours. Calculate the diffusivity of water vapor in air from these data.

This is the case of diffusion through a stationary gas layer discussed above. However, the water vapor pressure is so low compared to the air pressure that Eq. 11-2 can be used without significant error. The concentration of water vapor at the liquid surface is obtained by application of the perfect gas law. Thus,

$$P_w V = NRT = (m/M)RT$$

where P_w is the vapor pressure of water at 77°F, m is the mass of water in a volume V, and M is the molecular weight. Concentration is mass per unit volume, or

$$C_1 = m/V = MP_w/RT \text{ and } C_2 = 0$$

The average evaporation rate is the mass corresponding to the drop in level divided by the total time, or

$$\dot{m} = \rho A \Delta x/\theta$$

where A is the tube cross-sectional area and Δx is the difference between the initial and final levels. Substituting into Eq. 11-2, where x_{av} is the average diffusion pathlength

$$\dot{m}/A = \rho \Delta x/\theta = D(C_1 - C_2)/x_{av} = D(MP_w/RT)/x_{av}$$

Solving for diffusivity,

$$D = (\rho RT x_{av} \Delta x)/(\theta M P_w)$$

Numerical values of the quantities in the above expression are as follows:

$\rho = 62.3 \text{ lb}_m/\text{ft}^3$
$R = 10.73 \text{ (lb}_f/\text{in}^2)(\text{ft}^3)/(\text{lb-mole})(°R)$
$T = 77 + 460 = 537°R$
$x_{av} = 2.5 \text{ cm} = 2.5/30.5 \text{ ft}$
$\Delta x = 1.0 \text{ cm} = 1/30.5 \text{ ft}$
$\theta = 117 \text{ hr}$
$M = 18.0$
$P_w = 0.459 \text{ lb}_f/\text{in}^2 \text{ (from saturated steam table at 77°F)}$
Substituting into equation,

$$D = \frac{(62.3)(10.73)(537)(2.5)}{(30.5)(30.5)(117)(18.0)(0.459)} = 1.0 \text{ ft}^2/\text{hr}$$

Convection

Transport of mass by convection takes place by the same mechanism as the transport of heat. In turbulent flow, eddies are equally effective in transporting molecules of different temperatures and different chemical species. Natural convection currents would ordinarily be dependent on the existence of a temperature difference but, once established, would also be equally effective in transporting heat or mass. Concentration differences can also create density differences that will cause natural convection. By analogy to convective heat transfer, it is possible to express convective mass transfer rates in terms of a mass transfer coefficient as follows:

$$\dot{m}_a/A = k_c(C_1 - C_2) \qquad \text{Eq. 11-3}$$

In Eq. 11-3, the subscript on the mass transfer coefficient indicates that it refers to concentration as a driving force. As discussed subsequently, it is possible to express the driving force for mass transfer in terms of other units than concentration. It is important that the symbol for mass transfer coefficient not be confused with thermal conductivity. In this text, the mass transfer coefficient symbol will always have a letter subscript with it. Mass transfer coefficients depend on system parameters in the same manner that heat transfer coefficients do, but specific correlations are much fewer and less well established.

Transport Phenomena

The material discussed above forms part of the general subject of transport phenomena, which includes heat transfer and momentum transfer. Momentum transfer refers to the transport process that results in fluid friction. As explained the the Fluid Flow chapter, viscous flow behavior results from random molecular motion between portions of the fluid having different velocities. When a molecule moves into a region having a lower forward velocity it is necessarily slowed and thereby transfers some of its forward momentum to the stream. This transfer of momentum creates a forward force on the fluid at that point. Similarly, when a molecule moves into a region with higher velocity, it gains momentum from the stream and creates a retarding force. Similar considerations apply to the motion of turbulent eddies in turbulent flow.

Newton's viscosity law as given by Eq. 7-1 of the Fluid Flow chapter is readily interpreted in terms of momentum transport.

$$F/A = \tau = -\mu dV/dx \qquad \text{Eq. 11-4}$$

Newton's second law of motion states that force is equivalent to the rate of change of momentum, or momentum per unit time. The shear stress, τ, which is force per unit area, can be considered to be the momentum flow rate per unit area from a higher velocity to a lower velocity layer. It should be remembered that this flow of momentum is perpendicular to the stream velocity V. Thus, for a fluid in steady flow in a pipe, there is a flow of momentum in a radial direction from the center to the wall. Since a positive flow of momentum is associated with a decreasing velocity, or negative velocity gradient, the minus sign is included in Eq. 11-4 in order to make the two sides consistent. Equation 11-4 may be divided by density as follows:

$$\tau/\rho = -(\mu/\rho)(dV/dx) = -\nu(dV/dx) \qquad \text{Eq. 11-5}$$

The ratio μ/ρ or ν is called the kinematic viscosity of a fluid. Since μ has dimensions of $(M/L\theta)$ and ρ has dimensions of (M/L^3), kinematic viscosity has dimensions of length squared divided by time. By analogy to Eq. 11-1, it might logically be called a diffusivity for momentum.

To develop the corresponding analogy for heat, Eq. 8-1 of the Heat Transfer chapter (Fourier's law) can be divided by ρc_p and written as follows:

$$(q/A)/(\rho c_p) = -(k/\rho c_p)(dt/dx) = -\alpha(dt/dx) \qquad \text{Eq. 11-6}$$

where α is the thermal diffusivity as defined in the section on transient heat conduction. In that section, it was noted that α also has dimensions of length squared divided by time.

We now have the analogous Eqs. 11-1, 11-5, and 11-6 representing transport of mass, momentum, and heat in which the flux of a quantity is equal to the gradient of a driving force multiplied by a coefficient having the same dimensions for all three. The term "flux" is commonly used to indicate the transport rate of some quantity per unit area. It is interesting to note that the ratio (ν/α) or $(\mu/\rho)(\rho c_p/k)$ is simply the Prandtl number, $c_p\mu/k$. The corresponding dimensionless ratio for mass transfer, ν/D, is called the Schmidt number, designated by the symbol Sc.

These similarities or analogies among the transport processes have been applied primarily to gaseous systems. Air will usually be the major constituent with some substance such as water vapor present in small concentrations. This secondary constituent will usually not be present in large enough concentration to affect significantly the bulk properties such as viscosity, thermal conductivity, etc., and its only effect will be to determine the mass diffusivity, D. Average numerical values of the transport properties for the air-water vapor system at ordinary temperatures are as follows:

$\nu = 0.62 \text{ ft}^2/\text{hr}$

$\alpha = 0.86 \text{ ft}^2/\text{hr}$

$D = 1.0 \text{ ft}^2/\text{hr}$

$Pr = \nu/\alpha = 0.62/0.86 = 0.72$

$Sc = \nu/D = 0.62/1.0 = 0.62$

It is seen that, while the transport properties do not have equal values, they are of the same order of magnitude.

Similar comparisons can be made for convection. To be specific, let us

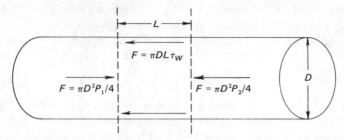

FIG. 11.1. CYLINDER OF FLUID, LENGTH L, IN A PIPE OF DIAMETER, D

consider the case of flow of gas inside a pipe. Mass can be transported between the pipe wall and the gas, heat can be transferred to or from the wall, and there will be fluid friction. For mass transfer, we can write

$$\dot{m}_a/A = k_c(C_{av} - C_{wall}) \qquad \text{Eq. 11-7}$$

For heat transfer, Eq. 8-9 of the Heat Transfer chapter can be written

$$q/A\rho c_p = (h/\rho c_p)(t_{av} - t_{wall}) \qquad \text{Eq. 11-8}$$

By comparing Eqs. 11-7 and 11-8 with Eqs. 11-1 and 11-6, it can be seen that the coefficients k_c and $(h/\rho c_p)$ correspond to the molecular diffusivities divided by length and thus have the units of velocity.

For momentum transfer, or friction, we will first develop a simple relationship between shear stress and pressure drop. Consider a cylinder of fluid contained in a length of pipe L with a diameter D, as shown in Fig. 11-1. At the upstream end, a force equal to the pressure at that point times the cross-sectional area acts in the forward direction. At the downstream end, a similar force acts in the opposite direction. The net forward force resulting from fluid pressure is thus $(\pi D^2/4)(P_1 - P_2)$. By Newton's laws of motion, there can be no net force on a body moving with constant velocity. Therefore, the forward pressure force must be exactly balanced by the retarding force at the wall of the pipe. This force is simply the shear stress at the wall multiplied by the cylindrical surface of the fluid cylinder, or $\tau_{wall}(\pi DL)$. Equating the two forces,

$$\tau_{wall}(\pi DL) = (\pi D^2/4)(P_1 - P_2)$$

or

$$\tau_{wall}/\rho = D\Delta P/4L\rho \qquad \text{Eq. 11-9}$$

Equation 7-12 can be arranged as

$$D\Delta P/4L\rho = fV_{av}^2/2 \qquad \text{Eq. 11-10}$$

The factor g_c has been omitted in Eq. 11-10 to be consistent with the expressions involving shear stress, which are written on the basis of proportionality constant of unity in the force-mass dimensional relationship (refer to chapter on Dimensions and Units). Substituting from Eq. 11-9,

$$\tau_{\text{wall}}/\rho = (fV_{\text{av}}/2)(V_{\text{av}} - V_{\text{wall}}) \qquad \text{Eq. 11-11}$$

The velocity at the wall is, of course, zero. The velocities are separated in this manner so that Eq. 11-10 will be comparable to Eqs. 11-7 and 11-8.

In Eqs. 11-7, 11-8, and 11-11, we have similar expressions for convective transport of mass, heat, and momentum in which the flux of the transported material is given by the product of a coefficient and a driving force. In each case, the coefficient has the units of velocity. In a highly turbulent system, convective transport proceeds by the same mechanism regardless of what it is that is being transported. It might be expected, for example, that the ratio of the heat flux to the temperature difference would be quantitatively equal to the ratio of the mass flux to the concentration difference. In other words, the three coefficients in Eqs. 11-7, 11-8, and 11-11 should be equal. Writing this equality and dividing through by velocity, we have

$$h/\rho V c_p = k_c/V = f/2 \qquad \text{Eq. 11-12}$$

Equation 11-12 is an expression of what is known as Reynolds analogy, named after the originator of these ideas on turbulent transport. It should be emphasized that this is not an exact physical relationship, but is rather an expression of some semi-quantitative principles involving the nature of turbulent flow. Furthermore, the development here is quite brief in the interests of simplicity, and many aspects of the problem are not discussed. The objective has been to give a general descriptive background and appreciation of the subject rather than to develop a quantitative working tool. Various extensions of this analogy have been made by allowing more specifically for combined effects of molecular and turbulent transport, with a corresponding improvement in agreement with experiment.

Experimental data are readily obtained to check the validity of the heat transfer-friction analogy. For this purpose, it is preferable to make both measurements in the same system. Thus, it is quite possible to measure heat transfer rate and pressure drop simultaneously for a fluid flowing in a tube. Mass transfer experiments are less convenient, both because of problems in devising suitable experimental procedures and because there is no simple instrument for measuring concentration. A frequently used device is the wetted-wall column, in which a thin film of liquid runs down the inside wall of a vertical tube and evaporates into a gas stream flowing through the tube. Mass transfer coefficients can be calculated from the results of such experiments. The conditions in actual processing equipment involving heat and mass transfer, such as dehydrators, cooling towers, packed columns, etc. are more complex than in simple tube flow, but the general principles of the analogies are still valid.

It is interesting to note from Eq. 11-12 that $h/\rho k_c = c_p$, or $h/\rho k_c c_p = 1.0$. In the development of the wet bulb temperature concept in the section on Psychrometry, we saw that h/k_y for the air-water system is approximately equal to c_s. The subscript on the mass transfer coefficient here indicates that the driving force is humidity rather than concentration. Noting that concentration has units of lb water/ft^3 air and humidity has units of lb water/lb air, we can write

$$Y = c/\rho_{air}$$

$$\dot{m}_w/A = k_c(C_1 - C_2) = k_y(Y_1 - Y_2) = k_y(C_1 - C_2)/\rho_{air} \qquad \text{Eq. 11-13}$$

$$k_c = \dot{k}_y/\rho \qquad \text{Eq. 11-14}$$

Thus, the Reynolds analogy result that $h/\rho k_c = c_p$ is equivalent to the wet bulb condition that $h/k_y = c_s$. Small effects such as the difference between c_s and c_p are not of concern. We can therefore say that if Reynolds analogy is valid, the wet bulb relationship is satisfied. This does not mean that experimental verification of the wet bulb relationship necessarily proves the general validity of Reynolds analogy. The dimensionless ratio $h/\rho k_c c_p$ is called the Lewis number (Le) and plays an important role in the treatment of combined heat and mass transfer operations.

The above discussion concerning concentration and humidity driving forces brings out an important point in mass transfer. In heat transfer, the driving force is always temperature. In mass transfer, in addition to the two already mentioned, we can have partial pressure, activity, fungacity, or other thermodynamic potentials. Accordingly, it is important that the driving force be clearly specified whenever a mass transfer coefficient is used.

Most process applications involve interphase mass transfer, that is, transfer of substances among solid, liquid, and gas phases. If one of the phases is a pure substance, as in psychrometric applications, the transport problem is actually only that of a single phase. Many times, however, transport in both phases must be considered. An example would be an absorber in which sulfur dioxide is removed from an air stream by a water spray. The basic assumption made in treating interphase mass transfer is that there is a condition of thermodynamic equilibrium at the interface between the phases. Information is thus required as to the equilibrium concentrations of constituents in the two phases. In heat transfer, by contrast, the equilibrium condition is simply equality of temperatures. The subject is introduced at this point to emphasize that, although the basic transport principles of heat and mass are the same, there are many more complications in the applications of mass transfer. Furthermore, most mass transfer applications will also involve heat transfer so that it may be necessary to solve the two sets of relationships simultaneously in order to obtain an answer.

Example 2.—Air at 100°F and 30% rh is flowing over a water surface with a velocity of 15 ft/sec. The water receives sufficient heat from other sources that its temperature remains at 100°F. Previous experiments show that a mass transfer coefficient k_c of 0.1 ft/sec can be expected under these conditions. Estimate the rate of evaporation per square foot of surface area.

$$k_c = 0.1 \text{ ft/sec} = 360 \text{ ft/hr}$$

From the psychrometric chart, Fig. 9.5, at 100°F,

$$Y_1 = Y_{sat} = 0.0432 \text{ and } Y_2 = 0.0124 \text{ (at 30\% rh)}$$

specific volume $= 1/\rho = 14.4$ ft³/lb at 30% rh

Using Eqs. 11-13 and 11-14,

$$\dot{m}_w/A = k_y(Y_1 - Y_2) = \rho k_c(Y_1 - Y_2) = (360/14.4)(0.0432 - 0.0124)$$

$$= 0.77 \text{ lb/(hr)(ft}^2)$$

It should be noted that the water will not come to the wet bulb temperature of the air since it is receiving heat from external sources to maintain its temperature at 100°F.

PROBLEMS

1. Water vapor diffuses from the water at the bottom of a 10-ft well to dry air flowing over the top of the well. Calculate the rate of diffusion assuming the air in the well is stagnant and that the entire system is at 77°F and 1 (one) atmosphere.

2. An open circular tank 5 ft in diameter contains ethanol exposed to the open air at 77°F and atmospheric pressure. Assuming there is a still layer of air 9 in. thick over the surface of the alcohol, calculate the weight of ethanol lost per day. The mass diffusivity of ethanol in air is 0.46 ft²/hr and the vapor pressure of alcohol is 1.12 psia at 77°F.

3. A capillary similar to that used in Example 1 is partially filled with pure benzene rather than water. Calculate the time required for the benzene level to drop from 2 cm to 3 cm from the top when held at 54°F. The properties of benzene at 54°F are as follows: vapor pressure = 0.97 psia; density = 55.5 lb$_m$/ft³; mass diffusivity in air = 0.34 ft²/hr.

4. How long will it take for ½ gm of iodine crystals at 104°F to sublime from a bulb that is connected to the atmosphere by a short tube 1 in. long

and $\frac{1}{4}$ in. in diameter? The mass diffusivity of iodine vapor in air at 104°F is 1.0 ft^2/hr. The vapor pressure of iodine at 104°F is 0.0175 psia. The molecular weight of iodine is 253.8.

SYMBOLS

A area perpendicular to direction of diffusion (or heat flow), ft^2
C_a, C_1, C_2 concentration of component a, 1, or 2, respectively, lb/ft
c_p specific heat at constant pressure, Btu/(lb)(°F)
c_s humid heat, Btu/(lb)(°F)
D diameter, ft
D coefficient of diffusion, ft^2/hr
F force, lb$_f$
f friction factor in fluid flow, dimensionless
g_c conversion factor, 32.2 lb$_m$ft/lb$_f$sec^2
h surface coefficient of heat transfer, Btu/(hr)(ft^2)(°F)
k thermal conductivity, Btu/(hr)(ft^2)(°F/ft)
k_c coefficient of convective mass transfer, ft/hr
k_y coefficient of convective mass transfer, lb$_{air}$/(ft^2)(hr)
L length, ft
M molecular weight, lb-moles
m mass of water, lb
$\dot{m}_a$ diffusion rate of component a, lb/hr
$\dot{m}_w$ diffusion rate of water, lb/hr
N number of lb-moles
P_w partial pressure of water vapor, psia
P_1, P_2 pressure at points 1 and 2, respectively, lb/ft
ΔP change in pressure (pressure drop), lb/ft^2
q heat flux, Btu/hr
R universal gas constant, 10.73 ft^{3}lb/(in.^{2})(lb-mole)(°R)
rh   relative humidity
T absolute temperature, °R = °F + 460
t temperature, °F
V volume, ft^3 or velocity, ft/sec
x distance in direction of diffusion (or heat flow), ft
x_{av} average diffusion path, ft
Δx change in liquid level, ft
Y_1, Y_2 humidity at 1 and 2, respectively, lb H$_2$O/lb dry air
α thermal diffusivity, ft^2/hr
θ time, hr
μ absolute viscosity, lb/(ft)(sec)
ν kinematic viscosity, ft^2/hr
ρ density, lb$_m$/ft^3
τ shear stress, lb$_f$/ft^2

CHAPTER 12

Dehydration[1]

INTRODUCTION

Although man has used dried foods for thousands of years, artificial dehydration of foods dates back only about two centuries. By artificial dehydration, we mean that some artificial source of heat is provided to take the place of direct exposure to the sun. Sometimes, the term "dehydration" is used to indicate artificial drying as contrasted to sun drying. In this text, the terms dehydration and dehydrated foods will be used synonomously with drying and dried foods. The equipment in which the moisture is removed is usually called a dryer, although the term dehydrator can also be used.

Specific types of dryers are discussed later in the chapter, but it will be helpful at this point to indicate some general classifications. Some types of dryers are intended for solid materials. In these, the material may be loaded onto a shelf, tray, or moving belt. With proper provision, liquids can also be handled in this type of equipment. On the other hand, spray and drum dryers are suitable only for liquids. Another useful classification is atmospheric pressure vs. vacuum drying. In atmospheric pressure drying, the necessary heat is usually brought to the material by a circulating air stream, which also carries away the moisture. In vacuum drying, the material must be placed inside a closed chamber, and heat is provided by radiation or conduction from a hot surface. Finally, there are continuous and batch dryers. Continuous drying is obviously desired for economy in high volume operations. For small scale or some limited seasonal operations, batch drying can be appropriate. Also there are complications in adapting vacuum drying to continuous operation. A semi-continuous operation is common in which material is introduced and removed intermittently rather than as a steadily flowing stream.

Hot air dryers for handling solid materials comprise by far the greatest number of applications, and most of discussion that follows is devoted to these. Somewhat different principles are involved in vacuum dryers and spray and drum dryers, and these types are considered separately.

Many of the basic principles on which drying theory depends have been developed in previous chapters. Chapter 2 on Mass Balance includes a specific discussion of drying applications. The subject of psychrometry is

---

[1] The symbols used in this chapter are listed and defined at the end of the chapter.

intimately involved in the treatment of dehydration. Finally, the application of combined principles of heat and mass transfer is required in a complete analysis of the problem. As pointed out in Chapter 11 on Mass Transfer, the quantitative application of combined heat and mass transfer relationships to dehydration is an engineering subject of considerable complexity that goes beyond the scope of this text. However, an understanding of the basic principles together with application of empirical or approximate methods will go far toward solving problems encountered in practice.

For more complete discussions of the entire subject matter of this chapter, reference should be made to the excellent two volume work *Food Dehydration,* Avi Publishing Co.: *Vol. I, Principles,* Van Arsdel (1963); and *Vol. II, Products and Technology,* Copley and Van Arsdel (1964).[2]

MOISTURE IN SOLIDS

Moisture can be held within a solid in a variety of forms. Purely mechanical forces related to surface tension may hold it in pores or in interstitial spaces between particles or as a film on a solid surface. Moisture in a bed of wet sand is of this nature. Adsorbed moisture is held on a solid surface by weak intermolecular or "van der Waals" forces, which may extend for a distance of a few molecular diameters. In addition to this physical adsorption, there may be chemical adsorption, in which water is held in the solid by chemical bonds over a wide range of strengths. Water of hydration of an inorganic salt such as calcium sulfate is an example of a reversible chemical reaction. Moisture may be present as either a liquid or solid solution. Finally, moisture may be contained within the chemical structure of the solid, as in carbohydrates. The loss of this moisture is irreversible and results in the decomposition of the solid. In ordinary dehydration operations, the removal of this last category of moisture is an undesired result.

There are no sharp dividing lines between these different forms in which moisture is held. As pore size decreases, the capillary force arising from surface tension that holds liquid in the pores increases. At sufficiently small pore sizes, the capillary forces will become comparable to the van der Waals forces of adsorption. Likewise, depending on the chemical nature of the solid, there may be a gradual transition from van der Waals attraction to actual chemical bonds.

Measurements of water vapor pressure as a function of moisture content provide information as to the state of the water in the solid. Moisture in interstitial spaces or large pores exerts the normal vapor pressure of water.

---

[2] The *2nd Edition* of *Food Dehydration, Vols. 1 and 2* by Van Arsdel, Copley and Morgan was published by Avi Publishing Company in 1973.

By a well known thermodynamic relationship, the vapor pressure above a curved liquid surface depends on the radius of curvature. For a convex surface, such as a liquid drop, the vapor pressure increases as the radius decreases. Capillary forces produce a concave surface on water in small pores, with a corresponding decrease in vapor pressure as the diameter decreases. Thus, as water is removed in dehydration, the remaining water is held in pores of increasingly smaller size, and the vapor pressure decreases. The vapor pressure of adsorbed moisture is still lower and continues to decrease as successive layers of molecules are removed. Finally, chemical bonds give the lowest vapor pressures of all. Another indication of the state of the moisture in a solid is the heat of vaporization. Moisture in large spaces, that shows the normal vapor pressure, requires only the normal latent heat of vaporization. If the moisture is more tightly held by capillary or adsorptive forces or by chemical bonds, vaporization requires energy to overcome these forces in addition to the normal latent heat. Moisture present as a solution will have a lowered vapor pressure, but the heat of vaporization will not be increased unless there is also a heat of solution.

The terms "unbound" and "bound" are commonly used to distinguish moisture in relatively large spaces from that held more tightly by the forces described above. As the discussion indicates, there is a continuous transition from unbound to bound moisture, and it is not possible to make a precise dividing line. Unbound moisture is frequently defined as that which exerts the normal vapor pressure, while bound moisture has a lower vapor pressure.

This situation of bound moisture leads to uncertainties in measurement of moisture content, particularly in the low moisture range. The usual primary method of moisture determination is some kind of oven drying process. The amount of moisture lost in such a process depends on the severity of the drying conditions. Conditions that will remove all the bound moisture may also cause some chemical decomposition and its resultant weight loss. Reports of moisture content measurements should include a reference to the analytical procedure used.

Equilibrium Moisture

The relationship between the moisture content of a material and the equilibrium water vapor pressure discussed above can be expressed as curves of vapor pressure vs. moisture content at constant temperature. For material in contact with air, the pressure of water vapor can be given in terms of air humidity, and the equilibrium vapor pressure relationship can be expressed as moisture content of the solid vs. air humidity. If the moisture content of a solid is higher than the equilibrium value for a given air humidity, water will evaporate into the air until equilibrium is achieved. If we define unbound moisture as that which exerts the normal water vapor pressure, all unbound moisture must evaporate before equilibrium can be achieved with air that is less than saturated. In other words, water will evaporate until the equilibrium vapor pressure of the water in the solid is equal to the partial pressure of water vapor in the air.

If the moisture content of the solid is initially less than the equilibrium condition for the surrounding air, the solid will gain moisture. For a condition of true thermodynamic reversibility, the equilibrium moisture content would be the same regardless of whether it is approached from a higher or lower moisture content. With complex materials such as foods, however, it will usually be found that the equilibrium moisture content is higher when approached from above than from below. There are various possible explanations for this phenomenon, depending on the nature of the binding forces holding the moisture. Most solid food products undergo irreversible changes on dehydration, as discussed later, so that an equilibrium moisture content approached from below is actually for a different material. In ordinary dehydration operations, we are concerned with moisture contents obtained by desorption. In considering possible regain of moisture by dried products in storage, absorption moisture contents are of interest.

Many results of equilibrium moisture content measurements are reported in the literature. The data may be plotted as moisture content vs. relative humidity at constant temperature. To be useful for dehydration calculations, data must be available for a wide range of temperatures. In such plots, the slope is steep at the origin of zero relative humidity, decreases in the intermediate range, and becomes steep again at higher relative humidities. In the preceding paragraph, mention was made of the effect that changes in a solid material during drying may have on equilibrium moisture contents. The extent of these changes depends to some degree on conditions such as the temperature history and rate of water removal, and an equilibrium moisture content observed in an actual drying operation may not agree with a value obtained in a laboratory measurement.

The equilibrium moisture content is the lower limit that can be obtained in a dehydration operation. The difference between the total moisture and the equilibrium moisture represents the amount that can be removed and is called the free moisture content.

Moisture Movement Through Solids

Before moisture can be carried away in an air stream, it must first get to the surface of the solid. There are several mechanisms by which moisture which is not initially at the surface may move through the solid. In any actual drying operation, there will usually be a combination of mechanisms, and drying rate data do not ordinarily provide sufficient information to distinguish among them. Furthermore, as described below, the mechanisms will usually change as drying proceeds.

1. Capillary movement. This is the same mechanism by which a drop of water spreads through a piece of blotting paper. As moisture is removed from the surface by evaporation, unbound moisture is drawn from the interior by capillary forces. Capillary forces are effective in beds of granular solids such as sand as well as in solids with an interconnected structure. This is the primary mechanism for movement of unbound moisture.

2. Solid shrinkage. Most solids of biological origin shrink on dehydration. This shrinkage has the same effect as squeezing a sponge, and moisture is forced to the surface.

3. Solid diffusion. Either bound or unbound moisture may diffuse through a solid. Diffusion of moisture through cell walls is a well-known phenomenon. Solid diffusion is important in drying gelatinous materials such as soap or glue.

4. Surface diffusion. Adsorbed moisture can diffuse along a solid surface from a higher to a lower moisture content region. This is an important mechanism that is not related to capillary forces and applies only to bound moisture.

5. Gaseous diffusion. After a solid is partially dehydrated, either unbound or bound moisture may evaporate below the surface and pass through a porous dried shell by gaseous diffusion. This is the predominant mechanism in freeze drying, in which capillary and shrinkage forces are not effective, but it occurs to some extent in the later stages of all dehydration.

6. Pressure gradient flow of vapor. This is similar to gaseous diffusion but occurs as a result of a difference of total pressure of the gas rather than a difference in partial pressure of water vapor. It can occur in vacuum drying when the total pressure surrounding the solid is maintained at a lower value than the vapor pressure of the water within the solid. This mechanism cannot be effective in atmospheric pressure drying.

Many research studies have been made on the subject of moisture movement in order to provide a better understanding of the drying process. The mechanism has a direct bearing on the magnitude of drying rate constants, which are discussed subsequently. Drying rate constants must always be determined empirically, however, and the particular mechanism is relatively unimportant from a practical point of view.

MATERIAL CHARACTERISTICS

Many early drying studies were made with beds of sand. This is an ideal material for experimental work. It is completely inert and can be reused indefinitely to study the effects of different variables. Unfortunately, most applications involve more complex materials. Usually, if moisture is distributed throughout a solid structure rather than simply being held in spaces between inert particles, the material will shrink or expand with removal or addition of moisture. Such changes in volume may be reversible, as with clays. With materials of biological origin, however, irreversible changes will probably occur on drying. The material is now different than it was originally, and it is not possible to verify experimental results by adding moisture and repeating the measurement. Furthermore, the extent of the change will probably be affected by the conditions under which the moisture was removed, such as temperature, rate of drying, size of piece, etc. In addition, it will in general not be possible to duplicate precisely a raw material, introducing uncertainties in comparing experiments made at different periods of time or at different locations. Because of these many uncertainties, quantitative treatment of food dehydration problems will usually depend strongly on experience and empirical relationships.

The most pronounced changes that take place in food materials on dehydration are associated with shrinkage. As water is removed from cells of vegetable or animal tissue, the cells shrink and cell walls may rupture. Adjacent fibers may fuse together and may be cemented by residues of soluble constituents. The extent of these changes depends on the rate of drying. It is well known, for example, that if green wood is dried too rapidly, the outer layer will shrink around the undried core and develop cracks. Cracks can be avoided by drying at a low enough rate to permit uniform shrinkage throughout the volume.

Similar effects occur in dehydration of vegetable dice, but here initial rapid drying is usually desirable. A rigid outer dry layer is formed while the wet interior has its original volume. During the latter stages of drying, the interior shrinks back against the rigid shell, leaving a porous structure of cracks and voids that facilitates rehydration. If drying is slow so that shrinkage is uniform throughout the volume, the result is a hard, dense product that rehydrates with difficulty. In addition to product quality considerations, rapid drying has the economic advantage of giving higher dehydrator throughput.

As moisture moves toward the surface as a result of capillary or shrinkage forces, any dissolved matter is carried with it. Evaporation of moisture at the surface may leave these dissolved solids deposited as a layer having low permeability to water vapor. In this event, the drying rate can drop to a very low value while the interior is quite moist. The extent of both this migration of dissolved solids and the shrinkage effects described in the preceding paragraph depend on the size of the piece or, more specifically, on the surface-to-volume ratio. The effects are relatively less important with small pieces, which have a high ratio of surface to volume.

The sensitivity of food products to damage by high temperatures imposes limitations on the drying conditions that can be used. In the earlier stages of drying, rapid evaporation of moisture provides sufficient cooling that relatively high air temperatures can be employed without adverse effects. Care must be taken during the later stages to avoid overheating the dry

DEHYDRATION 247

material. Accordingly, drying conditions must be milder and drying rates lower than for an inert material. Two additional phenomena that affect the quality of dried food products are loss of volatile flavor and odor constituents and browning. The loss of some volatiles along with the moisture is unavoidable, but the effects can be reduced by raw material selection and optimum drying conditions. Sulfur dioxide or sulfite treatment is the standard method for minimizing browning. All of these effects relating to product quality are highly specific to the individual product, and the proper drying conditions must be selected on the basis of experience. The student should refer to other sources for a more detailed consideration of these aspects of product quality.

DRYING RATE BEHAVIOR

In an actual dehydration operation, the air temperature and humidity change as the air moves past the moist material, and the moisture content of the solid varies from one point to another in the bed. Although data from such operations are essential in developing design methods, they cannot easily be analyzed to provide fundamental information relating the effects of process variables to rates of dehydration. Constant condition batch drying experiments are better suited for this purpose and, more generally, for providing an understanding of the mechanism of the drying process. In such an experiment, a sample of material is dried in an air stream having a constant temperature, humidity, and velocity. If the material consists of reasonably large pieces, such as vegetable dice or fruit slices, drying of a single piece may be studied. Results will be more applicable to actual dehydrator operation if a thin bed or layer of material is used rather than a single piece. The sample must be small enough, however, that the air temperature and humidity do not change appreciably between the inlet and outlet and that the moisture content of the solid stays uniform over the depth and width of the bed.

Basically, constant condition batch drying experiments will consist of measurement of moisture loss with time at various constant values of air temperature, humidity, and velocity. Drying rate constants obtained from such data give a direct expression of drying rate in terms of instantaneous point values of process variables. In principle, equations utilizing these constants for instantaneous drying rates can be integrated over the total bed volume and desired range of moisture content to obtain the required drying time either for batch or continuous operation. Such a procedure is quite valid for inert materials, for which the drying rate depends on the instantaneous moisture content and not on the previous drying history. For example, grain drying falls into this category.

In batch drying experiments, results are related to average moisture contents. The drying rate at any time, however, will depend on the distri-

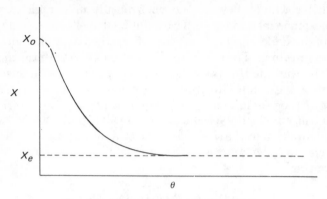

FIG. 12.1. MOISTURE CONTENT VS TIME

bution of moisture within the solid, which depends in turn on the previous drying conditions. Furthermore, as previously discussed, physical changes in the solid occur that are dependent on previous drying history and that strongly affect drying rate. These effects are so significant that it is usually not possible to make a reliable prediction of drying time for continuous dehydration entirely on the basis of constant condition measurements. Accordingly, it is necessary to conduct experiments that represent the process to be used in the actual production operation. The real value of the more fundamental approach is that, once it is related to practice through large-scale experiments, it provides a basis to determine the effects of variations in operating conditions and to establish optimum drying schedules without the necessity of extended experimental programs for each individual situation.

The air in experimental studies may flow parallel to the surface of a layer of solid or may pass vertically through a bed of particulate matter to correspond to the arrangement of the commercial equipment. Because small experimental equipment involves a much larger ratio of exposed surface to volume than a commercial dryer, special attention is required to ensure that radiation heat transfer effects do not create an unrepresentative condition. Experimental data are conveniently plotted as curves of moisture content against time, as shown in Fig. 12.1. There will usually be a short initial period in which the solid is coming into equilibrium with the air, shown by the dashed portion of the curve. Following this transitory period, the curve will be relatively steep, indicating a rapid rate of drying while the moisture content is high. With the passage of time and the corresponding reduction of moisture content, the curve becomes less steep and finally approaches the equilibrium moisture content asymptotically.

As discussed in the Mass Balance chapter, it is convenient to express moisture content as X, the pounds of moisture per pound of dry matter.

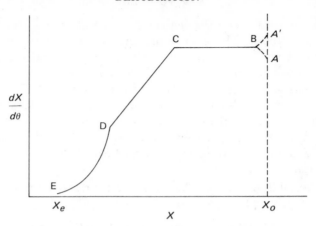

FIG. 12.2. DRYING RATE VS MOISTURE CONTENT

The slope of a tangent to the curve of Fig. 12.1 can be written as $dX/d\theta$ and represents the rate of drying of one pound of dry matter at a particular time or moisture content. From such slopes taken over the entire length of the curve, a plot can be made of drying rate vs. moisture content, as shown in Fig. 12.2. Since drying rate is intrinsically related to moisture content rather than time, Fig. 12.2 rather than Fig. 12.1 is the appropriate method of representing the fundamental drying behavior. Such plots typically can be divided into several distinct periods as discussed below. It should be emphasized that all of these periods do not always appear and that there may not be sharp dividing lines between periods. It should be further noted that the moisture contents at the ends of these periods are not fixed constants for a material but depend on drying conditions, particularly air velocity and temperature.

Initial Period

As pointed out, there will be a brief initial (AB of Fig. 12.2) period while the material is coming into balance with the drying conditions. Usually, the temperature of the solid will rise during this period, and the drying rate will rise accordingly. This period would seldom have any practical importance and, except under unusual circumstances, its effects can be ignored.

Constant Rate Period

There may initially be an excess of unbound moisture at the surface of a wet solid, and transport of moisture to the surface by capillary or shrinkage forces may be sufficient to replenish the loss from evaporation for a period of time (BC of Fig. 12.2). This situation is similar to that of the wet bulb temperature, and if heat transfer by radiation and conduction are small, the temperature of the wet solid will equilibrate at the wet bulb temperature of the air. The temperature driving force for heat transfer from air to solid is therefore the difference between the dry and wet bulb temperatures, or wet bulb depression, which remains constant. The drying rate is equal to the heat transfer rate divided by the latent heat of vaporization and is also constant. It is more accurate to use the term "saturated surface drying" to describe this period. The drying rate may decrease because of the reduction of surface area from shrinkage, but the mechanism remains the same. Allowance for this shrinkage can be made in analysis of experimental data.

The constant drying rate can be expressed in terms of either temperature or humidity driving force as follows:

$$-L_s(dX/d\theta) = h_c(t_1 - t^*)/\lambda = k_y(Y^* - Y_1) \qquad \text{Eq. 12-1}$$

In this equation, L_s is the pounds of dry matter per sq ft of tray area. The product $L_s(dX/d\theta)$ thus represents the rate of moisture loss from 1 sq ft of tray area. It should be remembered that the transport coefficients h_c and k_y are therefore based on the tray area and not on the actual surface area, which is not known for a bed of particulate matter. As in the Psychrometry section of Chapter 9, the asterisk represents the wet bulb temperature condition and the relation $h_c/k_yc_s = 1.0$ is considered to be valid. Since the effects of air temperature and humidity on drying rate are given directly by Eq. 12-1, experimental studies are focused on the behavior of the transport coefficients. For air flow parallel to the surface, these coefficients vary approximately as the 0.8 power of the velocity. For flow through a bed of particulate matter, the dependency on velocity will drop to the 0.6 power or less. With particulate matter, both the true surface area and the air flow patterns near the surface will depend on the size of the pieces and the manner of loading in the dryer. Also, higher velocities can cause air flowing parallel to the surface to penetrate somewhat into the bed, leading to a velocity effect greater than the 0.8 power.

In some dehydrator operation, the solid may gain heat by conduction from a hot tray. There may also be radiation from hot surfaces, either incidentally or by specific provision. If these heat transfer mechanisms are present, they must be included in the heat transfer term of Eq. 12-1. Although a constant rate period may still exist, the temperature of the solid will come to a constant value that is higher than the wet bulb temperature of the air.

In many food drying applications, there is no constant rate period. In drying of grains or uncut fruit such as prunes, for example, the surface is never saturated with moisture. Even with high moisture content cut vegetables, the constant rate period may be of minor importance.

Example 1.—In a tray drying experiment, the moisture content of diced potatoes was reduced from 75% to 66% in 18 minutes. The 2 ft by 3 ft rectangular tray was loaded with 8 lb of wet potatoes. The dry bulb and wet bulb temperatures of the air were 180°F and 100°F. Air flow was parallel to the tray at a velocity of 800 ft/min, and drying took place only from the top of the bed. Past experience has shown that the drying rate will be constant under these conditions.

(a) Calculate the heat transfer and mass transfer convection coefficients, based on the tray area.

(b) Estimate the drying time if the air dry bulb temperature is reduced to 150°F with the same wet bulb and the air velocity is increased to 1200 ft/min.

From the problem statement,

Initial moisture ratio, $X_1 = 75/25 = 3.0$

Final moisture ratio, $X_2 = 66/34 = 1.94$

Total weight of dry matter $= 0.25(8) = 2$ lb

Tray area $= 2(3) = 6$ ft^2

Tray loading $= 2/6 = 0.333$ lb dry matter/ft^2

Drying time $= 18/60 = 0.30$ hr

Applying Eq. 12-1 to constant rate period,

$$L_s(X_1 - X_2)/\theta = h_c(t_1 - t^*)/\lambda = k_y(Y^* - Y_1)$$

$\lambda = 1037$ Btu/lb (at 100°F from steam tables)

$Y_1 = 0.0239$ (from psychrometric chart)

$Y_2 = 0.0432$ (from psychrometric chart)

Substituting into equation,

$$0.333(3.0 - 1.94)/0.30 = h_c(180 - 100)/1037 = k_y(0.0432 - 0.0239)$$

$h_c = 15.3$ Btu/(hr)(ft^2)(°F)

$k_y = 61.0$ lb/(hr)(ft^2)(ΔY)

Check value of Lewis number

$c_s = 0.24 + 0.45Y = 0.24 + 0.45(0.0239) = 0.25$

$h_c/k_yc_s = 15.3/(61.0)(0.25) = 1.0$

Since a Lewis number of 1.0 is implicit in the psychrometric chart, this result simply serves to confirm that the calculations are consistent.

Assuming that the transport coefficients vary as the 0.8 power of velocity,

$$h_c = 15.3(1200/800)^{0.8} = 15.3(1.383) = 21.2$$

Equation 12-1 shows that drying time is inversely proportional to the product of the heat transfer coefficient and the wet bulb depression. Since all other factors are the same,

$$\frac{\theta_2}{\theta_1} = \frac{h_1(t - t^*)_1}{h_2(t - t^*)_2} = \frac{15.3(180 - 100)}{21.2(150 - 100)} = 1.16$$

$$\theta_2 = 1.16(18) = 20.8 \text{ minutes}$$

Falling Rate Period

At some point, moisture can no longer be transported from the interior rapidly enough to keep the surface saturated, and dry spots will begin to appear. From this time, the rate will decline continuously as long as the drying process is continued (CDE of Fig. 12.2). All the mechanisms of moisture movement discussed previously may be effective during some part of the falling rate period. In the first part of the period, a continuously decreasing portion of the surface will remain saturated (if there had been saturation initially), and both capillary and shrinkage forces will be active. It is possible that most of the drying will take place from this saturated area and that the drying rate will decline in relation to the fraction of the total area that remains saturated. Throughout the falling rate period, there will be a gradual transition toward the mechanisms of surface, solid, and gaseous diffusion. One or more break points as indicated by point D on the curve in Fig. 12.2 either may or may not appear. With inert granular materials, the drying rate may maintain a measurable value until it suddenly drops to zero when the moisture is gone. If appreciable bound moisture is present, as is usually the case with food products, the drying rate can be expected to approach zero asymptotically as the moisture content approaches the equilibrium value.

The moisture content at point C in Fig. 12.2, the division between the constant and falling rate periods, is commonly called the critical moisture content. It should be noted that the critical moisture content is not entirely a property of the material, but depends on the manner of loading in the bed and on conditions in the constant rate period. A greater bed depth and a higher constant drying rate will both cause the constant rate period to terminate at a higher moisture content.

The literature contains reports of many experimental drying investigations in which the data have been analyzed mathematically on the basis of some particular mechanism of moisture movement through the solid. The complex nature of the process, however, makes it impossible to attach any fundamental significance to rate constants obtained from such analysis. The fact that experimental data do not conflict with a theory does not prove the validity of the theory. Essentially all the moisture movement mechanisms described above lead to the same general form of drying rate curves. Drying rate constants can be looked upon only as empirical expressions of the rate of moisture loss during dehydration. Because of the empirical nature of the constants, experimental data must be obtained over a much wider range of variables than would be necessary if there were a dependable theory.

Many times it will be found that at least a portion of the curve CDE in Fig. 12.2 can be approximated by a straight line that crosses the zero drying rate axis at the equilibrium moisture content. Such a straight line can be represented by the equation

$$-dX/d\theta = K(X - X_e)$$ Eq. 12-2

This equation can be integrated to give

$$-\ln \frac{X - X_e}{X_0 - X_e} = K\theta$$ Eq. 12-3

The ratio in the logarithmic term of Eq. 12-3 represents the fraction of unaccomplished drying. It is interesting to note the similarity to the transient heat transfer relationship shown in Fig. 8-14. In that figure, it is seen that the logarithm of the unaccomplished temperature change has a straight line variation with time over a wide range. Such a similarity seems reasonable in view of the analogy between conduction of heat and diffusion of mass discussed in the Mass Transfer chapter. As discussed previously, however, the constant K represents the combined effect of all the mass transport mechanisms and cannot reliably be interpreted in terms of a specific diffusivity.

In the constant rate period, all resistance to mass transfer is external, that is, between the surface of the solid and the air, and the drying rate depends only on external variables such as air temperature and velocity. In the falling rate period, the total transport resistance is the sum of external and internal resistances. At the beginning of the falling rate period, the resistance to internal movement is relatively small, and most of the resistance is in external transport. We can thus say that the external resistance is controlling. In the later stages of drying, the internal resistance becomes very large and the external resistance is relatively unimportant, and the process is internal resistance controlling. External variables do not directly affect the internal resistance, and the influence of such variables on the drying rate will change continuously throughout the falling rate period. For example, initially the air velocity will have the effect described in the constant rate section. Toward the end, the air velocity may have no effect on the drying rate. It is thus not possible to make any kind of a generalized correlation for the dependence of overall drying rate constants on process variables.

Example 2.—It has been found that tray drying of prunes takes place entirely within the falling rate period and that, with constant drying conditions, the drying rate can be considered proportional to the difference between the total moisture and the equilibrium moisture ratios. In one experiment, prunes initially at 68.7% moisture were dried to 46.2% after 5 hr and 24.3% after 12 hr. Estimate the equilibrium moisture content and the time required to achieve a total moisture of 18%.

$X_0 = 0.687/0.313 = 2.20$
$X_5 = 0.462/0.548 = 0.86$
$X_{12} = 0.243/0.757 = 0.321$
$X_{final} = 0.18/0.82 = 0.2195$

Applying Eq. 12-3 to the 5-hr results,

$$\ln \frac{2.20 - X_e}{0.86 - X_e} = 5K$$

For the 12-hr results,

$$\ln \frac{2.20 - X_e}{0.321 - X_e} = 12K$$

Eliminating K between the two equations above,

$$\ln \frac{2.20 - X_e}{0.321 - X_e} = (12/5) \ln \frac{2.20 - X_e}{0.86 - X_e}$$

By trial and error solution, $X_e = 0.17$. To find K, substitute this value into either the 5-hr or the 12-hr equation. Using the latter,

$\ln(2.03/0.151) = 12K$
$K = 0.217$

Substitute into Eq. 12-3 to obtain final drying time

$$\ln \frac{2.20 - 0.17}{0.2195 - 0.17} = 0.217\theta$$

$\theta = 17.1$ hr

It should be noted that there is no general method for predicting the effect of air velocity or wet bulb depression on the drying rate constant K. For design calculations, it is necessary to have experimental data or empirical correlations covering the range of variables involved.

DRYING EQUIPMENT

A large number of types of dryers are manufactured for various applications in process industries. This section discusses a few of these that are of particular importance in food processing.

Truck and Tunnel Dryers

In this equipment, trays of wet material are stacked on trucks, which are then moved through a long drying tunnel. The arrangement is illustrated in Fig. 12.3. The trays may be of either wood slat or open metal construction, with typical dimensions of 3 ft × 6 ft. The loaded trays are stacked to a height of about 5 to 7 ft with sufficient spacing to permit the necessary passage of air. There must be a close clearance around all four sides between the stacked truck and the tunnel so that air is forced to flow between the

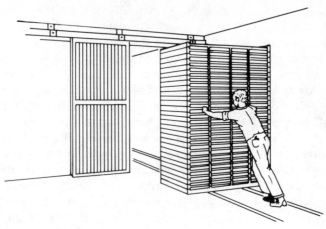

FIG. 12.3. TRUCK AND TUNNEL DEHYDRATOR

trays. The trucks move on tracks set into the floor of the tunnel. The necessity of keeping doors at the tunnel ends closed in order to confine the air flow requires that the trucks be moved intermittently rather than continuously. When a truck-load at the dry end is completed, it is removed, the line of trucks is advanced one position, and a fresh truck is pushed into the wet end. Tunnels may be long enough to hold from 4 to 5 trucks up to about 20, with the greater lengths being used for products having a longer drying time.

Air circulation may be provided by either axial flow or centrifugal fans. Heat is most commonly supplied by direct combustion of natural gas in the circulating air stream. If the available fuel produces contaminants that cannot be permitted to come into contact with the food, the air must be heated indirectly in some type of heat exchanger. If a very dry air supply is desired, indirect heating by steam can be used so as to eliminate the moisture from the fuel combustion. Air temperatures and velocities required for efficient rates of drying are usually such that there would be substantial wasted drying capacity if the air were used on a once-through arrangement. Accordingly, it is common to make provision for recycling a portion of the discharge air to mix with the fresh air intake.

There are two basic air flow arrangements in a tunnel dehydrator: parallel and countercurrent. Various combinations of these can be provided in multistage units. The situation is somewhat analogous to the flow arrangements in heat exchangers, but there are important differences. Countercurrent flow produces the lowest moisture contents, since the material leaving the tunnel is exposed to the dry incoming air. However, this air is also hot, and there is a serious problem with overheating the dry product. At the wet end of the tunnel, the product temperature will not rise significantly above the wet bulb temperature of the air. At the dry end, where the rate of drying is so low that there is very little evaporative cooling, the product temperature can approach the dry bulb temperature of the air. The air temperature that can be used, and therefore the dryer capacity, may be limited by the necessity of avoiding product damage. Furthermore, the air in the wet end with a countercurrent arrangement is relatively cool and moist, and the drying rate is correspondingly limited. In fact, it is possible for moisture to condense out onto a truck load that has just entered the tunnel before it has had time to be heated to the equilibrium temperature. This appreciable period of a warm, moist environment at the wet end provides excellent conditions for growth of microorganisms, and serious deterioration of product quality can result.

With parallel air flow, much higher entering air temperatures can be used since the product temperature will not rise above the air wet bulb. The high drying rate greatly reduces the length of time that the wet material acts as a microbial incubator. In the dry end, where evaporative cooling is no longer effective in limiting the product temperature, the air temperature has dropped sufficiently to avoid the danger of overheating. The disadvantage of parallel flow is that it may not be able to achieve a low enough final moisture content.

One way of avoiding the difficulties described above is to use a 2-stage operation, with parallel flow in the first stage for rapid removal of the bulk of the moisture and countercurrent flow in the second stage for a low final moisture content. This arrangement obviously involves a more complex installation and more labor for handling trucks. As an alternative to the second stage, low cost bin dryers may be used to achieve the final moisture content. The material is dumped into the bulk bins through which a gentle stream of heated air is passed. The moisture content is low enough at this stage that microbial growth is not a problem.

The selection of the optimum arrangement depends on a combination of factors related to product characteristics and costs. If an operation is strictly seasonal, such as prune dehydration, higher operating costs can be tolerated in order to reduce fixed capital costs. With year-round operation, more elaborate equipment arrangements can be justified in order to reduce operating costs. In general, the shorter drying times obtainable with parallel flow will favor this for the primary method. A very low inherent drying rate or a low initial moisture content would favor countercurrent flow. Also, there can be product quality characteristics that can dictate the choice of one method over another.

World War II provided a strong impetus for the production of dehydrated vegetables and fruit in the U.S., and during the following years, tunnel dehydrators were by far the predominant type of installation. This equipment involves no complex mechanical construction and is easily installed to meet the needs of large or small operations. The relatively moderate capital investment makes it possible to operate a dehydrating plant economically on a seasonal basis. Tunnel dehydrators have the disadvantage of high labor costs for handling the trays and trucks. Tray maintenance is a substantial expense. Drying conditions can not be as uniform or as closely controlled as in continuous belt dryers, and the product quality may not be as dependable.

Fruit drying is a seasonal operation and tends to be done in local installations of moderate size. These circumstances, together with the relatively long drying times required, favor tunnel dehydrators, and by far the greatest tonnage of fruit that is not sun-dried is processed in this type of equipment. Vegetable dehydration, on the other hand, tends to be concentrated in large, centrally located plants that process a variety of vegetables on almost a year-round basis. The economics in this situation favor the continuous belt dehydrators discussed below, and tunnel dehydrators are being phased out.

Continuous Belt Dryers

This equipment is very simple in principle. The solid material is dried by heated air while being conveyed on a continuous belt through a long horizontal chamber. Belts are made of woven steel mesh or linked plates, and the air passes up or down through the belt and bed of solid rather than parallel to the surface. In a typical machine, the belt may be from 6 to 10 ft wide and have a working length from 30 to 60 ft. Circulation through the material gives higher drying rates than circulation parallel to the material surface and permits the use of deeper beds of material. Alternate up and down flow can be used to obtain greater product uniformity. Air is supplied by a number of fans located on one side along the length of the dryer. The dryer is divided into sections, in each of which one or more fans discharges air into a plenum chamber either above or below the belt. The air then passes through the belt and into another plenum on the opposite side, and back to the fan suction. There is no flow of air in either direction along the dryer. The change in air humidity in one passage through the belt is relatively small, so a large proportion of recirculation is used. Dampers are provided to discharge the necessary amount of air and bring in fresh, dry air. If desired, air discharged from a section toward the dry end can be admitted as make-up in a wetter section. Each section is provided with its independent heat supply, either gas burners or indirect heaters.

As drying proceeds, a bed that was originally of substantial thickness will become much thinner as a result of shrinkage. An important saving in equipment and floor space can be made by terminating the first belt at some intermediate point in the dryer and discharging the material onto a second belt, where it is piled to a greater depth. This second belt must operate at a lower lineal speed in order to keep the pounds per hour of dry matter the same in both stages. A large belt dryer may have several such stages. This multistage operation has the further advantage that the material is redistributed at each transfer and a uniform product results.

The fact that air velocity, temperature, and humidity can be controlled independently in each section gives a high degree of versatility in matching conditions to the requirements of the product. Thus, the advantages of a high air temperature at the wet end and dry air of moderate temperature at the dry end can be combined in a single machine. This high degree of flexibility, however, can create difficulty in selecting optimum conditions, either in design or in operation. Extensive experience with different products, either in full size or experimental equipment, is the only satisfactory basis for making a selection.

Continuous belt dryers are complex and expensive machines, requiring a high level of specialized engineering and fabrication talent. Unlike tunnel dryers, they cannot be adequately designed and constructed on a local basis. The high capital investment makes it uneconomical for this equipment to be idle over any extended period of time. Accordingly, they are most effectively used in large integrated plants where they can be operated on essentially an annual basis. The high drying rates obtainable make them desirable for materials such as cut vegetables that can utilize this capability. They would be inappropriate for drying unpeeled fruit such as prunes or raisins.

Deep Bed Dryers

In this batch drying method, air is passed upward through a bed of material that is piled in depths up to several feet in a bin or chamber. The material must have a large enough particulate size to permit adequate passage of air and must have a sufficiently high compressive strength to maintain the open structure. This method is suitable for materials that are initially of relatively low moisture and that have such inherently low drying rates that the capabilities of high-drying-rate equipment are not advantageous. Because of this low drying rate that is governed by internal movement of moisture within the solid, air velocities can be kept low so as to avoid excessive costs of forcing air through a high resistance. The long drying time at moderate temperatures requires that moisture contents be low enough to avoid microbial growth.

Drying in a deep bed starts at the bottom, and there will usually be a substantial moisture gradient between the bottom and top. This gradient can create a problem in determining when the desired average moisture has been attained. In some cases, it may be necessary to redistribute the material from bins in order to equalize moisture through the mass after completion of drying.

Deep bed dryers are simple and inexpensive to construct and are widely used for grain drying in local farm applications. In a vegetable dehydration plant, they are ideally suited for the final drying stage, thus supplanting a far more costly continuous dehydrator installation.

Rotary Dryers

A rotary dryer consists essentially of a rotating cylindrical metal shell that is set on a small incline. Particulate material enters at the upper end, and air flow may be either parallel or countercurrent. The interior surface is equipped with flights, which are longitudinal fins extending inward toward the center. The solid material is continuously carried up by the rotation of the flights until it spills off and cascades through the air. As well as providing excellent contact between solid and air, this action of the flights acts as a sort of screw that conveys the material down the incline. With parallel flow, the air stream also assists in the forward motion. In order to avoid loss of product and pollution of discharge air, some type of dust separator or collecting device is necessary.

The high degree of turbulence and excellent contact between air and solid provide very high rates of drying for materials that have this capability. Small particulate matter and leafy material are especially well suited. Material that would tend to mat or pack on a tray or belt may easily be handled in a rotary dryer. The abrasion caused by the tumbling action rules out rotary dryers for many food materials. Furthermore, the particle size is frequently large enough that full advantage of the rapid drying potential cannot be realized. Accordingly, rotary dryers are little used for human food products but have important applications for animal feed or by-products such as tomato or apple pomace, where product quality requirements are less stringent. One important application is in drying of chopped alfalfa. The extremely rapid drying rate permits use of inlet air temperatures as high as 1500°F. Rotary dryers are used in two places in beet sugar processing: drying the finished sugar crystals from the centrifuges and drying the spent beet pulp for cattle feed.

Spray Dryers

Spray dryers are used to produce dry powder from liquid solutions or suspensions. Concentration of liquid materials by boiling is termed evaporation, and treated in Chap. 5 & 10. Like other drying processes, spray drying is simple in principle. The liquid is sprayed into a hot gas stream, and the liquid in the drops evaporates rapidly to leave a dry powder that falls out and is collected. Drying times are of the order of magnitude of seconds rather than minutes or hours. Even with high inlet air temperatures, the extremely rapid rate of evaporation provides cooling to keep the material from becoming overheated, and at no time is it necessary for either the wet or dry material to be in contact with a hot surface. The outward flow of water vapor from the drops apparently inhibits inward diffusion of oxygen, and very little oxidation occurs during drying. These characteristics of spray drying lead to important product quality advantages.

In addition to standard items such as fans, heaters, etc., there are three essential elements of a spray drying system: an atomizer, a drying chamber, and a system for collecting dry particles. Each of these elements involves special considerations that are dependent on the material to be dried.

Atomizers.—Two types of atomizers are in common use: pressure swirl nozzles and centrifugal. Pneumatic atomizers, as are used in paint sprayers, are convenient for small-scale applications but have only limited use in commercial operations. With pressure nozzles, the fluid is forced through a circular orifice with pressures ranging from a few hundred to a few thousand pounds per sq in. A chamber immediately preceding the orifice is designed to impart a swirling motion to the fluid. Nozzles have the advantage of simple construction with no moving parts. They are low in cost and easy to replace. On the negative side, they are subject to plugging and are not well suited for handling suspensions. Abrasive particles in the fluid can cause rapid wear of the orifice. An individual nozzle has a limited range of effective capacities, and a multiple nozzle installation may be necessary to obtain the desired flexibility of operation.

In a centrifugal atomizer, the fluid is fed into the center of a spinning flat rotor and is atomized by interaction with the surrounding air as it leaves the periphery. A variety of rotor designs are used, with vanes, slots, or other features to assist the dispersion of the fluid. Rotors may range from 6 to 14 in. in diameter and be driven at speeds up to 15,000 rpm. Centrifugal atomizers handle suspended solids with ease and have a wide capacity range.

An important desired feature of an atomizer is that it produces a narrow range of drop sizes. With a wide range, small particles can become overheated in the time required to dry the larger drops. Also, a wide range of sizes may create problems with powder collection and result in excessive carryover of small particles. The drop size range for any atomizer depends on the rheological characteristics of the fluid, and considerable experimentation may be necessary to make a satisfactory choice.

Drying Chambers.—The purpose of the drying chamber is to maintain the particles in suspension in the air stream for a sufficient length of time to complete the drying. Many arrangements are available, and the proper selection depends to a large measure on the nature of the product. The chamber may be horizontal or vertical, and air flow may be parallel, countercurrent, or mixed. Both cylindrical and rectangular, or box, chambers are used. A typical construction is a cylindrical chamber with a conical bottom, as shown in Fig. 12.4. Horizontal dryers are always parallel flow.

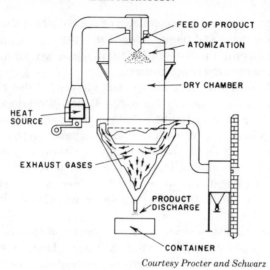

Courtesy Procter and Schwarz

FIG. 12.4. SPRAY DRYER

Dry powder falls to the floor and is continuously removed by scrapers. In vertical dryers, air may enter at the top with the liquid and exhaust at the bottom, or it may reverse direction and exhaust at the top. Both air and spray may enter at the bottom with all streams leaving at the top, or countercurrent flow can be used with upward flow of air and downward movement of powder. Placement of spray nozzles and air inlets and exhaust ducts can be arranged to give a variety of mixed flow patterns.

It is important that the powder be dry before it settles out of the air stream. Hygroscopic materials are difficult to dry to the point where they are not soft and sticky, and they tend to ball up and to stick to the walls of the chamber. Devices that continuously thump or scrape the walls are frequently provided to prevent an accumulation of powder. Basically, the chamber must be large enough to provide time for completion of drying. For this reason, it is difficult to conduct representative experiments in laboratory or pilot-scale equipment. Conditions must be altered by changing air rates and temperatures and drop sizes so as to make the drying time compatible with the size of the chamber. These altered conditions may create problems in scaling up to full-size equipment.

Powder Collection.—The primary separation may take place within the drying chamber by normal settling or as a result of reversals in air flow direction, or this same mechanism may be utilized in a separate chamber. Cyclone separators are widely used as external devices. This equipment has an inverted conical shape. The powder laden air enters tangentially at the top, and powder is thrown by centrifugal force against the conical surface. Powder spirals down and collects at the bottom of the cone, while air reverses in direction and passes out at the center of the top. Cyclone separators may be built up to about 10 feet in diameter, but multiple smaller units give more complete separation.

Some additional separation equipment is always needed to follow settling chambers and, many times, cyclones as well. Bag filters are efficient for this purpose. Fabric bags up to about 1 ft diameter and several feet long are arranged in a battery to provide sufficient capacity. Arrangements can be made for automatically shaking the bags and withdrawing the powder from the bottom. Wet scrubbers, in which the air is contacted with water to remove the remaining dust, can be used as an alternative to bag filters. The water discharge stream from the scrubber would ordinarily be recycled to the dryer feed.

By far the greatest food industry application of spray drying is in production of non-fat dry milk powder. Although drum dryers are used for some specialized dry milk solids, spray drying is the method of choice. Spray drying is also important in production of dried egg products and soluble coffee. Application of spray drying to fruit and vegetable juices has been less successful. These materials tend to form sticky, hygroscopic particles that stick to the chamber walls and are not free-flowing for easy collection and removal.

Drum Dryers

The drum, or roller, dryer is a standard piece of equipment for producing a dry solid from a liquid slurry or solution. Liquid is spread in a thin film on the surface of a hollow drum, which is heated internally. Before completion of one revolution, the dry product is scraped off with a blade. Drum dryers are constructed in both single and double or twin drum units. In the latter arrangement, the parallel drums may rotate either toward or away from each other. There is a variety of methods for distributing the feed over the surface and for handling the dry product.

Drum dryers can handle a wide range of liquids, including slurries that are much too thick to be sprayed. At one time, they were used for most dry skim milk production, but spray drying has largely taken over this application. In general, better quality food products can be obtained by other methods. They are extensively used, however, in production of dried potato flakes.

Freeze-Drying

Freeze-drying is the process of drying by sublimation, directly from the frozen state with no thawing. Maintaining the frozen state means, in effect, keeping the water vapor partial pressure in the space surrounding the material less than the vapor pressure of ice at 32°F, or 4.58 mm Hg. Most food materials have effective freezing points less than 32°F, so the water partial pressure in practice must be at a lower value. The usual way of accomplishing this result is to conduct the process in a vacuum chamber with the total pressure below the critical value. On the other hand, freeze-drying can proceed in the presence of dry air at atmospheric pressure. Residents of cold climates can observe that a frozen washing will dry on a clothes line without thawing on a clear cold winter day. "Freezer-burn" of food held in frozen storage is freeze-drying of the surface as a result of inadequate packaging.

In freeze-drying, the only significant mechanism for movement of moisture through the solid is vapor transport under either a concentration or total pressure gradient. The capillary and shrinkage mechanisms that are predominant in ordinary dehydration require a liquid state. Accordingly, as freeze-drying proceeds, the ice boundary recedes from the outer surface and vapor escapes through the porous outer shell of dry matter. During the drying process, there are thus two regions within the solid: a gradually receding ice core and a surrounding dry shell. There is no region of partially dry matter. The porous solid remaining after the ice phase has disappeared will have a significant content of adsorbed moisture. This moisture does not affect the physical properties of the solid or interfere with the normal drying mechanism, but it usually must be reduced for adequate storage life of the dry product.

The most apparent feature of freeze-dried solid foods is the absence of shrinkage. The material cannot shrink while it is frozen, and there is no tendency for it to shrink when dry. The absence of liquid movement means that there is no migration of soluble constituents. This condition, together with the low temperature, permits the retention of biological activity in dried product. The low temperature also results in better retention of volatile flavor and odor constituents. The open, porous structure of the dry product permits almost instant rehydration. In general, any food that can be satisfactorily frozen can be freeze-dried and will closely resemble the undried material on reconstitution. The porous nature of freeze-dried foods makes them susceptible to oxidation, and they must be packaged to exclude oxygen. The only real disadvantage of freeze-drying is its relatively high cost compared to air drying.

Although the moisture remains in the frozen state, it is still necessary to provide the heat of sublimation of over 1200 Btu/lb. In a vacuum chamber, this heat cannot be supplied by a hot air stream, and some indirect method must be used. The usual method is to have trays of frozen material placed alternately between flat heating platens that radiate to both top and bottom. The source of heat is usually hot brine that circulates through the platens. An effective commercial equipment arrangement is to have separate carts fitted with platens which can be loaded with trays of frozen food in a cold room. Quick-connect couplings are provided for the hot brine lines.

The absence of a circulating air stream in freeze-drying also means that some provision must be made for removing the water vapor that is evolved. The most common method is to freeze out the vapor on refrigerated condensers inside the vacuum chamber. The condenser temperature obviously must be well below that of the frozen food. The ultimate vacuum is maintained by a mechanical vacuum pump that removes air leaking into the chamber. In principle, the water vapor could also be removed by the vacuum pump, but this procedure has a completely uneconomical pumping requirement. If an adequate supply of low cost steam is available, steam ejectors can be used in place of the pump-condenser combination to remove both the water vapor and air leakage.

Depending on the nature of the product, drying times will usually be about 8 to 10 hr and sometimes much longer. Although continuous equipment has been devised, batch operation is customary. A large freeze-drying operation will have a battery of units on staggered cycles so as to make effective use of the vacuum, refrigeration, and heating equipment. At the end of a cycle, the cart is withdrawn to a packaging room and the condensers are defrosted to prepare for a new charge.

During the drying process, water vapor moves from the ice boundary to the outer surface by some combination of diffusion and total pressure gradient flow. With a very high vacuum operation, so little air is present in the system that the diffusion mechanism is unimportant. At higher pressures, the concentration of water vapor is small compared to that of air, and transport is entirely by diffusion. As the vapor flows out through the dry shell, the heat of sublimation must flow in from the outer surface to the ice boundary through the same shell. The porous dry shell is an excellent thermal insulator, and getting the heat in is the bottleneck in the drying process. The thickness of the shell increases as drying proceeds, and heat flow rate decreases proportionately.

In contrast to other types of drying, the theory of freeze-drying is well understood. It is basically a question of transport of heat and vapor through a porous solid, subjects that have been extensively studied both theoretically and experimentally. In fact, it is possible to make satisfactory predictions of drying time from experimental measurements of properties of dried solids. In essence, the process is somewhat analogous to the wet bulb temperature condition. The rate of outward flow of vapor through the resistance of the shell is balanced by the rate at which the latent heat of sublimation flows in through this same resistance. If the external conditions of chamber pressure and temperature of the outer surface are fixed, the ice will assume a temperature that is dependent on the ratio of the heat and mass transfer resistances. Although these resistances increase as the thickness of the shell increases, they are both proportional to the thickness, and the ratio does not change. In the usual operating absolute pressure range of freeze dryers, transport of both mass and heat depends on pressure in a rather complex way, and the theory is more complicated than might be indicated by previous discussions of transport behavior.

The ice core temperature is closely related to the vapor-pressure curve for ice and is thus strongly dependent on the chamber pressure. Chamber pressure is therefore the process variable that is controlled to maintain the desired ice temperature. Depending on the product, pressures from 1–2 mm Hg down to a few tenths of a millimeter may be used. Materials such as fruits, which have low freezing temperatures because of the high sugar content, require the lower pressures.

Both theory and experiment show that the drying time is approximately proportional to the square of the thickness of the material. If a ½-in. thick steak required 8 hr, then a 1-in. thickness would require 32 hr. When drying times rise above 10 or 12 hr, the equipment throughput is reduced to the point that the process starts to become uneconomical. It is the long drying time coupled with the high cost of a vacuum drying operation that makes freeze-drying so much more costly than air drying. Efforts to reduce the cost have been primarily directed toward shortening the drying time by developing more effective means of getting the heat of sublimation to the ice core.

Freeze-drying of foods received a strong impetus in the U.S. during World War II and the Korean conflict in providing rations for front line troops. During the intervening years, a large variety of products has been manufactured for civilian consumption. Aside from a few specialty items and some campers meals, most of these have not been able to develop sufficient markets to justify the high cost. A notable exception is freeze-dried soluble coffee, which has sufficient quality advantage over the spray dried variety to have captured a major share of the market. In Europe, where there has been less extensive use of domestic refrigeration and a greater dependence on dried foods, there has been a wider market for freeze-dried products.

DRYING TIME CALCULATIONS FOR CONTINUOUS DEHYDRATION

In view of the similarities between heat and mass transfer, one might be led to believe that sizing a dehydrator is a somewhat comparable task to sizing a heat exchanger. In a heat exchanger, we are given the flow rates and terminal temperatures of two streams and wish to obtain the required area. With a dehydrator, the problem is to determine the required size for specified flow rates of air and solid and the terminal moisture contents. Previous discussions have shown, however, that mass transfer is a much more complex phenomenon that heat transfer. Information on thermal conductivities and heat transfer coefficients is readily available, and the materials do not undergo fundamental changes during the process. In most drying applications, we do not have a clear understanding of the mechanism and the material is continuously changing. Furthermore, a complete solution to the drying problem requires simultaneous solution of both heat and mass transfer equations. It is well within the scope of this text to present basic design methods for heat exchangers and give illustrative examples. The engineering theory for an equivalent approach to a typical food dehydration problem does not exist, and an essentially empirical method is required. The objective of this section therefore, is not to present any complete method for sizing continuous dehydrators but rather to illustrate the type of approach that is used. The discussion is based on drying solid material that is moved or conveyed mechanically with either parallel or countercurrent flow of air. It will be assumed that there are no heat losses to the surroundings and that the solid receives heat only by convection from the air, i.e., there is no radiative heat transfer. Actually, it is not difficult to account for the effects of heat losses and radiation if their magnitudes are known.

If drying takes place entirely within the constant rate period, there is a very simple solution for drying time. As discussed previously, this is not a case of practical importance in food dehydration, but it will be instructive to go through the solution. As noted above, the surface of the solid remains saturated with unbound moisture during the constant rate period, and the heat and mass transfer coefficients do not change. In continuous dehydration, the drying rate will change as the material moves through the dryer because of the change in air temperature and humidity. The situation corresponds to adiabatic humidification of the air as described in the chapter on psychrometry. The air temperature drops as it moves through the dryer and picks up moisture, but its adiabatic saturation (or wet bulb) temperature remains constant. After the brief initial warm-up period, which has an unimportant effect, the temperature of the material remains at the wet bulb temperature. This wet bulb temperature relationship constitutes the simultaneous solution of heat and mass transfer equations mentioned above. The remainder of the problem is simply a simultaneous solution of Eq. 12-1 together with the mass balance equation for the dehydrator.

Referring to Fig. 12.5, S and G are the pounds per hour of solid and air, both expressed on a moisture-free basis. The subscript 1 designates the wet end and the subscript 2 the dry end. Thus, Y_1 is the humidity of the entering air with parallel flow and the discharge air with countercurrent flow. The overall moisture balance is

$$S(X_1 - X_2) = \pm G(Y_1 - Y_2) \qquad \text{Eq. 12-4}$$

In this equation, the plus sign is used for countercurrent flow and the minus sign for parallel flow. On a differential basis, we can write

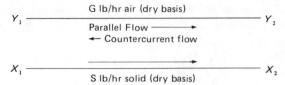

FIG. 12.5. MATERIALS (G AND S) AND STATE (1 AND 2) CONVENTIONS FOR CONTINUOUS DEHYDRATION

$$SdX = \pm GdY$$ Eq. 12-5

Eliminating dX between Eqs. 12-1 and 12-5,
$$dX = \pm(G/S)dY = -(k_y/L_s)(Y^* - Y)d\theta$$
$$\mp dY/(Y^* - Y) = (Sk_y/GL_s)d\theta$$
Integrating over the length of the dryer,

$$\pm\ln(Y^* - Y_2)/(Y^* - Y_1) = (Sk_y/GL_s)\theta$$ Eq. 12-6

In Eq. 12-6 the plus and minus signs still indicate countercurrent and parallel flow as before. The drying time θ is the residence time required for the material to move from the entrance to the exit of the dryer. The total quantity of solid, expressed on a dry basis, that is contained within the dryer at any time is simply the product of the residence time and the solid flow rate, or

$$L_t = S\theta$$ Eq. 12-7

The following example illustrates the use of these equations.

Example 3.—Diced potatoes are to be dried in a parallel flow tunnel dehydrator from a moisture ratio of 3.0 to 1.0. The potatoes will be spread on 3 ft × 6 ft trays at a loading of 1.5 lb of wet material per sq ft. Each truck will hold 18 trays, and the tunnel is to accommodate 8 trucks. Outside air is 80°F and 40% rh will be heated to 200°F before entering the dehydrator at a rate of 2200 lb/min (dry basis). It will be assumed that the drying is entirely within the constant rate period with a transfer coefficient $k_y = 50$ lb/(hr)(ft^2)(ΔY). Determine the drying time and the solids handling capacity of the dehydrator.

In this situation, the air rate is selected so as to give the desired linear velocity for good transfer coefficients. The rate thus is based on the tunnel cross-sectional area rather than on the solids rate. If an outlet air temperature is selected, the outlet humidity can be obtained by following a constant wet bulb line on the psychrometric chart from the entering condition. The solids rate can be calculated from Eq. 12-4 and Eq. 12-5 then used to obtain the drying time. The number of trucks in the tunnel is then obtained by application of Eq. 12-7. If the answer is not equal to 8 trucks, a new outlet air temperature must be chosen and the calculation repeated. It is possible that the final air temperature thus obtained will represent an unrealistic or uneconomic condition. In this case, it would be necessary to modify the design conditions.

From psychrometric chart,

$Y_1 = 0.0087$ (air at 80°F and 40% rh)

After heating to 200°F,

$t^* = 92.6°F$

$Y^* = 0.0341$

From problem statement, $X_1 = 3.0$ and $X_2 = 1.0$

$L_s = 1.5/X_1 = 0.5$ lb dry matter/sq ft.

Assume air outlet temperature = 110°F. Following 92.6°F wet bulb time to this temperature, $Y_2 = 0.0297$

From Eq. 12-4,

$S = G(Y_2 - Y_1)/(X_1 - X_2) = 2200(60)(0.0297 - 0.0087)/(3.0 - 1.0)$

$= 1387$ lb/hr

Substituting into Eq. 12-6,

$$\ln \frac{0.0341 - 0.0087}{0.0341 - 0.0297} = \frac{1387(50)\theta}{2200(0.5)} \text{ and } \theta = 1.67 \text{ hr}$$

From Eq. 12-7,

$L_t = S\theta = 1387(1.67) = 2310$ lb dry matter in dehydrator.

The dry matter per truck is the tray loading times the total tray area, or $0.5(3)(6)(30) = 270$ lb. The number of trucks is the total dry matter divided by the dry matter per truck, or

$n = 2310/270 = 8.56$

A higher outlet temperature will give a shorter drying time and a smaller number of trucks. For the second trial, assume an outlet temperature of 115°F. Following the wet bulb line to 115°F, $Y_2 = 0.0286$. As before,

$S = 2200(60)(0.0286 - 0.0087)/(3.0 - 1.0) = 1320$ lb/hr

$$\ln \frac{0.0341 - 0.0087}{0.0341 - 0.0286} = \frac{1320(50)\theta}{2200(0.5)}$$

$\theta = 1.53$ hr

$n = 1320(1.53)/270 = 7.5$ trucks

Interpolating between these two trials give a temperature of 113°F and a dry matter rate of 1350 lb/hr. The accuracy of the calculation does not justify another trial to get a closer answer. The wet solids rate is 1350(3) = 4050 lb/hr.

The above example does not constitute a realistic drying situation. A drying time of 1.5 hr with 8 trucks means that a truck change would have to be made almost every 10 minutes. Actually, a constant rate period would hardly exist even at the outset, and the final moisture content would be brought to a much lower value in any practical tunnel. The drying time would be substantially longer and the tunnel throughput less.

The example illustrates an application of the "point condition" integration method. This general method can be applied, even in the falling rate period, if drying rate constants at any instant depend only on the existing moisture content and not on the previous history of the material. Complete information would be needed on convective heat and mass transfer coefficients as well as drying rate constants over the entire range of operating conditions. The general problem is much more complicated than the example because the temperature of the solid will not ordinarily remain at the air wet bulb temperature during the falling rate period. Although various approximations can be made to simplify the calculations, this entire method is not valid for any significant food applications. The Van Arsdel reference, mentioned earlier in the chapter, gives details of a method, based on extensive experimental correlations, for calculating drying times for several cut vegetables in truck and tunnel dehydrators.

The only really valid general approach to this problem that is applicable to all materials under all conditions is experimental. Instead of using constant drying conditions, a sample of material is dried with a continuously changing air temperature and humidity so that it experiences the same treatment that it would receive if it were moving through a continuous dehydrator. The experimental procedure involves changing the air temperature and humidity at intervals on the basis of a stepwise heat and mass balance that represents the desired terminal dehydrator conditions. The time required for the sample to reach the final moisture content is the drying time for the continuous dehydrator. The only drawback to this approach is the time and effort required. Each drying time determination for a specific set of external conditions requires an experiment that lasts at least as long as the drying time. In the absence of previous dehydration experience for a particular material, however, there may be no adequate alternative to making at least some measurements of this type. It should be noted that this method is equally adaptable to the through-circulation, cross-flow arrangement of continuous belt dryers.

SYMBOLS

c_s specific heat
G mass flow rate of air
h_c convective heat transfer coefficient
K combined drying rate constant for all types of mass transport.
k_y convective mass transfer coefficient
L_t mass of product solid within dryer at time t
L_s mass of dry matter per unit area of tray
ln natural logarithm
S mass flow rate of product solid
t temperature
t^* wet bulb temperature

X dry basis moisture content
Y moisture content of dry air
Y^* moisture content of dry air at wet bulb temperature
θ time
λ latent heat of vaporization of water

Subscripts

0 & 1   initial condition, usually for $\theta = 0$, or wet end
2   final condition or dry end
e dry basis moisture content when drying rate has dropped to zero, e.g. equilibrium moisture content.

Useful Tables

TABLE A.1

SELECTED SI (SYSTEM INTERNATIONAL) BASE UNITS,
PREFIXES AND PHYSICAL QUANTITIES

Basic SI Units

Physical Quantity	Unit Name	Symbol
Electrical current	ampere	A
Mass	kilogram	kg
Thermodynamic temperature	kelvin	K
Length	meter	m
Amount of substance	mole	mol
Time	second	s

Prefixes

Negative Exponent	Prefix	Symbol	Positive Exponent	Prefix	Symbol
10^{-1}	deci	d	10	deka	da
10^{-2}	centi	c	10^2	hecto	h
10^{-3}	milli	m	10^3	kilo	k
10^{-6}	micro	μ	10^6	mega	M
10^{-9}	nano	n	10^9	giga	G
10^{-12}	pico	p	10^{12}	tera	T
10^{-15}	femto	f	10^{15}	peta	P
10^{-18}	atto	a	10^{18}	exa	E

TABLE A.2

SELECTED SI UNITS THAT ARE DERIVED

Physical Quantity	Name of SI Unit	Symbol	Definition
Energy	joule	J	$kg\, m^2/s^2$
Power	watt	w	$kg\, m^2/s^3 = J/s$
Force	newton	N	$kg\, m/s^2 = J/m$
Electrical charge	coulomb	c	As
Electrical potential difference	volt	V	$kg\, m^2/s^3 A = J/As$
Electric resistance	ohm	Ω	$kg\, m^2/s^3 A^2 = V/A$
Frequency	hertz	Hz	$1/s$
Pressure	Pascal	Pa	$kg/ms^2 = N/m^2$
Area	square meter		m^2
Volume	cubic meter		m^3
Density	kilogram per cubic meter		kg/m^3
Velocity	meter per second		m/s
Acceleration	meter per second squared		m/s^2
Kinematic viscosity	square meter per second		m^2/s
Dynamic viscosity	Pascal second	Pas	$kg/m_s = Ns/m^2$
Surface tension	newton per meter	N/m	kg/s^2

TABLE A.3

SELECTED PHYSICAL QUANTITIES WITH SPECIAL NAMES AND
EXACT SI UNIT DEFINED VALUES

Physical Unit	Unit Name	Symbol	Definition
Gravitional acceleration			9.806650 m/s^2
Length	angstrom	Å	10^{-10} m
Length	inch	in.	2.54×10^{-2} m
Length	micron	μm	10^{-6} m
Volume	liter	l	10^{-3} m^3
Mass	pound (avoirdupois)	lb	0.45359237 kg
Mass	tonne	t	10^3 kg = Mg
Force	dyne	dyn	10^{-5} N
Force	kilogram force	kgf	9.80665 N
Pressure	atmosphere	atm	101325 Pa
Pressure	torr	Torr	$(101325/760)$ Pa
Pressure	millimeter of mercury	mmHg	$13.5951 \times 980.665 \times 10^{-2}$ Pa
Pressure	bar	bar	10^5 Pa
Pressure	pascal	Pa	N/m^2
Energy	erg	erg	10^{-7} J
Energy	kilowatt hour	kwh	3.6×10^6 J
Energy	thermochemical calorie	cal (thermochem.)	4.184 J
Energy	I.T. Calorie	cal$_{IT}$	4.1868 J
Temperature (t)	degree Celsius	°C	t°C = (TK) − 273.15
Temperature (t)	degree Fahrenheit	°F	t°F = (TR) − 459.67
Kinematic viscosity	stokes	St	10^{-4} m^2/s
Dynamic viscosity	poise	P	10^{-1} kg/ms

TABLE A.4

SELECTED MEASUREMENT UNITS AND SI EQUIVALENTS

Length, Area, and Volume

	SI
1 in. =	2.54 cm
1 ft = 12 in. =	0.3048 m
1 acre = 43,560 ft^2 =	4046.86 m^2
1 ft^2 = 144 in.^{2} =	0.092903 m^2
in.^{2} =	6.4516 cm^2
ft^3 = 1728 in.^{3} =	0.0283168 m^3
in.^{3} =	16.38706 cm^3

U.S. Liquid Measure
1 gal. = 231 in.^{3} = 0.13368 ft^3 = 0.0037854 m^3
1 qt = 57.75 in.^{3} = 0.033420 ft^3 = 0.00094635 m^3
1 oz = 1.8047 in.^{3} = 29.574 cm^3
1 gal. = 4 qt = 8 pt = 128 oz
1 barrel = 31 gal. or more depending on law or usage

U.S. Dry Measure
1 bushel = 4 pecks = 32 qt = 64 pints
1 bushel = 1.244456 ft^3

British Imperial Liquid and Dry Measure
1 gal. (Imp) = 0.00454609 m^3 = 0.160544 ft^3
1 qt (UK) = 0.00113652 m^3 = 0.0401360 ft^3
1 oz fl (UK) = 28.4131 cm^3 = 1.73387 in.^{3}
1 bushel (UK) = 0.0363681 m^3 = 1.28433 ft^3

TABLE A.4 (*Continued*)

Acceleration

1 ft/s² = 0.3048 m/s²

Mass

1 kg = 2.20462 lb
1 lb = 16 oz = 453.5929 g = 0.4535929 kg
1 g = 15.4324 gr (grain)
1 slug = 32.172 lbf = 14.593 kg
1 ton (2000 lb) = 907.185 kg
1 ton (metric — 2240.00 lb) = 1016.05 kg

Density

1 lb/ft³ = 16.0185 kg/m³
1 lb/in³ = 27.6799 g/cm³
1 lb/gal (Imp) = 0.0997763 kg/dm³
1 lb/gal (US) = 0.1198264 kg/dm³
1 slug/ft³ = 515.379 kg/m³

Force

1 N = 0.224809 lbf = 7.23301 pdl (poundal)
1 lbf = 4.44822 N
1 pdl = 0.13825 N

Pressure and Stress

1 atmos = 760 torr = 101.325 kPa
1 atmos (Tech 1 kgf/cm²) = 98.0665 kPa
1 bar = 100 kPa
1 lbf/ft² = 47.8803 Pa
1 lbf/in.² = 6.89476 kPa
1 pdl/ft² = 1.48816 Pa
1 ft H₂O = 2.98907 kPa
1 in. H₂O = 249.089 Pa
1 in. Hg = 3.386 kPa

Work — Heat (Energy), Power, Heat Rate

1 hp h = 2.68452 MJ
1 Btu = 1.05506 k J
1 ft lbf = 1.35582 J
1 Ws = 1J = 0.737562 ft lbf
1 kJ = 0.277778 Wh
1 Kwh = 3.6 MJ
1 hp = 745.700 W/(Js) = 550 ft lbf/s
1 Btu/hr = 0.293071 W
1 ft lbf/s = 1.3558 W
1 Btu/lb °F = 4186.8 J/kgK
1 Btu ft/ft² h°F = 1.73073 W/mK
1 Btu in/ft² h°F = 0.144228 W/mK
1 Btu in/ft² s°F = 519.220 W/mK

Dynamic Viscosity

1 cP = 1 mPas
1 Pas = 0.0208854 lbf s/ft² = 0.671969 lb/fts

Kinematic Viscosity

1 m²/s = 10.7639 ft²/s

Food Engineering Task Force
Recommended Course Outline

Recommendations on subject matter outlines for food-oriented courses. Proposed in the Minimum Standards for Undergraduate Education in Food Science and Technology,[2] submitted by the IFT Council Committee on Education. Only the Food Engineering Task Force recommended course outline is given here.

FOOD ENGINEERING
TASK FORCE ON SUBJECT MATTER FOR THE COURSE
FOOD ENGINEERING

Chairman—D. F. Farkas, USDA Western Utilization R&D Div.; J. C. Harper, U. California-Davis; V. A. Jones, No. Carolina State U.; M. Karel, Massachusetts Inst. Technology; M. P. Steinberg, U. Illinois.

THE OBJECTIVE of Food Engineering courses is to introduce a limited number of engineering fundamentals. The student interested in in-depth aspects of food engineering would be expected to elect a course sequence in engineering independently of the courses discussed here.

The proposed outline (that follows) contains material for a full year's work, preferably the junior year. The first course covers thermodynamics, fluid flow and heat transfer. The second course covers evaporation, refrigeration, psychrometry, drying, distillation, and optional topics.

Prerequisites for the first course in Food Engineering are 1 year of calculus and 1 year of physics. It is recommended that Physical Chemistry be taken concurrently with Food Engineering.

Effective instruction in Food Engineering cannot be carried out without some parallel laboratory work. Therefore, a list of experiments, which might serve as a basis for a laboratory text, is included in the outline.

FIRST COURSE (½ YEAR)

Lecture Material

UNITS/DIMENSIONS—Consistency of dimensions; mass-force concept.

THERMODYNAMICS—First Law (closed and steady-state systems); Material balance; Energy balance; Thermodynamic properties of materials (steam, refrigerants).

---

[2] *Food Technology.* March 1969, *23*, pp. 33–37.

FLUID FLOW—Mechanical energy equation (Bernoulli); Laminar and turbulent flow; Reynolds number, Friction factors; Flow measurement; Newtonian and non-Newtonian liquids; Compressible fluids.

HEAT TRANSFER—Conduction, steady and unsteady state (series and parallel); Thermal conductivity; Heat capacity, Diffusivity, Gurney-Lurie charts; Thermal processing/process engineering; Convection, Coefficients (film, overall, and analysis of selected systems); Radiation (fundamental equation; emissivity-qualitative aspects); Heat exchangers (counterflow, parallel flow, significance of log-mean temperature differences).

Laboratory Experiments

MEASUREMENT—Pressure/vacuum; temperature; liquid flow; gas flow; heat transfer by radiation.

CHARACTERISTICS—Of pumps; fans, blowers, compressors; vacuum pumps.

HEAT TRANSFER—Heat exchangers (evaluation of overall heat transfer coefficient; Comparison of different types of exchangers).

OPTIONAL EXERCISES—Heat transfer in transient conduction; Energy transfer, e.g. by dielectric devices and radio-frequency ovens.

SECOND COURSE (½ YEAR)

Lecture Material

EVAPORATION—Mass and energy balance; Rate calculations; Principles of operation.

REFRIGERATION—Thermodynamics of compression cycle; Principles of operation; Liquefied gases as contact refrigerants.

PSYCHROMETRY—Properties of air-water mixtures; Psychrometric charts; Examples (other than drying).

DEHYDRATION—Drying during constant and falling rate periods; Mass transfer coefficients, diffusion mechanisms; Principles of operation of dryers.

DISTILLATION—Equilibrium; Batch and continuous distillations; Equilibrium flash distillation; McCabe-Thiele diagrams (optional).

CONTROL—Principles of instrumentation and process control

Laboratory Experiments

EVAPORATION
REFRIGERATION
PSYCHROMETRIC MEASUREMENTS
DRYING—Rate studies; Evaluation of continuous process
INSTRUMENTATION AND CONTROL

APPENDIX

The following topics are optional Lecture Material. An asterisk (*) designates those topics for which laboratory experiments may be included at the discretion of the instructor.

SIZE REDUCTION*

SEPARATIONS*—Filtration; Mechanical; Density; Membrane processes; Extraction*, Leaching; Ion exchange; Adsorption.

MATERIALS HANDLING—Including mixing, Homogenization*.

ELECTRICAL*—Circuits, power, motors.

COST ANALYSIS

Addendum

Following is a list of books in which the reader may be interested in further study of the subject of food engineering.

BALL, C. O., and OLSON, F. C. 1957. Sterilization in Food Technology. McGraw-Hill Book Co., New York.

BIRD, R. B., STEWARD, W. E., and LIGHTFOOT, E. N. 1960. Transport Phenomena. John Wiley & Sons, New York.

CHARM, S. E. 1971. The Fundamentals of Food Engineering, 2nd Edition. Avi Publishing Co., Westport, Conn.

CHARM, S. E., and KURLAND, G. S. 1971. Blood Viscosity and Microcirculation. Academic Press, New York.

DAVIES, J. T., and RIDEAL, E. K. 1963. Interfacial Phenomena. Academic Press, New York.

DICKERSON, R. W. JR. 1965. Thermal properties of foods. *In* The Freezing Preservation of Foods, 4th Edition, Vol. 2, D. K. Tressler, W. B. Van Arsdel, and M. J. Copley (Editors). Avi Publishing Co., Westport, Conn.

EARLE, R. L. 1966. Unit Operations in Food Processing. Pergamon Press, Elmsford, N.Y.

EIRICH, F. D. 1958. Rheology: Theory and Applications, Vol. 2. Academic Press, New York.

FERRY, J. D. 1961. Viscoelastic Properties of Polymers. John Wiley & Sons, New York.

FROST, A. A., and PEARSON, R. G. 1961. Kinetics and Mechanisms, 2nd Edition. John Wiley & Sons, New York.

GOLDBLITH, S. A. 1967. Basic principles of microwaves and recent developments. *In* Advances in Food Research, Vol. 15, C. O. Chichester, E. M. Mrak, and G. F. Stewart (Editors). Academic Press, New York.

HALL, C. W., and HEDRICK, T. I. 1971. Drying of Milk and Milk Products, 2nd Edition. Avi Publishing Co., Westport, Conn.

JOSLYN, M. A. 1961. Concentration by freezing. *In* Fruit and Vegetable Juice Processing Technology, 2nd Edition, D. K. Tressler and M. A. Joslyn (Editors). Avi Publishing Co., Westport, Conn.

JOSLYN, M. A. 1961. Physiological and enzymological aspects of juice production. *In* Fruit and Vegetable Juice Processing Technology, 2nd Edition, D. K. Tressler and M. A. Joslyn (Editors). Avi Publishing Co., Westport, Conn.

JOSLYN, M. A., and HEID, J. L. 1963. Food Processing Operations, Vol. 1, 2, and 3. Avi Publishing Co., Westport, Conn.

KING, C. J. 1973. Freeze-Drying *In* Food Dehydration, 2nd Edition, Vol. 1, W. B. Van Arsdel, M. J. Copley, and A. I. Morgan, Jr. (Editors). Avi Publishing Co., Westport, Conn.

KREITH, F. 1965. Principles of Heat Transfer, 2nd Edition. International Textbook Co., Scranton, Penn.

MCCABE, W. L., and SMITH, J. C. 1967. Unit Operations of Chemical Engineering, 2nd Edition. McGraw-Hill Book Co., New York.

MERYMAN, H. T. 1966. Freeze-drying. *In* Cryobiology, H. T. Meryman (Editor). Academic Press, New York.

MOORE, W. J. 1962. Physical Chemistry, 3rd Edition. Prentice-Hall, Englewood Cliffs, N.J.

NEUMANN, B. S. 1953. Powders. *In* Flow Properties of Disperse Systems, J. J. Hermanns (Editor). John Wiley & Sons, New York.

ORR, C., JR. 1966. Particulate Technology. Macmillan Co., New York.

PERRY, J. H. 1963. Chemical Engineer's Handbook, 4th Edition. McGraw-Hill Book Co., New York.

RICCI, J. E. 1966. The Phase Rule and Heterogeneous Equilibrium. Dover Publications, New York.

ROLFE, E. J. 1968. The chilling and freezing of foodstuff. *In* Biochemical and Biological Engineering Science, N. Blakebrough (Editor). Academic Press, New York.

RUBIN, E. E., and GADEN, E. L., JR. 1962. Foam separation. *In* New Chemical Separation Techniques, H. M. Shoen (Editor). Interscience, New York.

SKELLAND, A. H. P. 1967. Non-Newtonian Flow and Heat Transfer. John Wiley & Sons, New York.

SMITH, A. U. 1961. Biological Effects of Freezing and Supercooling. Edward Arnold, London, England.

TALBURT, W. F., and SMITH, O. 1975. Potato Processing, 3rd Edition. Avi Publishing Co., Westport, Conn.

TREYBAL, R. E. 1968. Mass Transfer Operations, 2nd Edition. McGraw-Hill Book Co., New York.

VAN ARSDEL, W. B., COPLEY, M. J., and MORGAN, A. I., JR. 1973. Food Dehydration, 2nd Edition, Vols. 1 and 2. Avi Publishing Co., Westport, Conn.

WALKER, H. L. 1961. Volatile flavor recovery. *In* Fruit and Vegetable Juice Processing Technology, 2nd Edition, D. K. Tressler and M. A. Josyln (Editors). Avi Publishing Co., Westport, Conn.

WILKINSON, W. L. 1960. Non-Newtonian Fluids. Pergamon Press, Elmsford, N.Y.

WINTROBE, M. W. 1961. Clinical Hematology. Lea & Febiger, Philadelphia.

Index

INDEX 281